Bill Gillham

# Parisians' Paris

PALLAS ATHENE

# Contents

# Preface

Where to find Paris? Not an empty question, because the essence of the city is elusive but everywhere, in a thousand momentary details that vanish and re-appear in a different guise. A busy sight-seeing programme can mean that you miss what you'd hope for.

No guidebook, however hard it tries, can capture that dimension. You have to find it for yourself. But a guide can put you in the way of discovering those fragments that make up the whole. Leaning against the American bar in La Coupole I watched the barman preparing a multi-coloured cocktail: he caught my eye and shrugged, 'C'est toxique'; an *huîtrier* opening oysters with effortless skill outside a brasserie; an old lady helping herself to chocolate cake in Dalloyau and murmuring 'It is temptation, *monsieur*' – shades of Oscar Wilde.

I didn't set out to write a guidebook. In a sense it has written itself, growing out of the way I've planned my visits, over many years, in search of the Paris known to people who live there know. There is a world of difference between the Paris of tourism and Parisians' Paris.

So in these pages only summary reference is made to the obvious 'sights'. And there are no predictable picture-postcard views, but the kind of photographs that reflect the human face of the city: that is, where it is to be found.

B. G.

# Introduction

Paris can be a surprisingly disappointing experience: typically visitors try to do too much in too short a time and, in attempting to get the full picture, somehow see none of it. The city exists at several levels. The main sights are so dramatic, the many tourist traps so strident, that the web of detail often local in character can be overlooked; but this is where the distinctive quality of Paris is to be found. We suggest your stay should be locally based, living in one of the many village-like communities that make up the city with occasional forays outside to the major sights. Successive visits can be made each to a different quarter (their variety even when adjacent is infinite) and, gradually, the detailed picture will emerge.

This guide is made up of sections dealing with eighteen of the villages *(quartiers)* of which Paris is composed, scattered across the city. Sometimes conventional names have been used, although there is a little-known dimension even to such apparent clichés as Montmartre. Here, as elsewhere, within a few hundred metres of the tourist spots you can find an almost provincial sense of community, a community inhabited largely by people who spend their lives there.

With this in mind we have used names that better reflect the areas as they are defined (like Nouvelle Athènes and Batignolles-Monceau) rather than conventional arrondissement numbers, because these administrative divisions only partially fit their character (usually the more upmarket ones like the 8th and the 16th).

*Hurdy-gurdy man (and street singer) in the rue Cler*

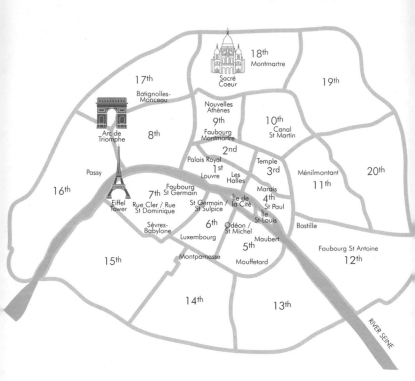

First an outline map of Paris which shows the approximate location of the different districts as we've defined them.

We have not included some 'obvious' districts (the Marais, les Halles, Ménilmontant and Bastille) as places to stay because a better base for visiting them is in immediately adjacent areas such as St Paul for the Marais, the Palais-Royal for Les Halles, Canal St Martin for Ménilmontant and the Faubourg St Antoine for Bastille. These alternative localities are either less crowded or less tourist-dominated; and with a strong character of their own.

The aim has been to delimit areas, manageable in size for exploration on foot, and where there is much of detail and interest to be discovered. No part of traditional Paris is without interest: there are a variety of reasons for not including everything. For example, much of the district around the Gare du Nord and Gare de l'Est is decidedly dreary. The 8th and 16th are excluded as far as hotels are concerned on grounds of cost; but they also have a rather antiseptic quality despite the grandeur of the buildings and the dazzle of riches. Passy, on the western edge of the 16th arrondissement, is an attractive 'village' with a distinctive bourgeois chic, but not enough to warrant more than a visit. Other parts of Paris, in the 13th, 19th and 20th arrondissements, do contain interesting pockets of often ethnic culture – like Belleville in the 20th or the Chinese quarter in the 13th – but they are not for the casually curious and do not provide convenient bases for other explorations. The distinctive, if somewhat self-conscious Buttes aux Cailles district in the 13th is excluded for similar reasons. The 15th arrondisse-

ment mainly lacks the qualities for inclusion: that part near the 7th arrondissement has something to commend it but if your experience of Paris were to be confined to that quarter you would feel, rightly, very much on the fringe of things.

Most people on a first visit head for the Latin Quarter perhaps because it has an exotic ring. If that's your inclination then the Maubert district is proba-bly the best base for an initiation into what the Left Bank has to offer. However, there is a good deal to be

*The class of '68, forty years on...*

said for starting in a less well-known part of the city, perhaps on the Right Bank for which there is no stereotype: a non-standard experience may be a truer one. The different quarters are described in enough detail for you to form your own judge-ment as to what might appeal.

## Right Bank (north of the river)

The *Rive Droite* is a byword for chic, aloof, expensive luxury. The breathtaking window displays of the elegant shops in the rue St Honoré, the rue de la Paix and the like are a distinctive part of the Paris experience. If you are very rich you will have an enjoyable time staying there; and it certainly warrants a day-trip. But typically even the more modest hotels are beyond our price-range, and reasonably-priced places to eat are hard to find.

However, the smart image of the Right Bank does not extend much beyond the magic circle of the 8th and the 16th, perhaps into the western half of the 17th. In fact much of the Right Bank is distinctly shabby yet with a quality of shabbiness that is infinitely appealing, reminiscent of the 1950s photographs of Robert Doisneau. It also includes some areas of Paris little known to tourists like Batignolles, the part of Montmartre that lies behind Sacré-Coeur, and the upper reaches of the 9th arrondissement below the somewhat sleazy Pigalle district. Here are the summary details:

**Faubourg St Antoine**: Close to the frenzied activity of Bastille, a first impression may be that the area is slightly seedy: but it is important to persist. There are no hotels of great charm but several decent ones at a modest price and many excellent bistrots. Add in such features as the Promenade Plantée – a garden walk along what used to be a railway line; the Viaduc des Arts underneath where designer-craftsmen make and sell their creations; the covered market of the place d'Aligre and the surrounding bric-à-brac stalls; the ethnic grocers, often African; the extraordinary décor of Le Train Bleu, the fin-de-siècle restaurant of the Gare de Lyon – and more, and you will revise those first impressions.

**St Paul/Ile St-Louis**: The St Paul area – between the rue St Antoine and the Seine, and opposite the Ile St-Louis – is in contrast to the crowded Marais district to the north. There is an air of provincial calm in its streets which have fewer hotels

*The provincial architecture of old Montmartre*

and shops, though an excellent range of antique shops in the rue St Paul. For such a central area it is remarkably traffic-free, and with the charm of antiquity everywhere in evidence.

The Ile St-Louis itself is a wonderfully preserved district of 17th century houses and elegant quais overlooking the Seine, where alas there are nowadays no hotels. There used to be a very basic one on the quai d'Anjou where I stayed in the 1960s for the equivalent of two euros a night: incredible but true. The main street down the middle of the island is crowded during the day but nonetheless has some peaceful, civilised hotels, two of which are just within our price-range; but if you want to stay there you book months ahead.

**Temple**: A very mixed area and one difficult to define: taken as those streets which lie either side of the rue du Temple,

*Canal St Martin*

running up from the Hôtel de Ville to the place de la République, its character changing from the wholesale clothing outlets at the lower end to the increasingly fashionable area south of République. Much less frequented by tourists than the immediately adjoining Les Halles/Beaubourg district, it lacks an obvious focus but repays careful exploration. It is, in fact, a district which encapsulates the purpose of the present book: good restaurants, hotels, shops and a distinctive ethos that you would probably not find without guidance.

**Canal St Martin**: The quarter around the Canal St Martin has become one of *the* places to live and socialise (for Parisians) but is still little penetrated by tourists. As defined here the area has been extended to the west to take in that part south of the Gare du Nord and Gare de l'Est which repays getting to know and gives a sense of the mixed character of Paris: like the Turkish quarter round the rue du Faubourg St Denis where you will find two excellent brasseries – Brasserie Flo in the cour des Petites Ecuries and Julien in the street itself.

**Nouvelles Athènes**: Properly this term applies to just part of the area included here – specifically the 'classical' bourgeois housing around the place St Georges – but it does set the tone for the quarter as a whole. Largely undiscovered even by the tourists who flock to the sex shows of nearby Pigalle, the character of the area and its comparatively modest housing prices have attracted younger Parisians who would otherwise have had to migrate to the outer suburbs. Particularly in the northern part, the buildings have the character of a Paris that is becoming harder to find as the gentrification of the inner city proceeds.

*Fire-station in Nouvelle Athènes*

**Faubourg Montmartre**: Very centrally-placed, this is a lively area with mercifully unsmart small shops, hotels and restaurants. The 19th century *passages* (shopping arcades) are alone enough justification but there are gems like Chartier – a *bouillon-brasserie* which remains true to its petit bourgeois roots and where it is difficult to spend much more than 20€ on a meal – and the magical confiserie, A la Mère de Famille with its original 19th century shop front and a comprehensive stock of traditional sweetmeats from all over France. Hotels include the Chopin in the passage Jouffroy, built as an hotel when the passage was constructed in 1846.

**Palais-Royal**: This is classic Paris at its best with the enormous range typical of a capital city. Apart from the Palace itself with its splendid gardens and arcades there are very smart, much restored shopping galleries such as Vivienne and

Véro-Dodat and a shabby but more interesting one, Choiseul; traditional bourgeois bistrots like Chez Georges; and one of the finest (and oldest) restaurants in the world: Le Grand Véfour at the top end of the Palais-Royal. For it is the latter that sets the tone for the district. A favourite hotel is nearby – the Molière in the rue Molière, one of those central side streets that attract no traffic.

**Batignolles-Monceau:** Batignolles is an area you won't go to or find unless you know it's there. It lies to the east of the more upmarket part of the 17th arrondissement and north of the Gare St Lazare. This is the place to get a sense of the work-

ing-class Paris of fifty years ago. With a strong 'village' ethos it is not yet designed or developed for tourists so there are fewer hotels but some excellent 'bistrots de quartier'. As defined here the area also takes in the elegant Parc Monceau to the west – a perfect place for a picnic lunch you've bought in the nearby rue de Lévis, one of the best market streets in Paris. If the city had won the bid to host the 2012 Olympics, the athletes' village would have been built near here, perhaps to the detriment of its character.

*Informal style in Montmartre*

**Montmartre:** What every tourist knows and yet doesn't, because tourist activity is focused on a small part of it. Montmartre has a strong local character, most easily apparent to the north and west of the hot-spots of the place du Tertre and Sacré-Coeur, territory little explored by visitors: since they 'know' what's there, they don't look. Bypassing the myth is not the least of the pleasures of discovering anew this part of Paris.

*Parc Monceau*

## Left Bank (south of the river)

The term *Rive Gauche* evokes associations of artists, intellectuals, students and the avant-garde in all its manifestations; and this is not too far from the reality. Here are the colleges and grandes écoles, the studios and galleries alongside antique shops and interior decorators. Some of the oldest parts of Paris are here, having escaped Baron Haussmann's relentless purge of the town planning in the 1860s. So you will find streets and buildings on a smaller scale than the *grands boulevards*; together with the varied street life and many of the famous cafés and bistrots (some now rather expensive). It is also – and always has been – an international area and perhaps this is why it has withstood the main pressures of tourism, although there are some streets like the rue de la Huchette and the immediate vicinity which are shunned by Parisians as a parody of the real thing.

**Montparnasse**: If its literary and artistic associations are largely a thing of the past, the area still retains a strong sense of character with (south of the boulevard) some of the best inexpensive hotels in the city. The brasseries are a living legend: La Coupole, the Sélect, the Dôme and Rotonde face each other across the boulevard, each with its own special character. And if you take the express lift to the top of the 1970s Tour Montparnasse you will have a unique view of the surrounding city.

**Luxembourg**: This is taken as the area to the east and south of the famous gardens (and you're never far from these with their extraordinary variety). Many of the institutions of Paris are to be found within the boundaries of the quarter, including some of the *grandes écoles*, Val-de-Grâce, the Panthéon. And it contains some small, civilised hotels.

**Mouffetard**: Defined by the famous market street with its share of tourist traps, it nonetheless manages to be resolutely local in character and the immediately surrounding area is ideally suited to a shopping expedition with many unusual

*The epitome of Montparnasse: La Coupole from the terrace of the Sélect*

small shops. As you penetrate further to the east you find relatively unexplored territory: by tourists, that is, a part of the city where you need to keep your eyes open for the unexpected detail; and to the north is one of the major Roman sites of Paris, the Arènes de Lutèce.

**Maubert**: The eastern half of what is usually described as the Latin Quarter, the oldest part of Paris with some surprisingly inexpensive hotels and an area which is rewarding to those prepared to go where their instinct takes them. Cutting through from the boulevard St Germain one day to get to the tourist-thronged quais by the Seine, I turned into the rue de Bièvre and came across a small and delightful public garden,

*Musée de Cluny*

deserted except for an old man carefully washing down a bench before sitting on it. You won't find the jardin de la Bièvre on any map; I have sat there many times since but have never seen a car or even a bicycle on the street.

**Odéon/St Michel**: Surely, with Montmartre, the ultimate cliché of Paris? It is certainly something of a magnet for young (studenty) tourists but, perhaps because of its history as the student quarter, retains its character and secrets. And despite the lively antics of those who do not sleep, there are pockets of calm even close to the place St Michel with its 24-hour bustle.

**St Germain/St Sulpice**: Like the Latin Quarter, this old and sometimes elegant part of the city is heavily visited but copes with it while retaining its carefully preserved ethos. If the atmosphere of the 'literary' cafés of the past – Flore and Deux Magots on the boulevard St Germain – is now thick with a variety of Anglo-Saxon accents (you'll find the French at the nearby Café Bonaparte), the quarter's cosmopolitan character is inured to reputation. In the rue Jacob there are some exceptionally quiet hotels, even if they are at the top of our price-range, and elsewhere some of the most famous bistrots and brasseries in the city.

St Sulpice is arguably the smarter place to live: Catherine Deneuve, an icon of Parisian high-style, has her apartment here near the church. It is a good deal more peaceful than St Germain but in the northern part near the boulevard hotels are beyond our defined price-range. Yet as is often the case in Paris, just two streets away (towards the Jardin du Luxembourg) you can find a big difference in price. As a whole a fascinating area of a style discreetly concealed.

**Sèvres-Babylone:** Just to the north of Montparnasse this sector has some distinctively interesting shops: from the food hall in the department store Le Bon Marché (the oldest in Paris and considered by many the best) to myriad smaller specialists in the rue de Sèvres and the rue du Cherche-Midi, to the excellent street market in the boulevard Raspail with its famous *marché biologique* (organic) on Sunday morning.

**Faubourg St Germain:** Dominated by embassies, government institutions and residences, this is not an area of the most obvious appeal but don't be deterred by the impression of a remote formality. Even if you cannot penetrate the façades of the many 18th century houses *(hôtels particuliers)*, you can still appreciate their architectural scale and detail; for example the Hôtel Matignon with its private park, the official residence of the Prime Minister – to be preferred to the President's Elysée Palace on the Right Bank.

**Rue Cler/Rue St Dominique:** The western part of the 7th arrondissement is more mixed in character. Apart from the domineering presence of the Eiffel Tower and the Invalides, it has its share of ministries and embassies and always seems to have bus-loads of security police lurking in side-streets (they are as tough as they look). But the rue St Dominique and the rue Cler, a lively market street, in themselves shift the balance. And with guidance (from this book) you can find other unexpected places of interest and get under the apparently impervious skin of the area.

# When not to go to Paris
# (and what to do if you have to)

From mid-July until the end of August there is a mass exodus of those who live in Paris when their city is given over to tourists who know no better. Most of the restaurants listed in this guide are closed for at least part of that time. That's one problem. But you probably wouldn't want to eat anyway because at the height of summer the temperature can reach debilitating levels: sometimes more than that, as in recent years large numbers of elderly people have died from heat exhaustion and related conditions.

The problem is that in addition to not wanting to eat (coq au vin when the temperature is 30°C and rising loses its appeal) you won't be able to sleep. One of the worst things about Paris in high summer is that the nights are not particularly cooler than the days: there are no cooling sea breezes and the streets and buildings (including your hotel room) seem to retain the day-time heat like a storage radiator. If you must go you should choose a hotel with air conditioning, and this applies any time from mid-June to mid-September.

Is this being too negative? Well, not because it isn't true. What qualifies the assertion is the way the authorities have responded to the almost unavoidable heat wave that descends on the city at this time of year. *Paris Plage* is the astounding enterprise that for just four weeks (last week in July, first three weeks in August) transforms two miles of the Seine embankment into a riotous faux sea-side and has recently been expanded to include the Port de la Gare and the Bassin de la Villette (see p. 227).

*A busy cross-roads opposite the Ile de la Cité*

# Families in Paris

And what about children? It would be idle to pretend that our guide was not primarily aimed at other than selfish adults. But the pattern we propose (living in a local area, shopping and picnicking in the park, going to small or unusual museums, occasional sight-seeing expeditions, visits to ice-cream specialists and so on) is well suited to children for whom a novel set of routines is of great interest.

Taking the longer view, it is never too early to introduce children to the intricacies of Paris and the French language. They will absorb these influences with an unconscious ease which mocks the efforts we made to master the language and culture at school. France is quite definitely another country: they do things differently there. And for children it is the detail of these differences that make up the fascination – from the street cleaners hosing down the pavements in the early morning or a policeman with white gloves and a whistle refereeing the traffic – to the satisfaction of being able to work out the *direction* and *correspondances* on the Métro map.

A few useful points:

1. If you are within reach of Eurostar, it is preferable to flying. The journey is simpler, so less tiring for younger children – and not much more expensive in terms of total time and cost.

2. Be prepared to spend more money on accommodation. Many hotels have 'family' rooms for three or four people and/ or can provide an extra bed or cot. The ideal is a 'suite' or an 'appartement' in a hotel, preferably with a 'cuisinette': there are suggestions on pp. 224-225, together with a list of flat rental agencies. However, rented flats are not usually in the more

interesting or economical areas, are no cheaper and not so flexible as to dates or lengths of stay. The kind of help you can get from a hotel reception (babysitters, doctors, general advice) tips the balance in their favour. To this should be added the helpfulness of chambermaids, particularly if suitably rewarded.

3. Whichever way, having your own cooking/dining facilities will save you a fortune. Even cheap restaurants become expensive when costs are multiplied (and even when there is a special menu for children). The real cost inflation, however, comes from café snacks which swallow up the euros. If you have a large and pleasant apartment you and the children can shop for food – going from one specialist to another. Doing this is also a way of coping with children's conservatism and emphatic tastes; but concessions are necessary so make sure you bring with you the Marmite, Cocopops or whatever! If they help with the shopping, children can choose what appeals to them, and these expeditions have added interest as you go from pâtisserie to charcuterie (often with an excellent range of prepared dishes) to fromagerie and so on.

4. The same applies to shopping for lunch in the park, to which you should make a daily visit because the children's play areas are excellent (see details of gardens in each quarter). And with that strange freemasonry that exists between young children they will soon form friendships – consolidated from day to day.

5. Although 'eating in' is more economical, eating at a restaurant is similarly part of children's experience of Paris. You will normally want to dine earlier than adult hours in the evening: but that makes it easier for restaurants to deal with. There is often a simplified *menu enfants* – or they can simply share yours.

6. The occasional outside-the-district trip will be as much as they want: the six best ones for children are listed on pp. 226-227. The weekly events-listing in *Pariscope* has a section devoted to 'enfants', or 'jeunes' in *L'Officiel des Spectacle*s.

7. The French have high standards and strong views on behaviour and childcare, so be prepared for criticism stated or implied. I once ordered coffee in a restaurant at the end of a meal for my elder son (then aged ten): the waitress refused to bring it, clearly regarding me as unfit to be a parent.

# Down to the detail: a summary

Each of these 'village' communities is covered in a separate section containing the following:

A more extended **introduction**.

Some of the main conventional '**sights**'.

**Quiet hotels** with most double rooms in the price range 75-175€ per night: those with air conditioning are indicated.

**Breakfast**: where to start the day in Parisian style instead of the hotel basement.

**Public gardens**: often not marked on maps and usually called *squares* (with a French accent) – ideal for planning your next itinerary or just to sit (Paris can be hard on the feet).

**Markets**: mainly selling food, these are of three kinds – covered markets, market streets and roving markets (moving along and only on certain days of the week).

**Cheesemongers** (*fromagers*): easily overlooked because they're often small and tucked away – an ideal source for an al fresco lunch. Good bread to go with the cheese is easy to find (see box on p. 35).

Specialist **ice-cream makers** (*glaciers*): everyone's heard of Berthillon but there are others as good or better – and more creative.

**Neglected museums**: a few major collections like the Musée d'Orsay or the Louvre are tiringly over-visited but Paris is full of small, often idiosyncratic museums of great charm and interest.

*Artist in the square beside the church of St Germain-des-Prés*

**Interesting or unusual shops**: Paris is the natural home of the specialist entrepreneur with a carefully assembled stock.

Traditional **bistrots** serving traditional dishes: as distinct from the contemporary variety dishing up 'cuisine inventive'.

**Brasseries**: usually large and a great Paris tradition – important because they are normally open all hours and every day, including Sundays when most other restaurants close.

And as a section on its own towards the end of the book (because they are not distributed evenly across the city): some **special restaurants** where you can have a memorable lunch on the day of departure to lift your spirits (see pp. 206-211).

## *Principal sights*

Under this heading are listed some of the main 'conventional' sights in each area, or in those immediately adjacent – including some of the famous art galleries and museums. This is standard guidebook territory and you can do no better than go to the Michelin *Green Guide* for comprehensive coverage. Some sights are so well-known as to be hardly necessary to identify. If you are one of the half million visitors a day who descend on the Champs Elysées you won't need to be told that the Arc de Triomphe is at the top end – known as l'Etoile because no fewer than twelve avenues radiate out from it.

## *Finding the right hotel (quiet, convenient, not too expensive)*

Paris is full of people who do not sleep (and prevent others from doing so); and some streets have incessant traffic. The emphasis here on quiet hotels is not because the author is insomniac, just that bad experiences have made him feel he might be. Like all European capitals Paris is a very demanding city and you will not cope with it (let alone enjoy it) if you can't get a good night's sleep. Even in the quieter hotels some rooms are better than

*Prices in hotels and restaurants*

*Hotels*: Almost all the room prices given in the hotels listed are in the range 75-175€ per night for a double; and most of the hotels will have cheaper rooms (not recommended) or more expensive ones (if you can afford them).

In the main you get what you pay for, although there are some hotels which represent excellent value for money. For these in particular you must book months in advance. Hotels that have rooms free at peak periods and at short notice are either (a) expensive or (b) badly situated. Hotels with air-conditioning are rarely below the 125€ level.

Many hotels, particularly those in the 'business' class – with IT facilities and so on – increase their rates during the periods of the *salons*, which are large trade fairs of international significance. Needless to say they are held when Paris is at its best – early summer (normally the second week in June) and almost continuously from early September to mid-November. So: book well ahead for these periods and be prepared to pay a surcharge. The off-peak months are January-February and July-August and rates can be much lower then.

*Restaurants*: The restaurants listed are in the range 15-55€ for a two or three-course meal, excluding wine. You should not expect too much at the lower end but the food you can get in the 35-45€ range is of a quality for price unmatched in the UK.

others. If you're not able to inspect the hotel rooms beforehand (normal practice in France) then you should ask for those on the top floor *(au dernier étage)* and at the back *(au fond)* – which are likely to have a view over that wonderful cityscape, the rooftops of Paris. As a general rule rooms on lower floors are noisier if they are at the front, and gloomier if they are at the back; however, in summer top floor rooms can be hot.

To be avoided are 'single' rooms *(chambres simples)* as these are always the worst and often intolerably small. Few rooms in our price range are going to be large and a 'double' room *(chambre avec un grand lit)* will do quite well for one person and doesn't cost much more than a single room (there is often a single occupancy rate anyway). Only very good friends should share a room and if you don't want to share a bed you ask for *une chambre avec deux lits jumeaux.* If your French is up to it or if the receptionist speaks English an initial telephone enquiry is a good idea. Guidance on what to say is given on pp. 214-215. The call needs to be followed up by a letter, fax or e-mail confirming the exact arrangements and giving credit card details as a form of deposit (known as *arrhes*). A letter format should follow the rather elaborate conventions the French still seem to prefer (*Veuillez agréer, Madame, mes salutations les plus respectueuses,* etc): see p. 215 for 'model' layouts. For peak periods (May/June and September/October) bookings should be made not less than three months in advance – at least six months for the more popular hotels – like the **Grandes Ecoles** in Maubert, those in the rue Jacob (6th) or on the Ile St-Louis.

## *Breakfast*

Most tourists take *le petit déjeuner* in their hotel. There's no obligation to do so and it is generally charged extra. It can be good (we say where this is the case) but usually it is not: hotels are obliged by law to offer breakfast and they are rarely enthusiastic about it. Breakfasts are often served in a windowless basement (no good for bedrooms); you get a better view and experience by going to a local café, but note that for the ordinary Parisian breakfast is normally a *tartine* (a length of the narrow baguette known as *ficelle* with butter) and coffee. Brasseries can be the best choice being large and characterful; and they can be very good value. The 9,50€ breakfast at La Coupole in Montparnasse includes freshly squeezed orange juice, enough coffee for three cups, a *pain boule* and two *viennoiseries* (for example a croissant with the French equivalent of an apple turnover or, if you're lucky, a slice of *kugelhopf*, the fruit brioche from Alsace).

Some branches of **Paul** – listed in each quarter where they are found – offer a range of breakfast formules, for example juice, coffee and croissant for less than 5€.

**Salons de thé**, which have become very fashionable and so are mostly found in the smarter arrondissements, sometimes offer breakfast (from 8.30 am) like Dalloyau near the Luxembourg Gardens: but most salons don't open until midday from when they serve light lunches, as well as pastries with teas in far greater variety than in the English equivalent. Much-favoured by well-heeled women of a certain age, they can be a pleasant experience: but they are not cheap.

Since the philosophy of this book is that a good breakfast (preceded by a good sleep) is what you'll need to enjoy your stay in Paris, careful attention is paid to that part of the day which is often neglected in guide books.

## *Public gardens*

There are apparently over 500 public parks and gardens in Paris; in which case I have found only a fraction of them. The mayor of Paris has recently announced plans to ensure that no-one will find themselves more than half-a-kilometre from a garden. In a city where almost everyone (including the rich) lives in a garden-less apartment these public gardens, often very small and known only to locals, are a focus of commu-

*One of the many cast-iron fountains donated by the francophile Sir Richard Wallace, 1840*

nity life. The window they provide on the everyday scene is a large part of their charm. Almost always there is a defined children's play area with seats for parents, and elsewhere seats for those who just want to eat a sandwich or read their paper. They are typically well-maintained, thoughtfully constructed and normally peaceful. The smaller ones are not usually marked on maps and may be located in the kind of side-street you wouldn't think to go down.

An incidental caution: it is a criminal offence to feed pigeons (just pigeons) in Paris and getting on the wrong side of the French police is not a pleasant experience, quite apart from the hefty fine.

## Markets

For many visitors these are the quintessential experience of the city. Parisians are not by nature one-stop shoppers, especially

for fresh food, and clearly enjoy the daily ritual of choosing the fruit and vegetables etc. they are looking for, moving from one stall to another. The displays ravish the eye: colour, style of presentation and the enormous variety appeal to tourists and locals alike.

Actually there are three kinds of markets:

**Market streets** – a concentration of specialist food shops which spill out onto the pavement.

**Covered markets**, not all of which have survived in their original form – the Marché St Germain is nowadays little more than a characterless urban shopping mall, while the Marché St Quentin near the Canal St Martin hasn't changed in over a hundred years.

*Langoustines on a market stall*

**Roving markets** where stalls are set up in the street on certain days of the week – you need to check the days (which are regular) and remember that they are usually open only in the morning, although there is an emerging trend for

## Flea markets, brocantes and vide-greniers

Along with the Latin Quarter, flea markets *(marchés aux puces)* are what everyone has heard about. The biggest and best known is the Marché de St Ouen (Métro: Porte de Clignancourt) but there are others: the Marché de Vanves (Métro: Porte de Vanves) and the Marché de Montreuil (Métro: Porte de Montreuil) – all, as the names suggest, at the outer limits of the city. Generally open weekends only they can be a dispiriting experience: vast quantities of junk and, when it's not, eye-watering prices.

The Marché de Vanves in the avenue Marc Sangnier is by a long way the best, neither too expensive nor too rubbishy. A good place for period household fittings, light shades, door locks, brassware and the like, but with a wide variety of other stalls to pick over. On a Sunday there is an excellent street market in the adjacent boulevard Brune where you can buy whatever you fancy for a picnic lunch. At the Marché de St Ouen – which as a whole is vast and confusing – the Marché Paul-Bert off the rue des Rosiers can be rewarding and provides a necessary focus. The Marché de Montreuil is not worth the effort of getting out there.

My experience is that in general the short-lived *brocantes* – essentially lower-middle level antiques fairs – are better value and more likely to yield something. You feel that the stall-holders (usually part-time professionals) have made an effort to offer items of interest at a fair price. They are listed in *Pariscope*. *Vide-greniers* (attic clearances) – the equivalent of car-boot sales in the UK – are not so widely advertised because, as one might expect, they are local and amateur (and cheap). You need to keep your eyes open in 'your' area for notices and flyers.

afternoon/early evening markets. It is to these markets that traders come in from all over the Ile de France. Standards are high, but so also are prices for the more specialised products.

## Fromagers

There are many good things to eat in France but the extraordinary range of cheeses of quality and character is, perhaps, pre-eminent. Those who produce cheeses and those who sell their products are not just experts but scholars of their domain. And this scholarly passion is evident in the formal sense: Roland Barthélemy (see p.00) is co-author of *Fromages du Monde* (Hachette, Paris, 2003). Marie-Anne Cantin (p.000) has produced her own authoritative guide to 150 cheeses, mainly French (*Guide de l'Amateur des Fromages*, Solar, Paris, 2000). What marks out these enthusiasts?

– A firm adherence to traditional methods of manufacture and the use of *lait cru* (unpasteurised milk). Barthélemy calls pasteurised milk 'dead'. When you compare, for example, a farm-produced camembert with the pasteurised factory product you will agree.

– Careful maturing of cheeses by fromagers in their own cellars on straw, until exactly ready to eat (they often display a list of 'today's best').

Cheeses are classified in various ways (Barthélemy in his book says nature knows nothing of classification), but for practical purposes a simple division from soft to hard is adequate. For the softest cheeses you will need a spoon: for the rest a knife is sufficient. There is a simple folding knife by Opinel which can be bought in hardware stores and tabacs that is ideal and inexpensive (but don't carry it in your hand-luggage on the return journey).

The firmer cheeses are easier to eat; and goats' cheeses are usually in this category and small in size (traditionally because goats give less milk than cows). Almost half the cheeses in a fromagerie will be made from either goats' or sheep's milk. Of the firmer cows' milk cheeses the following are recommended:

*Vieux Comté*: A cross between Gruyère and Cheddar, this is a cheese very popular with the English. It is long to mature (hence 'vieux') – at least 18 months for the best results. Not so good younger than this – a bit rubbery in texture.

*A modest frontage for a top fromager in the Faubourg St Germain*

*Bleu d'Auvergne*: Similar to Stilton and excellent with a dry white wine.

*Beaufort*: Similar to Comté but it doesn't need so long to mature (12-18 months).

*Cantal*: A mild cheese of firm texture, early maturing.

*Tomme de Savoie*: In appearance (and the way it is made) this is very similar to Saint-Nectaire but the texture is firmer and less messy to eat.

*Camembert*: The true *lait-cru* farm cheese from Normandy, properly ripened, is a revelation.

*Livarot*: Another great Normandy farmhouse cheese, a bit runny when mature (at two months) but a strong experience; good with a young, fruity red wine like Syrah.

Finally: do you eat the rind? The experts don't agree. I eat the rind on all the above except Beaufort, Cantal and Comté. It doesn't mean I'm right.

## Boulangers

We don't list these separately because there are so many and they are all more or less good. Indeed almost any experience of bread in Paris evokes enthusiasm among those accustomed to the cooked-from-frozen offerings of our supermarkets. Taste, texture and freshness are the things that strike you most. Actually bread in France has improved over the past two decades with 'artisanal' bread having the most esteem. What can be called *pain de tradition* or *pain de campagne* is specified in detailed legislation (the *Decrét Pain* of 13th September 1993) and subject to rigorous control. There are numerous varieties but bread made with 'sour' dough – *pain au levain* – is in general the most highly rated. Although all bakers offer a good choice, the bread from the top specialists is so delicious you may feel you need nothing else. **Lionel Poilâne** in the rue du Cherche Midi deserves much of the credit though his brother Max, in Montparnasse, doesn't get as much recognition as he deserves. Lionel was killed in a helicopter crash in 2002; his legacy, however, is enduring and the variety of breads from his well-trained staff, presided over by his daughter, is as good as ever.

One chain of bakeries deserves a mention. **Paul** is an international company (there are several branches in London); bearing that in mind the standard they achieve is remarkable. The genius behind the enterprise is Francis Holder, a baker turned businessman. Of particular relevance to picnickers is that they specialise in *petits pains* using a variety of ingredients. Some of the larger shops serve bargain price breakfasts of a high standard if not generous in amount; these are listed in the districts where you can find them. You can also check their website: www.paul.com.

Almost all bakeries sell excellent *sandwiches* – so different from our own as to warrant a French accent. These are usually half-baguette size with good-quality fillings (*rillettes*, ham, tuna, salad and so on); costing around three to four euros they are a meal in themselves.

## *Glaciers*

Ice-cream does not figure very much in French gastronomy and where it appears on restaurant menus, like cheeses it is generally bought in from a small number of specialist suppliers (for example, **Mister Ice** in the 17th arrondissement). To enjoy ice-cream at its best you have to seek out these specialists.

The renaissance of ice-cream dates from the establishment of **Berthillon** in 1954 on the Ile St-Louis, the most famous name of all and suffering a little from its popularity (endless queues).

There have always been outposts of excellence usually Italian in origin, like **Baggi** in the rue Chaptal, 9th, founded in 1850 and **Calabrese** in the rue d'Odessa, 14th, dating from the 1960s; sadly both now closed. But the fashion for ice-cream is a comparatively recent phenomenon and although, like fromageries, glaciers take some tracking down, if you are an enthusiast the effort is worthwhile. Notable is the range of unusual flavours: *thé vert* or avocado at **Le Bac à Glaces**, 7th (p. 185), while the luscious ice-cream at **Amorino** (in various locations, as well as in direct competition with Berthillon on the Ile St-Louis) is an infantilising experience – try their *crema* (vanilla). The imaginative forms almost amount to an artwork, like the ice-cream flowers at **Gelati d'Alberto** in the rue Mouffetard (p. 153); and at **Dammann** the 'spaghetti bolognese' ice-cream – appearance, not flavour!

Chocolate is a keynote in many French desserts so chocolate ice-cream is often exceptional: as at Robert Linxe's **La Maison du Chocolat** – various branches and big business these days (and over-priced); the serious competitor is **Cacao et Chocolat** which I prefer – it's also better value (p. 64-65).

## *Neglected museums*

Nowhere are the lemming-like characteristics of the mass of tourists more evident than in the way that a few museums are besieged by visitors, while others often of greater appeal and personality are, by comparison, hardly visited at all. Examples are the Musée de la Curiosité et de la Magie in the St Paul district

(plenty of children, it is true); the Gustave Moreau museum in the Nouvelles Athènes quarter (Moreau's monument to himself); the superlative elegance of an *hôtel particulier* in the Monceau area, the Musée Nissim de Camondo (dedicated to the aviator son of a famous collector, killed in the First World War); and the Musée de la Chasse et de la Nature in the 7th arrondissement (for those interested in hunting, and with some great paintings). Elsewhere, artists' studios, famous individual art collections, dress and fashion, posters, postage stamps and postal history, photographers, public health, the police force, even boxing – all and many more are to be found. This is one route into what constitutes the distinctive character of Paris life and social history. Opening hours can be idiosyncratic (details are given but check with *Pariscope*).

## *Interesting shops*

There are a number of guides to Paris shops, usually written by women who see shopping as an exclusively female occupation – for example, giving advice on what to do with your husband, poor thing. If your taste is for department stores (the 19th century *grands magasins*) then there is a good choice: Galeries Lafayette and Au Printemps in the boulevard Haussmann (8th), La Samaritaine in the 1st arrondissement with an excellent rooftop vista over the Seine, the Bazar de l'Hotel de Ville (BHV) nearby; and the only one south of the river, Le Bon Marché, in the 7th arrondissement and with the best food hall in Paris. But the most interesting shops, and gender-free, are run by single-minded enthusiasts covering an almost infinite range of specialisms.

There is a shop in the Maubert quarter which deals exclusively with vanilla in its various manifestations; off the rue du Faubourg St Antoine one that specialises in advertising artefacts; in St Paul a specialist in wine antiques; opposite the Luxembourg Gardens a shop offering floral toilet waters of the old-fashioned

*Tradesmen's entrance in the avenue Denfert-Rochereau*

variety – and in the avenue de l'Opéra the aptly named Waaf
et Miaou, where you can buy a fancy-dress outfit for your
favourite pet. A few shops are included in each section as
examples, but you will find many more to your taste – one of
the benefits of getting to know a particular quarter well.

## Traditional bistrots

Our definition excludes those bistrot-type restaurants, of which
there are many, that serve 'cuisine inventive' – often intriguing but
usually the product of too much inventiveness as well as being
singularly unmemorable, even if you felt you enjoyed it at the time.
Incidentally, the term 'nouvelle cuisine' from which it developed
is now obsolete.

Typically the traditional bistrot:

– is small and privately owned;

– serves a limited range of traditional dishes (but sometimes
with an original twist);

– often has a particular regional affiliation and may, in fact,
be owned by a family still based in the Landes or Savoy or the
Auvergne or Normandy, and so on;

– has the kind of interior which owes nothing to the interior
decorator and often has a well-preserved shabbiness;

– will usually have a bar either zinc-covered or (from the '50s)
formica of a distinctly 'untrendy' character;

– will often have 'dishes of the day', the same from week to
week on the same day (hachis parmentier at Polidor on Tuesday;
petit salé aux lentilles at Aux Charpentiers on Wednesday; mijoté
de porc aux pruneaux at Allard on Thursday and so on – we list
them in the relevant entries);

– will usually have regional wines served by the glass or *en
carafe* or *en pichet* (from a ¼ litre upwards);

– often has paper tablecloths and napkins (certainly at the
lower end of the price range);

– rarely costs more than 40€ for a very full meal, and can cost
less than 20€.

The classic bistrot and brasserie dishes are described on

*A retro business card for a bistrot that doesn't take itself too seriously*
*(p. 67)*

pp. 44-45; whether they appear on the *carte* on any particular day normally depends on what is available at the market.

## Menu French

The French for a 'menu' is *carte* – so the latter term is used in that sense in this guide. When the word *menu* is used we mean the *prix fixe* of limited choice. This is usually at two price levels, for two courses or three from:

– *entrée* (starter)
– *plat* (main course)
– *dessert* (pudding)

A drink is often included (*boisson comprise*).

The cheapest menu is normally only available at lunchtime, Monday to Friday (usually called a *formule* or a *midi-express* and very good value); bourgeois establishments like to use the term *menu d'affaires* (business lunch).

Over the past decade or so some restaurants have come to offer a *menu-carte* i.e. a fairly wide choice in the *menu* format with no separate *carte*. The use of this can be taken as a sign of quality and good planning on the part of the restaurateur.

## *Prêt à manger*

Here are some useful guidelines (which apply to brasseries as well):

1. Normally book a table: if a bistrot is small and good it will likely be full. There is nothing quite so flat as the experience of turning up on chance and being told they cannot fit you in. It's a courtesy anyway and you will get a better reception if you have reserved. If the table they offer you is unsatisfactory (too small, near the lavatories or service door) say so politely but firmly: *La table n'est pas satisfaisante*. It is common practice to offer the worst tables first, especially to tourists. Guidance on what to say when booking is given on p. 214 (including how to spell your name in French). The exception to booking is in the lower price ranges (Polidor in the 6th arrondissement, for example, has no time for such formalities) and in some brasseries (La Coupole doesn't accept dinner bookings).

2. Treat dinner as your evening's entertainment. The French normally eat quite late – 9.00 pm is the norm. If you turn up an hour earlier than that you may well find the restaurant empty: 8.30 pm is a reasonable compromise. If you want to eat earlier (and more quickly) go to a brasserie and take their *formule* – a cheap, set meal. Snacks in a café are expensive, often costing more than a proper meal.

3. Note that closing hours given are for last orders – not when they throw you out *(accueil jusqu'à…)*.

4. Particularly in the smaller, cheaper bistrots be prepared to pay cash (see p. 221).

5. Bistrots usually have an English language menu but these are not always clear and are sometimes more difficult to follow than the French version where you can usually work it out, the main exception being the names for different kinds of fish (*cabillaud*, *raie*, *daurade*). For problem menu words see pp. 46-47.

6. The French like their meat very rare and it's important not to have an inferiority complex about this if you don't. Translating the presumed equivalent term on the scale from *bleu* (effectively raw and just seared on the outside) through to *saignant*, *à point*, *bien cuit*, *très bien cuit* doesn't translate the reality.

Unless you were brought up in France, *à point* is likely the most you'll be able to cope with; *bien cuit* is often closer to what we mean by medium.

7. The service charge is by law included in the bill. Most people leave some small change if service is satisfactory, but not more than five per cent even if it is outstanding.

8. If you really like the restaurant go again: the French restaurateur responds well to this sign of approval. But do try out different restaurants: I usually find I like best the one I've just been to...

## Never on a Sunday

Quite simply it is difficult to find a restaurant (*any* restaurant) open on a Sunday; and many are closed on Monday, at least at lunchtime. This is partly tradition and partly a matter of legal requirement for staff. It is usually the larger establishments (like brasseries) that can cope with this; but again continuous opening is a brasserie tradition. In the individual entries DAILY opening is marked in capitals: there is at least one such in each area.

Note that all markets (and many shops) are closed on Monday – but open on Sunday morning.

## Brasseries

Dining in a major brasserie is the ultimate Parisian experience. It's the size – they are usually big, sometimes enormous (La Coupole seats 450) – the buzz of the atmosphere with waiters in black waistcoats and long white aprons dancing around with speed and accuracy, the lights and the glitter: brass, polished mahogany and acid-etched glass in the typical turn-of-the-19th century interior, wildly jazzy in the art deco equivalent (Marty in the Mouffetard area, Charlot in the place de Clichy at the other end of the city).

The ambience is the thing because the food is usually decent but unremarkable and not expensive: for example the 32,90€ dinner menu at Brasserie Flo; while the 30€ lunch menu at Charlot is one of the best quality-for-price in Paris.

Brasseries are normally open every day, mostly from midday and often until the early hours.

## Classic bistrot and brasserie dishes

For whatever reason the techniques of traditional French cuisine do not translate into other cultures so that the experience of the real thing is a revelation. Slow-cooking is a key characteristic: it preserves flavour and makes tough meat tender.

**Aligot**: an Auvergne speciality of potatoes, Cantal cheese and garlic

**Blanquette de veau**: a delicate stew of poached veal, the stock thickened with egg and white sauce; more strongly flavoured than one might suppose but not to everyone's taste

**Boeuf à la ficelle**: usually a cheaper cut of beef tied with string and poached in its own broth until tender

**Boeuf bourguignon**: the great dish from Burgundy, again beef slow-cooked with red wine, onions, mushrooms and bacon

**Boeuf en daube**: slow-cooked beef stew with red wine, onions and tomatoes – a southern French speciality

**Boeuf (à la) mode**: beef marinated in red wine and slow-cooked with vegetables

**Bouillabaisse**: Mediterranean fish stew

**Carbonnade**: beef stew made with beer and onions (from northern France)

**Cassoulet**: the basic ingredients are usually white beans and varying combinations of pork, lamb, sausages, duck and goose (the latter often *confit* – preserved in fat). A speciality of the South-West but widely available in Paris.

**Chateaubriand**: thick fillet steak

**Choucroute garnie**: almost universally found in brasseries (many of which have Alsatian allegiances) this is a mound of sauerkraut with a topping of sausages, pork and ham in various forms. You have to starve first. Excellent with cold Alsatian beer or a good dry Alsace wine

**Choux farci**: cabbage stuffed with sausage-meat, ham and rice

**Coq au vin**: many regions claim this as their own and there are numerous variations; but the basic ingredient is a strongly-flavoured rooster (traditionally a tough old bird) slow-cooked in red wine which is reduced so as to penetrate the flesh

**Garbure**: from the South-West, a variant of cassoulet but more soup-like, with the usual ingredients (preserved meats, beans, etc)

**Gigôt à sept heures**: leg of lamb cooked very slowly so that the fat disappears and the remaining strands of meat are meltingly tender

**Gras-double**: tripe baked with white wine, onions and tomatoes

**Hachis parmentier**: shepherd's pie but more delicious than the school-dinner style we remember. The meat is more unusual in flavour with many variations (pig's cheeks, for example), the potato more puréed and the cheese topping is not the supermarket variety

**Haricot de mouton**: a slow-cooked stew of strongly-flavoured mutton (not lamb) and haricot beans

**Lièvre à la royale**: jugged hare

**Mijoté de porc**: slow-cooked pork stew

**Navarin d'agneau**: lamb stew, often made with spring or summer vegetables

**Petit salé aux lentilles**: salt pork slow-cooked with lentils. Simple and delicious

**Pot-au-feu**: the great dish of the petit bourgeois; cheap cuts of beef simmered for hours with vegetables. The bouillon is often served separately; ditto the bone marrow

**Potée de porc**: hotpot of pork and cabbage

**Poule au pot**: a speciality of Béarn; traditionally a chicken stuffed and cooked with vegetables in its own broth

**Raclette**: hot melted cheese and potatoes with gherkins, a speciality of Savoy

**Rillettes**: coarsely shredded potted meat (usually pork)

**Salmis de pigeon**: pigeon stew

**Tablier de sapeur**: a speciality from Lyon – always on the carte at Moissonnier (p. 165) and Aux Lyonnais (p. 104). It is pig tripe which has been marinated to tenderise it, then breaded and grilled, served with a sauce such as gribiche. The name means 'fireman's apron'

**Tripes à la mode de Caen**: tripe stew from Normandy with cider, calvados and vegetables. You're a real Frenchman if you can eat this…

**Veau Marengo**: veal stew with tomatoes, garlic and mushrooms

FRENCH TRADITIONAL COOKING, NO VEGETARIAN FOOD

## Problem menu words

| | |
|---|---|
| abats | offal |
| aiglefin | haddock |
| ail | garlic |
| aïoli | garlic mayonnaise |
| airelle | cranberry |
| aloyau | beef sirloin |
| amuse-bouche | appetizer |
| ananas | pineapple |
| andouillette | tripe sausage |
| anguille | eel |
| bar | sea bass |
| barbue | brill (similar to turbot) |
| bavaroise | flavoured dessert of cream and gelatine |
| bavette | skirt steak (a bit tough) |
| beignet | fritter, doughnut |
| betterave | beetroot |
| biche | venison (from the female, so more tender…) |
| bigorneau | winkle |
| boudin noir | black pudding |
| boudin blanc | sausage made with 'white' meat (veal, chicken) |
| brochet | pike |
| bulot | whelk |
| cabillaud | fresh cod |
| caille | quail |
| calmar | squid |
| câpre | caper |
| cannelle | cinnamon |
| carbonnade | beef stew with beer and onions |
| carré de… | rack of (lamb etc.) |
| céleri rémoulade | grated celery root in mayonnaise |
| cervelles | brains (of what ever) |
| chevreuil | young venison |
| ciboule | spring onion |
| ciboulettes | chives |
| citron vert | lime |
| civet | game stew |
| clafoutis | baked batter tart (with fruit) |
| cochon de lait | suckling pig |
| coing | quince |
| colin | hake |
| contre-filet | sirloin steak |
| coquille St Jacques | scallop |
| crevette | shrimp |
| crudités | raw, chopped/ grated vegetables |
| daurade/dorade | sea bream |
| dinde/dindonneau | turkey |
| échalote | shallot |
| écrevisse | cray fish |
| entrecôte | rib steak |
| éperlan | whitebait |
| épinard | spinach |
| espadon | swordfish |
| étouffé | braised with little liquid |
| farci | stuffed |
| flétan | halibut |
| (au) four | baked |
| fourré | filled/stuffed |
| fromage de tête | pork brawn |
| gambas | big prawns |
| garbure | another name for the usual meat and bean cassoulet |
| gésier | gizzard |
| gibier | game |
| girofle | cloves |
| girolles | wild mushrooms (expensive!) |
| grenade | pomegranate (grenadine is the syrup made from it) |
| gribiche | sauce made with capers, gherkins, eggs, herbs |
| île flottante | pudding of meringue floating |

| | | | |
|---|---|---|---|
| | in custard *(crème anglaise)* | | tomatoes and peppers (a Basque |
| *jarret de..* | knuckle of ... | | speciality – |
| *joue* | cheek (no part of the animal is wasted) | *poireau* | horrible) leek |
| *kugelhopf* | (many spellings) fruit brioche originating in Alsace | *pommes de terre sarladaises* sliced potatoes baked in goose fat | |
| | | *praire* | small clam |
| *laitue* | lettuce | *pré-salé* | (literally 'salt marsh') – lamb |
| *langoustine* | Dublin Bay prawn (scampi) | | raised on the salt pastures of Nor- |
| *lapereau* | young rabbit | | mandy – a great |
| *lard(on)* | bacon (in cubes) | | delicacy |
| *laurier* | bay leaf | *prune* | plum |
| *lieu* | pollack | *pruneau* | prune |
| *limande* | lemon sole | *quenelle* | dumpling (but not |
| *lotte* | monkfish | | the suet and flour |
| *loup de mer* | sea bass | | lumps we're used |
| *marcassin* | young boar | | to) |
| *merlan* | whiting | *quetsche* | damson |
| *merlu* | hake | *râble* | saddle (of lamb, |
| *mignardises* | petit fours | | rabbit, hare etc.) |
| *(os à) moelle* | bone marrow | *raie* | skate |
| *morilles* | expensive mush rooms (morels) | *raifort* | horseradish |
| | | *ravigote* | vinaigrette sauce, |
| *morue* | salt cod | | often served |
| *mûre* | blackberry | | with fatty meats |
| *muscade* | nutmeg | *ris (de veau* or *d'agneau)* | |
| *myrtille* | bilberry/blue berry | | sweetbreads (the pancreas....) |
| *nature* | plain, ungarnished | *rognons* | kidneys |
| *navet* | turnip | *rouget* | mullet |
| *onglet* | flank steak (incli ned to be tough) | *rouille* | a thick mayon- naise of olive oil, |
| *palourde* | clam | | garlic and red |
| *pamplemousse* | grapefruit | | pepper (served |
| *panaïs* | parsnip | | with fish soup) |
| *parmentier* | made with potatoes (e.g. *hachis parmentier)* | *St Pierre* | John Dory |
| | | *sandre* | perch |
| | | *sanglier* | wild boar |
| *pigeonneau* | young pigeon | *sauge* | sage |
| *pintade* | guinea fowl | *soupe au pistou* | vegetable |
| *piperade* | a mixture of scrambled eggs, ham, onions, | | soup with basil |
| | | *soupion* | squid |
| | | *tourteau* | crab |

## Special restaurants

The very best Paris restaurants are of a level unequalled in my experience. You can dine as expensively in London but nowhere near as well for the price. The range 150-250€ a head (wine extra) will take you into almost all the top restaurants in Paris. And at least once in a while you should splash out and do just that.

But nearly all of these élite establishments (like the Tour d'Argent in the 5th and Le Grand Véfour in the 1st) have a lunch menu for around 70-90€ (still well above the price-range for the dinner restaurants we list and that doesn't include wine). Most of them are concentrated in the expensive, central arrondissements. What it does mean is that on your last day, if your return journey is late afternoon or early evening, you can take in an haute cuisine meal in a luxurious setting without frightening yourself with the bill. However, it is a seductive experience and you can easily lose your head: lunching at the Tour d'Argent I doubled the size of my bill because I couldn't resist finishing with a vintage green chartreuse.

There are other classic restaurants which, while not temples of haute cuisine, offer a good value lunch menu in a famous setting (like La Closerie des Lilas in Montparnasse). Especially delightful in the summer months – roughly late May to the end of September – is to eat outdoors on a terrace or in a garden. Top of my list is the 18th century garden of La Maison de l'Amérique Latine on the boulevard St Germain.

## Over to you

A guide should be just that: providing a lead, helping the reader to find a way through the complex experience of getting to know Paris, at least in the essential components of an enjoyable holiday. And if your interest is engaged by the approach we propose it will be the first of many visits: building on this framework (it is nothing else) through all those personal discoveries and insights to make up your own version of this wonderful city.

MILLET

IN MEMORY OF MY MOTHER,
WHO NEVER KNEW PARIS

PARISIANS' PARIS

*The Quartiers*

# 1. Faubourg St Antoine (and for Bastille)

Social fashions seem to be determined on the one hand by the very rich who occupy a world of their own from which new habits and styles filter down, and on the other by the young, without much money, but with firm ideas on what constitutes a good time. And the bourgeoisie in between follow when and where they can.

The Bastille phenomenon, which goes back some thirty years as far as I can tell, has gathered momentum until it has become well-known; and then, as is the nature of such things, the originators have tended to move on so that the fashionable territory has expanded in two main directions: north up to the Canal St Martin (see that section) and east/northeast around the Faubourg St Antoine and up to Ménilmontant.

The original focus remains in those streets to the east of the place de la Bastille, particularly the rue de la Roquette, the rue de Charonne and the rue de Lappe but also the many small adjoining streets and alleys. Subsequently the sector has spread and widened, penetrating old working-class districts. And these progressive changes affect the character of adjacent areas. If we have excluded the Bastille sector as a place to stay it is not so much because it is tourist-dominated but because, like nowhere else in the city, it is thronged by young (or youngish) Parisians who in localised areas keep going until the early hours. Even if you join in you need to be able to retreat to a calmer setting.

The quarter we have delimited is still largely unfashionable and quite cheap, particularly as you get nearer to the place de la Nation. It is also relatively undeveloped in the sense of social change and yet change is coming. For example, many of the better bistrots in terms of quality and value are to be found here; middle-class Parisians of modest means are now more likely to eat in the 11th and 12th arrondissements than in the 5th and 6th. Cheaper rents advantage the enterprising restaurateur; and the customers follow.

There are no major sights around the Faubourg St Antoine itself. But there is much of interest that doesn't qualify as a 'sight'. The district was the centre of furniture-making for centuries, and there are still many cabinet-makers (*ébénistes*) 'restoring' antiques for the trade. But retailers abound: if you want fake Second Empire furniture you'll find it here. And there is one of Paris' most characterful market areas in and around the place d'Aligre.

On the whole regular tourists don't come here to stay: they are missing something.

## Principal sights

**Place de la Bastille**: home to the Opéra Paris-Bastille (1989), perhaps one of President Mitterrand's less successful enterprises, and hotly debated then as now. It was officially opened on Bastille Day (14th July) to mark the Bicentenary of the storming of the infamous prison. The bronze Colonne de Juillet (1836) in the centre of the place overtops the surrounding buildings and catches the sun with its gilt winged figure of Liberty.

## Quiet hotels

### Ibis Bastille Faubourg St Antoine
*13 rue Trousseau, 75011*
*Tel: 01 48 05 55 55*
*Fax: 01 48 05 83 97*
*E-mail: h3577@accor-hotels.com*
*Métro: Ledru-Rollin*
*66 rooms*
*Price: 102€ for a double room;*
*135€ for an 'appartement'*
This hotel, part of a reliable good-value international chain (but French-based) replaces a former block of studios much beloved of the back-packing young. It is well-situated and half of the rooms overlook a garden at the back (and so are quieter). The place d'Aligre market is nearby.

### Hôtel des Trois Gares
*1 rue Jules César, 75012*
*Tel: 01 43 43 01 70*
*Fax: 01 43 41 36 58*
*E-mail: h3g@tiscal.fr*
*www.hotel-des-trois-gares.com*
*Métro: Bastille/Gare de Lyon*
*36 rooms*
*Price: 85€ for a double room*
*with shower, 90€ with bath;*
*some larger rooms AIR*
*CONDITIONED at 110€*
This has been an hotel for a very long time. I have a c.1915 guide-book by the Touring Club de France which lists it under the same name. Conveniently placed, it is a great bargain – particularly the most 'expensive' rooms – as air conditioning is rare anywhere near this price-level. In a surprisingly quiet street opposite the Port

de l'Arsenal, this is a not-much-visited part of central Paris even though it is an excellent base for whatever you might want to do.

### Hôtel des Pyrénées
*204 rue du Faubourg St Antoine, 75012*
*Tel: 01 43 72 07 46*
*Fax: 01 43 72 98 45*
*E-mail: reservation@hotel-pyrenees.net*
*Métro: Faidherbe-Chaligny*
*33 rooms*
*Price: 70€ for a double room with shower, 80€ with bath*
Despite being on the main road this is a quiet hotel, particularly if you take a back room overlooking the courtyard. A cut above most of the others in the locality, it is very well-maintained under the vigilant eye of the proprietor (female).

This is still a low price area to stay (and eat): the enterprising and good value bistrot Chez Ramulaud (p. 58) is almost opposite.

# Breakfast

### Le Square Trousseau
(see main entry p. 58)
*1 rue Antoine Vollon, 75012*
*Closed: the whole of August*
*Open: DAILY from 8.00 am*
A superlative place for breakfast, especially in mild weather when you can take it at the outside tables. There are no inclusive formules: reckon on 10-14€ depending on what you order. On balance, my first choice.

### Le Train Bleu
(see main entry p. 58)

*Gare de Lyon, place Louis Armand*
*Open: DAILY 8.00 – 11.00 am for breakfast*
Of course, travellers need sustenance at all hours and you can get snacks and drinks outside meal times in the large bar area. But, for present purposes you can come here for breakfast (fresh orange juice, café crème and 'viennoiseries') for 18€ in a fantastic (correct adjective) setting. If you're staying nearby you should do it at least once.

### Brasserie l'Européen
(see main entry p. 59)
*21 bis boulevard Diderot*
*Open: DAILY 6.30 – 11.00 am*
Good for an early breakfast, and on any day of the week when cafés are often closed or open later, on Sunday for example.

A bright start to the day, sitting in the window overlooking the façade of the Gare de Lyon. There is a formule at 5,50€ which includes coffee/chocolate/tea, a croissant and a tartine beurrée. But if you must have fresh fruit juice it'll add 4,20€ to the bill!

### Le Bistrot du Peintre
*116 avenue Ledru-Rollin*
*Closed: Christmas Eve and Christmas Day*
*Open: DAILY from 7.00 am (10.00 am Sunday)*
This art nouveau café has eye-catching appeal and as it's on the corner into the rue de Charonne it is in fashionable territory. Meals are served continuously from noon to midnight but you can get better value elsewhere.

Included here as a character-ful breakfast spot, especially if the weather allows you to sit outside. Inside is a bit smoky (a rearguard action will be fought here) but it's very popular with locals and has an attractive, slightly raffish style. Even if you sit at a table, a large café crème and a croissant will only cost 4,20€; or you could save more by leaning up against the zinc bar with the locals.

### Le Duc de Richelieu
(see main entry p. 58)
*5 rue Parrot*
*Closed: Sunday*
*Open: from 7.00 am*
The early opening hours mean that this café/bistrot is also a good place for a not-too-expensive breakfast in a relaxed atmosphere.

A large café crème and a crois-sant cost 5,10€ (no jam: that's for tourists).

## Public gardens

### Promenade Plantée/Jardin de Reuilly
This overhead walkway running along the avenue Daumesnil, and effectively part of a system that enables you to travel on foot from Bastille to the Bois de Vincennes, is a triumph of urban planning and regeneration. The four-kilometre promenade follows the course of the railway that closed in 1969. The transformation of the line into a walkway and the archways beneath into a series of upmarket arts and crafts studios and show-rooms (the Viaduc des Arts – see p. 00) was not completed until

1989. It has now achieved an established maturity, including sun-traps with seats, pergolas and ornamental ponds. Planted with both wild and cultivated trees and shrubs it is a not-too-challenging walk and the jardin de Reuilly at the far end – part of modern Paris, surrounded by new buildings – provides a contemporary setting for picnicking and with good provision for children. The nearby glacier (Raimo – see below) is an attractive extra.

You could easily spend a half-day walking and exploring with the Promenade as a focus. Strongly recommended.

### Jardin de Paris-Arsenal
*Location: between the boulevard de la Bastille and alongside the stretch of water known as Port de l'Arsenal.*
A neglected area as far as tourists are concerned, it has much to commend it, particularly if you like looking at yachts. There are three parallel longitudinal terraces: a treed walk with benches; a floral walk with pergolas and benches; and the quayside with a view of the marina.

A small children's play area is to be found about half-way along.

### Square Raoul Nordling
*Location: in the shadow of the Church of St Bernard between the rue St Bernard and the rue Charrière.*
Entirely given over to a children's playground, separated by a pedes-trian area (with trees and benches) from the:

### Square Louis Majorelle
*Location: between the rue de la Forge Royale and the rue St Bernard.*
Strictly for adults: trees and shrubs intersected by concrete paths. No grass but plenty of seats; a haven.

### Square Trousseau
*Location: on the southern side of the rue du Faubourg St Antoine near the Ledru-Rollin Métro station and between the rue Charles Baudelaire and the rue Antoine Vollon.*
The best garden in the area with the top-rated restaurant of the same name at the southwest corner. Not much grass but attractive flowerbeds and mature trees. A good play area for children and a fine central bandstand.

## Markets

### Place d'Aligre, 75012
This is really three markets:

– a **covered market** (**Marché Beauvau**) open the usual hours, 8.00 am – 1.00 pm and 4.00 – 7.30 pm, morning only on Sunday and closed Monday, with the best stalls for food – all high quality specialists;

– an **open air market** – fruit and vegetable stalls in the rue d'Aligre, bric-à-brac stalls in the place d'Aligre, normally mornings only;

– a **market street** (the rue d'Aligre) where individual shops have their own opening hours but roughly the same as for the covered market.

In many ways the most diverse and interesting market area in Paris and in a compact setting, notable for its multi-ethnic character – particularly North African. You'll find yourself being handed small advertisements for 'grands marabouts' (allegedly 'holy men') who will, amongst other things, rid you of those evil spells that have been troubling you. So now you know.

### Avenue Ledru-Rollin, 75012
*Open: Thursday 7.00 am – 2.30 pm and Saturday 7.00 am – 3.00 pm*
Located between the rue de Lyon and rue de Bercy. This is a good basic market but not as interesting as the Place d'Aligre.

See also the **street market** on the boulevard Richard Lenoir (Marché Bastille) on Thursday and Sunday mornings (p. 64).

## Fromagers

### Androuet
*15 rue d'Aligre, 75012*
*Closed: Monday, and Sunday afternoon*
*Closed : Tuesday to Friday, 9.30 am – 1.00 pm and 4.00 – 7.30 pm; Saturday 9.30 am – 7.30 pm; Sunday 7.30 am – 1.30 pm*
A branch of the entirely reliable chain of fromagers. Buy your bread from the famous organic bakery **Moisan** at 5 place d'Aligre.

### Fromager Lanquet
*Marché Beauvau (covered market in the place d'Aligre), 75012*

*Closed: Monday, and Sunday
afternoon*
*Open: market hours, as above*
This is a superlative fromagerie
and you won't find it in other
guidebooks. A fine range in
superb condition with some of
the rarer goats' cheeses like *tomme
de chèvre pyrénées* and *ardi gosna*
from the Basque country. They
even have (unpasteurised) English
cheddar.

## Glaciers

### Raimo
*59-61 boulevard de Reuilly, 75012*
*Closed: Monday*
*Open: 9.00 am through to 1.00 am*
Although just outside our area, as
an establishment dedicated to ice-
cream and its elaborations, for
enthusiasts it is worth the trip.
Founded in 1947, since when little
seems to have changed, it has an
extensive repertoire of flavours to
which it adds with discretion
(lychee is a recent one).

Most ice-cream parlours in
Paris are on the small side but
Raimo is large – plenty of tables
inside and along the terrace. The
range of parfaits and the like is
extensive and includes classics like
Poire Belle Hélène and their own
version of Melba (with red fruits).
As these can easily cost 8-9€ and
are high in calories you could
regard such self-indulgence as
lunch; or for the complete experience you could always have one of
their speciality cocktails such as
Porto Flip, a combination of port,
egg, cognac and Gordon's gin!

### Galler
*13 rue d'Aligre, 75012*
*Closed: Monday, and Sunday
afternoon*
*Open: 9.00 am – 7.00 pm
(Sunday to 1.00 pm)*
'Supplier to the Belgian Court': a
high class chocolatier which sells a
limited range of excellent ice-
creams (nine flavours) with
chocolate and coffee predominat-
ing. You get one boule for 1,90€,
two for 2,70€ and three for 3,50€.
You can also try their macaroons
and hot chocolate.

### Village Corse
*38 allée Vivaldi, 75012*
*Closed: Sunday and Monday*
*Open: 11.30 am – 7.30 pm*
I demand full credit for tracking
down this Corsican glacier. The
allée Vivaldi is part of the master
plan leading from the jardin de
Reuilly into a row of housing
blocks with a shopping parade
which, like such things, doesn't
appear to be a commercial success.
But the Village Corse offers Corsican dishes and speciality ice-cream
with flavours like marron (chestnut) and cédrat (sharp Corsican
lemon): excellent quality and cheap
at 1,50€ for one boule: whether it
survives is another matter.

## Neglected museum

### Musée du Fumeur
*7 rue Pache, 75011*
*Métro: Voltaire*
*Closed: Monday and public
holidays*
*Open: afternoons 2.00pm–7.00pm*

*Entrance: 4€*

A delightful museum of everything connected with the history of smoking in a slightly out-of-the-way location. Well worth a visit: you don't have to be an addict to enjoy.

## Interesting shops

### La Maison du Cerf-Volant

*7 rue Prague, 75012*
*Métro: Ledru-Rollin*
*Closed: Sunday and Monday*
*Open: 11.00 am–2.00 pm and 3.00–7.00 pm*

Near the place d'Aligre market this is an excellent example of the French specialist entrepreneur. Here they sell kites – of all kinds, sizes and complexity. Whilst some are suitable for children and amateurs, for many you have to be a dedicated enthusiast; and willing to spend the money.

They also sell a range of boomerangs, skateboards and the like – presumably on the principle that they also fly?

### Aladine

*12 rue Trousseau, 75012*
*Métro: Ledru-Rollin*
*Closed: Sunday and Monday*
*Open: 11.00 am–7.00 pm*

Here you can find advertising artefacts from the past hundred years and, for a small shop, the stock is remarkable. The dynamic owner also runs a nearby café so she may close at lunchtime. Prices are modest for the range and quality; and it's all original – no reproductions.

### Viaduc des Arts

*Avenue Daumesnil, 75012*
*Métro: Ledru-Rollin*
*Open: Monday to Friday:*
*variable hours.*

There are sixty arches here hosting designers/entrepreneurs, some more workshop-like in character than others. A veritable showcase of design-craft which you should allow time to explore.

Prices tend to be full and credit cards are only sometimes accepted. If you are a serious buyer you will need more than one visit – and will receive correspondingly serious attention. No time for time-wasters, however.

### Le Depôt-Vente Citeaux

*Rue de Citeaux (opposite*
*L'Ebauchoir, p. 00), 75012*
*Métro: Faidherbe-Chaligny*
*Closed: Sunday*
*Open: 11.00 am–7.00 pm*

With a narrow entrance this is a vast hall of 'antiques' and decorative items roughly from 1900-1960. Fascinating for a browse though not cheap (in Paris bargains are largely a myth) but it is certainly interesting. And you may find something that particularly appeals (for example those slatted folding garden chairs, suitably battered, at 38€).

## Bistrots

### Traversière

*40 rue Traversière, 75012*
*Tel: 01 43 44 02 10*
*Métro: Ledru-Rollin*
*Closed: Sunday, Monday and the first three weeks in August*

*Open: noon – 2.30 pm and
7.30 – 10.30 pm*
With a traditional range of dishes, including game in season, this medium-priced restaurant offers a lunchtime formule of two courses for 19,50€ and three for 23€. The dinner menus are priced at 30€ and 39,80€: à la carte (if you need it) will cost little more than the latter. Wine is available by the glass at 5€, en pichet at 8,50€ for a ¼ litre, and pro rata.

## A la Biche au Bois
*45 avenue Ledru-Rollin, 75012
Tel: 01 43 43 34 38
Métro: Ledru-Rollin
Closed: Saturday and Sunday
(Monday lunchtime), the
first three weeks in August,
Christmas to New Year
Open: noon – 2.30 pm and
7.00 – 11.00 pm*
Better value than many other restaurants in the more fashionable sector near Bastille, this bistrot as the name suggests has a speciality of game in season when it is advisable to book. The cooking is not sophisticated and the portions are substantial: a meal here is not to be rushed. There is a recommended prix fixe at 25€ but à la carte won't cost you more than 30€.

They have a speciality of aperitifs and good value, decent quality wines at around 15€ a bottle; a ⅔ litre pichet costs around 9-10€. The only drawback has been the sometimes rather smoky atmosphere which is set to change. In any case there is a terrace where smokers will doubtless congregate.

## L' Ebauchoir
*43-45 rue de Citeaux, 75012
Tel: 01 43 42 49 31
Métro: Faidherbe-Chaligny
Closed: Sunday, and Monday
lunchtime
Open: noon – 2.30 pm and 8.00 –
11.00 pm*
Traditional food and amazing value. The lunchtime menu is 13,50€ for three courses and 12€ for two. The 25€ menu is on a different plane (three courses and 22,50€ for two). There is no menu in the evening, so à la carte will cost around 40€.

Don't forget to try the rice pudding (*riz grandmère*). Wines cost 3-6€ for a glass, 16,50-34€ for a bottle.

## L'Encrier
*55 rue Traversière, 75012
Tel: 01 44 68 08 16
Métro: Ledru-Rollin
Closed: Sunday (Saturday lunch-
time) and the whole of August
Open: noon – 2.15 pm and
7.30 – 11.00 pm*
You need to book at this local bistrot run by a workers' cooperative. It is highly popular so otherwise you take your chance on getting a table. There is a formule express (pl + salade + dess) for 18€ and an even cheaper one at 14,50€. The 24€ menu of three courses offers an exceptional choice but if you want to go à la carte it will cost you 30€ at the outside. Wines are 3,80€ for a ¼ litre pichet, 6,90€ for a ½ litre.

This is a very convivial place so you have to be in the mood for it: not for solitary, reflective dining but recommended.

## Le Square Trousseau

*1 rue Antoine Vollon, 75012*
*Tel: 01 43 43 06 00*
*Métro: Ledru-Rollin*
*Closed: the whole of August*
*Open: DAILY noon – 2.30 pm*
*and 8.00 – 11.00 pm (and from*
*8.00 am for breakfast)*

A small belle époque restaurant with some of the best cooking in the area. Dishes are almost entirely traditional (gigot à sept heures, for example) but usually with a minor 'inventive' addition which enhances rather than detracts from the character. Price for quality is exceptional especially on the lunch menus at 21€ and 25€; à la carte dinner will cost around twice that. Wines are quite fully priced with nothing below 19€ a bottle: but it's good stuff.

## Le Duc de Richelieu

*5 rue Parrot, 75012*
*Métro: Gare de Lyon*
*Closed: Sunday*
*Open: 7.00 am through to 1.00*
*am (from noon for meals)*

Booking is not necessary at this recently established large café-bistrot where Meat is King. Located near the Gare de Lyon the carte typically includes staples such as pot au feu, steack au poivre and (for two) côte de boeuf. There is a bargain two-course menu for 14,50€, which is served at dinner as well as lunch, with three or four choices (e.g. céleri remoulade, boeuf braisé aux carottes). A la carte costs around 30€. A decent wine list (from around 20€ a bottle) but there are wines by the glass.

An excellent atmosphere – regulars are embraced by the patron. Witty touches: the carte for each day lists the saint whose day it is – 'but we are not a religious house'.
Recommended also for breakfast.

## Chez Ramulaud

*269 rue du Faubourg St Antoine,*
*75012*
*Tel: 01 43 72 23 29*
*Métro: Faidherbe-Chaligny*
*Closed: Saturday lunchtime and*
*Sunday; a week at Christmas;*
*and two weeks in August*
*Open: noon – 2.30 pm and*
*8.00 – 11.30 pm*

This newish bistrot offers a combination of traditional and innovative dishes with substantial portions and some well-priced menus, particularly at lunchtime when you can have a main course for 10€, two courses for 15€ and three for 17€.

There is a dinner menu–carte at 29€, à la carte being perhaps 50 per cent more than that – but you won't need it. The good value wine list is well balanced and includes little-known wines from the South-West which go well with dishes of that character.

Bottles are 18-140€ with many in the range 30-40€, but wines are available by the glass at 4€ or 12€ for a ½ litre pichet.

Booking is essential for dinner.

# Brasseries

### Le Train Bleu

*Gare de Lyon: place Louis*
*Armand, 75012*
*Tel: 01 43 43 09 06*
*Métro: Gare de Lyon*
*Open: DAILY 11.30 am – 3.00*
*pm and 7.00 – 11.00 pm (open*
*earlier for breakfast in the bar*
*area). See also entry for Sunday*
*brunch (p. 210)*

You enter the main concourse of the Gare de Lyon where the broad double staircase to the first floor restaurant is unmissable. The dining room itself beggars description. The gilt excesses, the paintings of the destinations (as they were) for travellers en route, the brass luggage racks and coat stands, the etched glass light shades, dazzle the eye.

It is hard to be objective about the food: it is certainly decent, substantial brasserie fare and entirely traditional. What lifts the experience – and cannot be dissociated from it – is the sumptuous belle époque interior dedicated to the theme of rail travel.

There is a prix fixe menu at 43€; à la carte costs at least half as much again. The carte includes many classic dishes with a strong emphasis on fish. A special 84€ menu offers four courses plus a glass of champagne plus a half-bottle of wine (and water). That is good value if it contains the dishes you want. There are few wines under 40€ a bottle, but there are some half-bottles and wines are available by the glass (5-9,50€). Best value is probably the buffet-style Sunday brunch for 35€.

If you're lucky you'll encounter the house cat – a large white and marmalade creature called Polo, who, when he's not stalking around with an air of self-possession, likes to lie stretched out on one of the leather armchairs in the bar area.

On food alone it doesn't warrant the expenditure: as a total experience it is worth every centime.

### Brasserie l'Européen

*21 bis boulevard Diderot, 75012*
*Tel: 01 43 43 99 70*
*Métro: Gare de Lyon*
*www.brasserie-leuropeen.fr*
*Open: DAILY 11.00 am through*
*to 12.30 am for meals (from 6.30*
*am for breakfast)*

Plats cuisinés (cooked meals) in brasseries are not usually their strength. Sometimes, as here, they are mediocre. So why is this brasserie included? For two reasons: it opens every day including Sunday, in an area noted for evil restaurants; and the shellfish is excellent and fresh – the vast turnover guarantees that. Recommended is the 32€ plateau des fruits de mer, very good with a ¼ litre pichet of riesling at 5,70€.

One tip: resist the blandishments of the waiters or you'll end up spending more than you intended or expected.

# 2. St Paul/Ile St Louis (and for the Marais)

There is something perverse, a kind of *snobisme* (the word doesn't quite translate) in referring to 'tourists' as if they were another race and you weren't one yourself. But the justification for that paradox is easily found by a visit to the Marais at peak periods (roughly 11.00 am to 5.00 pm) on any day of reasonable weather.

The enthusiasm for what one recent guidebook refers to as the 'magical Marais' has a lot to do, in cause and effect, with the vast and expensive renovation of the area. As a schoolboy over fifty years ago I recall going with a friend to visit an elderly retired general in a second-floor apartment in the place des Vosges. It is memorable because the general, speaking in the slow, measured tones of the French upper class, enabled me to understand every word he said. That and the unanalysed impression of an area with the gentle patina of age everywhere in evidence remain with me. Of course the district was in danger of dissolution but the subsequent restoration and cosmetic treatment have taken something subtle away.

The best time to see the place des Vosges (which *is* magical) is very early before breakfast. If you stay in one of the hotels in the St Paul area, you can slip across the rue St Antoine to sit in the central garden and absorb the experience, as the morning light enhances the rose-coloured brick of the old houses. Why all this about the Marais? Jane Austen would have understood. To value the less showy and dazzling sister you have to appreciate and recognise the charms of the celebrated beauty, because they are real enough.

The St Paul district is so much quieter than the Marais that, at all times of day, you can see it better. Its sights are not in the main dramatic, although I find the 15th century Hôtel de Sens one of the most visually stunning experiences in Paris.

The Ile St-Louis is a fine place to stay, provided you get

yourself out after breakfast and don't return until late afternoon. All the hotels are in the central street of St Louis-en-l'Ile; and almost all the shops, including Berthillon (p. 64), which attracts disproportionate custom. Actually the quais are relatively deserted and the end of the island which faces the Ile de la Cité provides a splendid breakfast spot (Le Flore en l'Ile). It is at this time of day that you see the island (and the view) at its best. In other words, you need to shape the pattern of your day round the realities of tourism; with that you will come away with some memorable images, and a sense of place.

## Principal sights

It is quite difficult to pick things out under this heading. The Ile St-Louis and the districts of St Paul (and the Marais) are full of 17th and 18th century houses and churches of a greater or lesser scale and corresponding distinction. The Michelin *Green Guide* provides excellent coverage and you are referred to that. What follows is a selection, by no means exhaustive:

**Eglise St-Paul St-Louis** (17th century), rue St Antoine.

**Hôtel de Sens** (15th century), rue du Figuier.

**Eglise St-Louis-en-l'Ile** (17th century), rue St-Louis-en-l'Ile.

And in the Marais:

**Place des Vosges** (early-17th century and originally the place Royale) with Victor Hugo's house (from 1832 to 1848) at no. 6.

**Hôtel de Sully** (17th century), rue St Antoine, with a fine courtyard and garden.

**Hôtel Carnavalet** (16th-17th century), rue de Sévigné: the museum of the city's history.

**Musée Picasso at the Hôtel Salé** (17th century), rue de Thorigny: a comprehensive collection in a superb setting.

**Musée Cognacq-Jay** at the Hôtel Donon (mainly late-16th century), rue Elzévir: the 18th century art collection of the founder of the department store Samaritaine.

**Synagogue** (1913) rue Pavée (off the rue des Rosiers in the traditional Jewish quarter): by Hector Guimard, its undulating façade more restrained than his better-known art-nouveau Métro entrances.

## Quiet hotels

**Hôtel St-Louis Marais**
*1 rue Charles V, 75004*
*Tel: 01 48 87 87 04*
*Fax: 01 48 87 33 26*
*E-mail: slmarais@noos.fr*
*www.saintlouismarais.com*
*Métro: Sully Morland/St Paul/Bastille*
*16 rooms*

*Price: 140€ for a superior double*
*room with bath; standard double*
*with shower 115€*
The sort of hotel (like the area)
which is easily overlooked because
of its slightly out-of-the-way loca
tion. Extremely well-maintained
and equipped it has a charm all its
own, being housed in what was
once a 17th century convent.

## Hôtel Castex
*5 rue Castex, 75004*
*Tel: 01 42 72 31 52*
*Fax: 01 42 72 57 91*
*E-mail: info@castexhotel.com*
*www.castexhotel.com*
*Métro: Bastille*
*30 rooms AIR CONDITIONED*
*Price: 150€ for a double room*
*(but see promotional offers)*
This very well-maintained hotel is
in a quiet street and in a building
which is mainly 17th century. The
proximity of the highly recommended Café de la Poste (p. 67)
and the major sights of the Marais
and the islands add to its value.
Air conditioning at this price and
in a hotel so central is another
point in its favour, especially in
the summer months.

## Hôtel du Septième Art
*20 rue St Paul, 75004*
*Tel: 01 42 77 04 03*
*Fax: 01 42 77 69 10*
*E-mail: hotel7art@wanadoo.fr*
*www.paris-hotel-7art.com*
*Métro: St Paul*
*23 rooms AIR CONDITIONED*
*Price: 100-145€ for a*
*double/twin room*
The Seventh Art is, of course, the
cinema and the theme is every-

where in evidence in this enormously popular hotel which
represents excellent value. Room
sizes are variable (reflected in the
price range); the bigger rooms are
worth the extra. However, you
need to book months ahead especially for peak periods and a
deposit equal to one night's stay is
required. Well-known to those on
the fringes of show business so
you can be sure of a diverse clientèle. Great fun.

## Hôtel des Deux Iles
*59 rue St-Louis-en-l'Ile, 75004*
*Tel: 01 43 26 13 35*
*Fax: 01 43 29 60 25*
*E-mail: hotel.2iles@free.fr*
*Métro: Pont Marie*
*17 rooms AIR CONDITIONED*
*Price: 170€ for a double room*
This is one of only two hotels
(same ownership) on the island in
our price-range. Rooms are not
large, but well-maintained and the
street is fairly quiet at night; and a
delight to wake up to in the morning before the day tourists arrive.
As this kind of hotel is everyone's secret find it is essential to
book months ahead.

## Hôtel de Lutèce
*65 rue St-Louis-en-l'Ile, 75004*
*Tel: 01 43 26 23 52*
*Fax: 01 43 29 60 25*
*E-mail: hotel.lutece@free.fr*
*Métro: Pont Marie*
*23 rooms AIR CONDITIONED*
*Price: 185€ for a double room*
Most of the same comments about
the sister hotel above apply here;
prices used to be the same but have
now edged higher at the Lutèce –

probably worth the difference. The rooms on the upper floors are slightly larger (and lighter) than those on the lower floors; those on the sixth floor are particularly recommended. For quality and location this is good value.

# Breakfast

### Le Flore en l'Ile
*42 quai d'Orléans*
*Open: DAILY from 8.00 am*
Breakfast here is almost twice the price of the hotel equivalent but you have a partial view (the best, rear view) of Notre-Dame, and that's worth the extra.

There is a choice of menus but the one called *Le Ludovicien* at 15€ comprises:
- coffee or tea or chocolate
- fresh fruit juice
- viennoiseries (croissants &c)
- butter and jam
- cereals

Sit outside in good weather, inside by the window when it's cold. A full price but worth getting up for.

# Public gardens

### Square Henri Galli
*Location: junction of the quai Henri IV and the quai des Célestins.*
This small garden is rather isolated by traffic and tends to be the province of those who practise intemperance. So: not particularly appealing, but it's there. Its claim to fame is that it contains the sole vestige of the old Bastille prison

remaining above ground; parts of the foundations are incorporated into the Métro station.

### Square Barye
*Location: the eastern end of the Ile St-Louis beyond the boulevard Henri IV.*
Cut off from the rest of the island by the boulevard, this small garden shaped like the stern of a ship with its narrowing terraced sections is never crowded. Not much grass but the mature trees and shrubs make up for it. There is a gate to one side (easily missed) which gives access to the riverside quais.

### Square Albert Schweitzer
*Location: between the Hôtel d'Aumont and the rue de l'Hôtel de Ville.*
Very small – just a children's playground - but there are tree-shaded seats around the play area. On the other side of the road there are a few stone benches overlooking the exquisite formal garden of the Hôtel de Sens – ideal for a quiet lunch or a thoughtful quarter of an hour.

If you continue past the Hôtel de Sens you come to the tiny **place Priou-Valjean** where there are a few tree-shaded benches. Very quiet: the birds make the most noise.

### Square de l'Avé Maria
*Location: between the rue de l'Avé Maria and the quai des Célestins.*
Nothing much: a few stone benches but neither so quiet nor as shady as the place Priou-Valjean above.

See also the **place des Vosges**

(p. 60): but note that the central garden can get very crowded.

# Market

## Place Baudoyer, 75004
*Tuesday 3.00 – 8.30 pm and Saturday 7.00 am – 3.00 pm*
Not very large but with a reasonable range of food stalls. Not as good as the **Marché Bastille** in the boulevard Richard Lenoir, 75001 which is not far away and stretches from the place de la Bastille up to the Métro Bréguet-Sabin in two double banks along the central reservation. One of the biggest open-air markets with many specialist stalls among the more usual offerings (Thursday and Sunday, mornings only).

# Fromager

## La Ferme St Aubin
*76 rue St-Louis-en-l'Ile, 75004
Closed: Monday
Open: Tuesday to Saturday, 8.00 am – 8.00 pm; Sunday 8.00 am – 1.00 pm and 3.00 – 8.00 pm*
Note the opening hours at this small, fastidious, delectable fromagerie (all adjectives necessary and appropriate). The quality and condition of the cheeses, and their presentation marks out the true fromager. Cheeses predominate, of course, but there is a range of wines to complement them (ask for advice). The slightly aloof service commands respect.

# Glaciers

There is no street in Paris with so many top-ranking ice-cream makers as the rue St-Louis-en-l'Ile. Of the three I would put Cacao et Chocolat first for quality and value. Berthillon's ice-cream is good but the queues (and the bored service – so would you be if you had their job) can be off-putting. Amorino is less busy and the italianate quality of their ice-cream is a recipe for self-indulgence.

## Berthillon
*29-31 rue St-Louis-en-l'Ile, 75004
Closed: Monday, Tuesday and six weeks from mid-July to the end of August
Open: 10.00 am – 8.00 pm*
It should be noted that there are other outlets on the island apart from this main one, the best being the café Le Flore en l'Ile (p. 63). However, to get the full range and the latest specialities you come here. Recommended is the wild strawberry sorbet *(à la fraise des bois)*; indeed their sorbets are generally the best in their range – try *thym-citron* and *pêche-menthe.* A single cornet *(une boule)* costs 3€ (and then upwards).

## Amorino
*47 rue St-Louis-en-l'Ile, 75004
Open: DAILY noon to midnight*
This is one of a number of branches in addition to the original one in the 14th arrondissement (rue Daguerre). Luscious ice-creams are their strength and the

less fancy the better. Cornets cost 3€, 4€ and 5,50€ for small, medium (as much as you need) or large (enormous).

## Cacao et Chocolat
*63 rue St-Louis-en-l'Ile, 75004*
*Open: DAILY 10.30 am– 7.30 pm*
The best of the three: their range is more restricted and chocolate predominates but the fruit sorbets are equally delicious and not too sweet: 2,10€ for one boule to 4,50€ for three, so they have the edge on price as well.

Chocolatiers in Paris take themselves (and what they sell) seriously. The message is that chocolate is as varied by origin as tea or coffee: the range offered here has sources identified and characterised. Chocolates, drinking chocolate, pâtisseries (their macaroons match those of Ladurée at less cost) are all to be found in this well-designed setting. There is a small bar where you can drink hot chocolate etc. and sample the macaroons.

# Neglected museums

## Musée Adam Mickiewicz
*6 quai d'Orléans, 75004*
*Métro: Pont Marie*
*Open: Thursday afternoon: tours at 2.15, 3.00, 3.45, 4.30, 5.15 pm; Saturday morning: at 9.00, 10.00, 11.00 am and noon.*
*Entrance: 5€ (includes guided tour)*
This 17th century building is home to the Société Historique et Littéraire Polonaise and houses the Polish Library, the Musée

Adam Mickiewicz, a small gallery devo-ted to Polish art, and an exquisite small salon of Chopin memorabilia.

You turn up at the selected time and press the button marked *Gardien*. At the time of my visit I was shown round by a charming (French speaking) Polish woman: I was the only client because this really does qualify as 'neglected' .

Mickiewicz was a Romantic poet and revolutionary – an equiv-alent to Byron – and there is a suitably Byronic portrait of him in the museum. The Polish community in Paris is proud of their great poet and of their long association with the city.

Recommended if you under-stand spoken French, but you can glean a great deal from the text accompanying the paintings, manuscripts and other memora-bilia – including Mickiewicz's death mask.

## Musée de la Curiosité et de la Magie
*11 rue St Paul, 75004*
*Métro: St Paul*
*Open: Wednesday, Saturday, Sunday, 2.00 – 7.00 pm; Thurs-day and Friday (same times) during school holidays*
*Entrance: 7€ adults, 5€ children*
*www.museedelamagie.com*
Always crowded with (French) children this is a unique assembly of working models and equipment relating to magic and conjuring with regular displays by masters of the art. There are also hourly performances by a magician which involve the juvenile members of

the audience, although the rapid-fire patter is hard to follow (for us, the children have no problem). However, adults do not feel out of place because the whole ethos is very professional and the way the performers command children's attention is something to marvel at.

# Interesting shops

### Calligrane
*4-6 rue du Pont Louis-Philippe, 75004*
*Métro: Pont Marie*
*Closed: Sunday and Monday*
*Open: 11.00 am – 7.00 pm*
There are effectively three shops here covering hi-design office accessories; a range of stationery; and fine papers, some of them hand-made (and not just for writing). Reminiscent of Smythson's in Bond Street but as French as that is English, the style is altogether more modern and everything has a clean, simple (= expensive) look about it.

### Les Magasins des Fraternités Monastiques de Jerusalem
*Metro: Pont Marie*
You don't have to be religious to feel spiritually uplifted by a visit to the shops described below. The warm welcome you receive is as genuine as the quality and value of the products they sell from monasteries all over France.
*Closed: Monday, and the whole of August*
*Open (in each case): Tuesday to Friday, 9.30 am – noon and 2.00 –*

*8.00 pm; Saturday from 10.00 am; Sunday 12.15 – 1.00 pm*

### Produits des Monastères
*10 rue des Barres, 75004*
This is the monastery larder: honey, jams, sweets and chocolates, herbal teas, cakes, biscuits, fine oils – all in great variety.

The adjacent **Librairie Sources Vives** (same address) sells religious books, CDs, notebooks, postcards, icons, nativity scenes, incense candles – many of them thoughtfully and beautifully made. Prices are reasonable and this shop (and Monastica below) are a marvellous source of presents.

### Monastica
*10 rue du Pont Louis Phillipe, 75004*
If I could pick out one item here it would be the toilet waters – traditional scents such as lavender and rose. As in commercial parfumiers there is a range of testers: the difference is in the price.

There are ceramics (not from monasteries I was told), leather sandals (monk-like), soaps and creams, and some fine table linen. Highly recommended.

### Galerie Alain Coran
*92 rue St-Louis-en-l'Ile, 75004*
*Métro: Pont Marie*
*Closed: Sunday and Monday*
*Open: 10.30 am – 1.00 pm and 2.00 – 7.30 pm*
This is a long way from the clichéd minerals and jewellery shop. The range is impressive and includes meteorites with prices from hundreds to thousands of euros

(450€ will buy one that would make a good paperweight); or you can buy a ring made from meteorites for 150€. More cheaply the use of, for example, slices of agate which have been turned into pendants (at 15€) is typical. But no simple entry here can do justice to everything they stock: you have to see for yourself.

The owner and his son are happy for you to look around but they ask please DON'T TOUCH – some objects are fragile.

## Bistrots

### Café de la Poste
*13 rue Castex, 75004*
*Tel: 01 42 72 95 35*
*Métro: Bastille*
*Closed: Sunday (Saturday lunchtime) and most of August*
*Open: 11.30 am – 3.00 pm and 7.30 pm – 2.00 am*
Off the tourist trails of the Marais and Bastille, it looks like the kind of café you wouldn't give a second glance. In fact this is a bistrot serving very good value traditional dishes which change from day to day: the offerings are on a blackboard.

Entrées cost from 3-8€, plats 11-13€; assiette de fromages (a generous selection) 6,50€; desserts 4-6€. Wine is available by the glass at 2,30–3,30€ and also en carafe (¼ litre 5,40–8€; ½ litre 10-15€). Chilled water (free) is brought to the table. You would struggle to spend more than 30€ on a complete meal including drinks.

Service is thoughtful and intelligent. The Café acts as a club for locals and things don't really start moving until after eleven. But you won't be made to feel an outsider. Not essential to book but it is small so they appreciate it if you do (and especially if you want to eat late).

### Vins des Pyrénées
*25 rue Beautrellis, 75004*
*Tel: 01 42 72 64 94*
*Métro: Bastille*
*Open: DAILY noon – 3.00 pm and 8.00 – 11.30 pm (for meals), the bar open until 2.00 am*
Describing itself as a 'restaurant-bar' this highly successful bistrot located in a quiet side-street offers a range of regional wines. The atmosphere of the place is a little OTT: their nostalgically illustrated 'business card' reads: 'When you put your arms around my neck I remember that day at the Vins des Pyrénées the little bistrot where you first smiled at me....'

Always animated, the bistrot becomes livelier as the evening wears on and the wines (not just from the Pyrénées) are imbibed. Many regulars but everyone is made welcome. There is a two-course lunchtime formule for 16€ but the carte (no menu in the evening) is reasonably priced: entrées about 8-13€; plats (in which fish is well represented) 13-22€; desserts 7-8€. A half-litre of one of several house wines is around 10€. Since the servings are generous my advice is to skip the entrée, in which case you could eat well for 20-30€.

Reservation advisable.

**Louis Philippe**
*66 quai de l'Hôtel de Ville, 75004*
*Tel: 01 42 72 29 42*
*Métro: Hôtel de Ville*
*Open: DAILY for meals, noon –*
*3.00 pm and 7.00 – 11.00 pm*
*(café service continuous)*
Serving standard bistrot fare this slightly faded café-restaurant is near the better-known **Trumilou** (at number 84) which you will only prefer if you enjoy passive smoking (and I doubt it will change). There is a small terrace, well-screened from the nearby traffic, and heated when necessary. The best spot in the area for an outdoor drink.

Louis Philippe is here for two reasons, apart from the fair-priced and usually reliable food. First, it is open on Sunday; second, if you book into the first-floor dining room (and specify a window table) you get a splendid view of Notre-Dame – at a good deal less cost than the Tour d'Argent.

There is a lunchtime menu (Monday to Friday) where you can have a main course (plat) for 12€, two from three courses for 15€, or the whole lot (e + pl + dess) for 18€ – great value. Wine by the glass is 3-4€ but a 1/3rd litre carafe is only 6€; 2/3rds of a litre i.e. approximately a bottle is 11,50€ – and it's adequate to good. A la carte is in the range 6-10€ for an entrée, 15-16€ for the substantial plat and 6-7€ for desserts. The plat du jour (recommended) is around 12€.

You may find that you like this place so much you'll go back there daily. If you do, admire the iron spiral staircase to the first floor: it was designed by Gustave Eiffel in his early days and they're very proud of it.

# Brasseries

### Brasserie de l'Ile St-Louis
*55 quai de Bourbon (corner of the rue Jean du Bellay), 75004*
*Tel: 01 43 54 02 59*
*Métro: Pont Marie*
*Closed: Wednesday (Thursday lunchtime), the whole of August and Christmas*
*Open: noon – 1.00 am (6.00 pm – 1.00 am Thursday) including SUNDAY*
The lovely dining room in an historic setting serves reliable, standard brasserie food which means you are safest ordering the more straightforward dishes. Entrées cost 6-9€, plats 16-26€ and desserts 7-11€. Main course portions are large so an entrée may be a course too much. Wines by the bottle cost typically less than 20€ but there is an excellent range of beers – good with the more Alsatian dishes.

The terrace facing the Pont St-Louis (closed to traffic) has a distant view of the dome of the Institut de France as well as nearby attractions. An excellent spot for a summer lunch; or just a drink. Booking essential for dinner.

### Bofinger
*5-7 rue de la Bastille, 75009*
*Tel: 01 42 72 87 82*
*Métro: Bastille*

*Open: DAILY 11.00 am through to 1.00 am*

Slightly out of our area this dazzling belle époque brasserie cannot be missed. Its origins go back a long way but the present format dates from 1919 before art deco took over. Inevitably it belongs to the Flo group with the element of standardisation that implies.

Seafood is best here but there are standard 'plats bistrots' on the menus: the lunch-time menu is particularly good value at 21,50€ and there is a dinner menu at 31,50€. A la carte will cost from 40€ depending on how far you go on the seafood. Reasonably priced wines in all formats.

*A well-known travelling pianist*
*(he turns up everywhere)*

# 3. Temple

The rue du Temple, the central spine of the area, is a street of successive contrasts and this is reflected in the fact that all the recommended hotels and restaurants are in the upper section. So what is the justification for including the whole stretch? The essential attraction of Paris lies in its diversity: that is true here. To get a proper sense of the district you have to see how it progressively changes and, as a first approach, simply walking the length of the street allows you to do this.

Leaving behind the formality of the place de l'Hôtel de Ville, and the faux-Renaissance edifice of the City Hall, you pass through the wholesale garment industry sector as far as the rue Rambuteau. There is a certain surreal fascination in seeing windows full of tailors' dummies that owe nothing to window dressing; shops with hats stacked high; rolls of fabric in a kaleidoscope of colours and dizzying patterns; crates full of extravagant costume jewellery that ravish the senses (the verb is exact). And all this runs – at a mere street's distance – alongside the Centre Pompidou from where there is a slightly tacky backwash.

Then, quite soon, you are into increasingly fashionable territory, an area which caters much more for Parisians than tourists so that though decent hotels are few, you can find some of the best value bistrots in the city and a brasserie (Chez Jenny) which is truer to its Alsatian roots than any other (p. 77). Next to this glittering temple (no pun intended) to choucroute garnie is the stylish Café Jenny with an excellent terrace overlooking the place de la République – traditionally an assembly point for political demonstrations.

Quite simply, this is one of those diverse quarters where it is important to avoid a stereotyped response when you're deciding where to stay. Much of it is within a stone's throw of Les Halles/Beaubourg but, as an experience, the style and tempo are of another world.

# Principal sights

**Eglise St-Nicolas-des-Champs**
(12th-century origins but mainly
15th-century), 254 rue St Martin:
the original character has been
somewhat overlaid by reconstruction over the centuries and it takes
a practised eye to discern their
successive revisions. Access restricted, but there is a fine 17th-
century altarpiece as well as paintings from the same period and
later.

**Musée des Arts et Métiers,** rue
St Martin: the ground floor of this
wonderful museum incorporates
the 12th century church of St
Martin-des-Champs, and the
monastery refectory is now the
library of the Conservatoire. (See
p. 73 for museum details.)

# Quiet hotels

**Hôtel du Vieux Saule**
*6 rue de Picardie, 75003*
*Tel: 01 42 72 01 14*
*Fax: 01 40 27 88 21*
*E-mail:*
*reserv@hotelvieuxsaule.com*
*www.hotelvieuxsaule.com*
*Métro: Filles du Calvaire*
*30 rooms (11 non-smoking) AIR*
*CONDITIONED*
*Price: 140€ for a double room*
*('chambre confort'); 160€ for a*
*'chambre supérieure'*
With a pleasant little courtyard
garden, here the best and quietest
rooms are on the top (4th) floor.
Facilities are good, including a free
sauna. The 10€ buffet breakfast is
recommended.

**Hôtel Saintonge Marais**
*16 rue Saintonge, 75003*
*Tel: 01 42 77 91 13*
*Fax: 01 48 87 76 41*
*E-mail: hotelsaintonge*
*@wanadoo.fr*
*www.hotelmarais.com*
*Métro: Filles du Calvaire*
*23 rooms*
*Price: 115€ for a double room*
Despite its title this hotel,
furnished in period style, is not
actually in the Marais – although
well-placed for visiting. In a quiet
situation it has the advantage of
being in the same street as Chez
Nénesse (p. 76).

**Austin's Arts et Métiers Hôtel**
*6 rue Montgolfier, 75003*
*Tel: 01 42 77 17 61*
*Fax: 01 42 77 55 43*
*E-mail: austins.amhotel*
*@wanadoo.fr*
*www.austins-paris-hotel.com*
*Métro: Arts et Métiers*
*29 rooms*
*Price: 148€ for a double room*
*(cheaper for single occupancy)*
A hotel of exceptional quality
which is located in a less obvious
area of Paris. In a street off the rue
de Turbigo, ignored by traffic, it is
opposite the recommended Musée
des Arts et Métiers. The buffet
style breakfast is good value at 9€.

# Breakfast

**Paul**
*Corner of the rue Renard and
the rue de Rivoli
Open: DAILY from 7.30 am
(8.00 am Sunday)*

You find this as you approach the narrow entrance of the rue du Temple (next to the **Bazar de l'Hôtel de Ville – BHV**, pronounced *bay-ash-vay* and where the basement is a mecca for DIY enthusiasts). One of the best branches of Paul with a large and pleasant café and terrace and the usual wide range of breakfast formules. And you can buy bread and pastries for later on the way out.

### Espace Gourmand
*27 rue des Archives*
*Closed: Sunday and the first*
*three weeks in August*
*Open: from 7.30 am*
There are a number of cafés in this section of the street but this pâtisserie with a few tables outside, and a row of sit-up-and-beg stools running along the counter inside, wins on charm, quality and courtesy – and price. One of their excellent croissants and a café crème will come to 4,20€.

## Public gardens

### Square Emile Chautemps
*Location: between the boulevard de Sebastopol and the rue St Martin.*
A typically French formal garden with straight paths lined with chestnut trees provides a retreat from the busyness of surrounding streets. Facing the much-cleaned and restored Conservatoire, and the two fountains with formal *bassins* add to the sense of order and peace. Not much grass but plenty of tree-shaded benches.

### Square du Temple
*Location: between the rue Perrée and the rue de Bretagne next to the Mairie of the 3rd arrondissement.*
Although not large this park has much in a limited space: exotic species of trees and shrubs, open water, rocks and even a small waterfall. The site was formerly within the large fortified precinct belonging to the Knights Templar in the 12th century; today it is one of the finest small parks in the city with pleasant walks and a beautiful shaded duck pond (much enjoyed by the variegated ducks).

## Markets

### Marché des Enfants Rouges
*39 rue de Bretagne, 75003*
*Closed: Monday, and Sunday afternoon*
*Open: Tuesday to Thursday, 8.30 am – 1.00 pm and 4.00 – 7.30 pm; Friday and Saturday, 8.30 am – 8.00 pm; Sunday 8.30 am –2.00pm*
A long established covered market that has recently been renovated but without loss of character. Notable here are the café areas with a choice of different cuisine – Japanese, Italian, Moroccan, for example.

It is essential to take account of the long lunch-break earlier in the week: the stall-holders can be seen taking a leisurely meal – don't try to interrupt them.

### Marché du Temple
*Rue E. Spuller (north-east of the*

square du Temple), 75003
*NEVER OPEN*
So why is it here? Because this was once one of the finest covered markets in Paris; and if you have morbid instincts you should peer through the surrounding grilles or wander round the shabby and derelict shuttered stalls – a strange, ghostly experience. Part of the floor area is used for temporary exhibitions, otherwise for clothing sales of the non-fashion variety; all of which only serve to heighten the sense of pathos.

## Fromager

### Jouanault (Fromagers de France)
*39 rue de Bretagne, 75003*
*Closed: Monday, and Sunday afternoon*
*Open: 8.00 am – 1.00 pm and*
*4.30 – 8.00 pm (Sunday to 1.00 pm)*
Adjacent to the Marché des Enfants Rouges, the shop name tells it all. An intelligent selection of cheeses from across France including (a matter of pride for fromagers) some rarities. Cheeses from Eastern France – the Savoy region – are a speciality. The Vieux Comté (at least 22 months old) is exceptional.

## Glacier

### Spécial Comptoir
*123 rue Oberkampf, 75011*
*Open: DAILY noon – 3.00 pm*
*and 6.00 pm – midnight*
You have to go out of the area for this one: about a fifteen minute walk up the rue Oberkampf which will sharpen your tastebuds.

If you didn't know it was there you would never find this small glacerie, the source of many original flavours including *pêche de vigne*, rose petal, violet and even *tatin calvados* ice-creams. A secret location for those in the know!

## Neglected museums

### Musée des Arts et Métiers
*60 rue de Réaumur, 75003*
*Métro: Arts et Métiers*
*Closed: Monday and public holidays*
*Open: 10.00 am – 6.00 pm (to 9.30 pm Thursday)*
*Entrance: 6,50€ (FREE to under 18s)*
*www.arts-et-metiers.net*
Housed in a dignified former 18th century priory this museum is dedicated to the practical side of science and technology and, to say the least, is a tribute to human ingenuity. Wonderful models. The range of exhibits covers transport (including Blériot's monoplane), scientific instruments (with the 18th-century laboratory of Lavoisier, who discovered oxygen), early forms of telecommunication and inventions where Foucault's famous and dramatic pendulum has pride of place. Fascinating.
Good shop and café.

### Musée de la Chasse et de la Nature
*Hôtel Guénégaud*
*60 rue des Archives, 75003*

*Métro: Hôtel de Ville*
*Closed: Monday and public*
*holidays*
*Open: 11.00 am – 6.00 pm*
*Entrance: 6€*
*www.chassenature.org*
In a beautifully restored 17th century mansion, this is for enthusiasts of hunting, shooting and fishing. Apart from various implements of destruction there are some superb paintings as well as trophies and 'objets d'art'. Children will enjoy the information cabinets about individual animals - including casts of their tracks and droppings; not to mention magnificent stuffed animals and a room with a ceiling of owl feathers.

## Musée d'Art et d'Histoire du Judaïsme

*Hôtel de Saint-Aignan*
*71 rue du Temple, 75003*
*Métro: Hôtel de Ville*
*Closed: Saturday*
*Open: 11.00 am – 6.00 pm*
*(from 10.00 am Sunday)*
*Entrance: 9,50€ (FREE to*
*under 18s)*
*www.mahj.org*
The permanent exhibition covers the historical evolution of Jewish communities from the Middle Ages to the present, and particularly in France. This is a serious scholarly centre with a library and documentary archives from which exhibits are selected for display. Of particular interest are those related to the Dreyfus affair. There are also paintings by 20th century Jewish artists like Chagall and Modigliani.

Temporary exhibitions are held, for which there is a separate charge. Audio-guides (in five languages) are provided free; and there are special areas for children.

## Musée de la Serrurerie Bricard

*Hôtel Libéral-Bruant*
*1 rue de la Perle, 75003*
*Métro: Rambuteau/St Paul*
*Closed: Saturday and Sunday*
*Open: 10.00 am – noon and*
*2.00 – 5.00 pm*
*Entrance: 5€*
Locks, keys and all the tools for making them in this fine old house on the fringes of the Marais (and of our area). With exhibits dating from Roman times and up to the 20th century, the strength is in the elaborate lock-cases from the 14th-17th centuries and the ingenious mechanisms for securing valuables of one kind or another. There is a detailed reconstruction of a traditional locksmith's workshop.

## Musée de la Poupée

*Impasse Berthaud, 75003*
*Métro: Rambuteau*
*Closed: Monday and public*
*holidays*
*Open: 10.00 am – 6.00 pm*
*Entrance: 6€ adults, 3€ children*
*www.museedelapoupeeparis.com*
In the easily overlooked impasse Berthaud (where there is also a pleasant restaurant) this museum is worth a detour, containing as it does some 500 French dolls dating from around 1800 to the present day. The faintly sinister quality of those perfect, impassive faces always evokes for me Agatha

Christie's short story *The Dress-maker's Doll*.

See below the entry for the linked shop.

## Interesting shops

### Boutique du Musée de la Poupée
*Impasse Berthaud, 75003*
*Métro: Rambuteau*
*Open: same hours as the museum*
This is *the* place to buy traditional dolls, and dolls' house furniture of high quality and equivalent prices. Adults can also buy antique dolls and there is a clinic for those 'injured'.

### A la Poupée Merveilleuse
*9 rue du Temple, 75003*
*Métro: Hôtel de Ville*
*Closed: Sunday and Monday*
*Open: 10.00 am – 7.00 pm*
There are plenty of places in Paris selling dolls and their accessories but this shop stands out as a supplier of children's fancy dress costumes and magicians' equipment suitable for beginners.

### Les Archives de la Presse
*51 rue des Archives, 75003*
*Métro: Hôtel de Ville*
*Closed: Sunday*
*Open: Monday to Friday, 10.30 am – 7.00 pm (Saturday from 2.00 pm)*
Opposite the National Archives this is a large shop with a vast range of magazines, primarily the popular variety, including fashion, and covering the whole of the 20th century and earlier ('the way we

were'). Good for a browse, if nothing else.

### Jadis et Gourmande
*37 rue des Archives, 75003*
*Métro: Hôtel de Ville*
*Closed: Sunday*
*Open: Tuesday to Friday, 10.00 am – 7.30 pm (Saturday from 10.30 am; Monday from 1.00 pm)*
Here is the main branch of this famous chocolatier with many of their specialities on display; for example, the presentation boxes with a simple message made up of individual chocolate letters (see also p. 147).

## Bistrots

### L'Ambassade d'Auvergne
*22 rue du Grenier St Lazare, 75003*
*Tel: 01 42 72 31 22*
*Métro: Arts et Métiers/Rambuteau*
*Closed: mid-July to mid-August*
*Open: DAILY noon – 2.00 pm and 7.30 – 10.00 pm*
Another starve-before-you-come address. It is difficult not to overeat here (you consume bread and pâté while you choose your meal). Food from the Auvergne is well-known to the British but is not widely available in Paris. The cooking is straight-forward and substantial – lamb and beef figure largely and usually accompanied by the Auvergnac speciality of *aligot* (not to be confused with the similarly spelt wine). Made of mashed potato, garlic and Cantal cheese curds, it adds character and calories.

The lunch formule of two courses (no choice) plus a glass of wine is fine value at 20€ if the daily special is to your taste. There is also an excellent value three-course menu of limited choice (recommended) at 30€; à la carte will cost around 45€. Wines from the Auvergne cost approximately16-18€ a bottle.

**Le Pamphlet**
*38 rue Debelleyme, 75003*
*Tel: 01 42 72 39 24*
*Métro: St Sébastien-Froissart*
*Closed: Sunday (Saturday and Monday lunchtime) and two weeks in August*
*Open: 12.30 – 2.30 pm and 7.30 – 11.30 pm*
A rather smart place serving food which draws mainly on the South-West but also from Lyon and the Auvergne. The cooking is a class above the average bistrot but the emphasis is traditional with inventive flourishes. Much thought and flair goes into the comparatively short menu offered as a three course *menu-carte* at 30€, and *menu dégustation* at 45€ per head for a whole table comprising: amuse-bouche, fish, meat, cheese, dessert, mignardises – fantastic value for a party with large appetites.

**Au Bascou**
*38 rue Réaumur, 75003*
*Tel: 01 42 72 69 25*
*Métro: Réaumur-Sébastopol/ Arts et Métiers*
*Closed: Saturday, Sunday, the whole of August, Christmas to New Year*

*Open: noon – 2.00 pm and 8.00 – 10.30 pm*
This is the leading Basque restaurant in Paris; it is also on the inventive edge but with its roots firmly in the region of origin.

The carte is not large and reflects what is available by season, for example the roast suckling lamb (from autumn to spring only). But in making your choice it is wise to be guided by the patron, Jean-Guy Lousteau, who is immensely knowledgeable. And provided you know what you don't like, you should follow his advice.

There is a two-course lunchtime formule for 18€ – dishes written on the *ardoise* (blackboard). On the carte you can expect to pay around 40€ for a four-course meal; this will defeat most people so two courses at around 25€ will normally suffice. Some excellent wines from the South-West by the glass: a half bottle will cost around 17€, and up to 90€ for a full bottle of their best.

A snug, narrow restaurant which is well-known and widely appreciated, so booking is essential.

**Chez Nénesse**
*17 rue de Saintonge, 75003*
*Tel: 01 42 78 46 49*
*Métro: Filles du Calvaire/ Temple*
*Closed: Saturday, Sunday, public holidays, the whole of August, Christmas to New Year*
*Open: noon – 2.30 pm and 7.45 – 10.30 pm*
A family-run 'bistrot de quartier'

with a 1950s formica bar – smart in its day and now back in 'retro' fashion. The food here is a million miles from cuisine inventive: firmly traditional with substantial portions, but not boring; dishes such as fish terrine and fricassée de volaille aux morilles are expertly delivered. It is packed out at lunchtime; in the evening offerings are more elaborate with corresponding prices, but even then you will pay no more than about 35€ à la carte.

### Le Valet de Carreau

*2 rue Dupetit Thouars, 75003*
*Tel: 01 42 72 72 60*
*Métro: République*
*Closed: Sunday (and Saturday lunchtime)*
*Open: noon – 3.00 pm and 7.00 – 10.00 pm*

In direct competition to Le Sablier next door, the standard is higher and the prices almost identical: a 12€ formule of two courses at lunchtime; a two-course formule in the evening for 19€ or three courses plus a half-bottle of wine or water for 29€ – excellent value – and only a little more if you go à la carte.

A bistrot in a peaceful setting with an unassertive character.

## Brasserie

### Chez Jenny

*39 boulevard du Temple, 75003*
*Tel: 01 44 54 39 00*
*Closed: from mid-June to mid-August*
*Open: DAILY noon to midnight (to 1.00 am Saturday)*

This eye-catching brasserie occupies a slightly elevated position at the top end of the boulevard. As a measure of its success, it sells more choucroute than any other and, if you like it, there is a formule which includes a ¼ litre of wine (Alsatian) and coffee for 19€ (three courses for 28€).

Next door (same owners) is the highly fashionable **Café Jenny** with a terrace overlooking the place de la République – restful on open-air days (the interior has loud music). Serving a vast range of snacks they also offer a bargain lunch of a main course, a drink and coffee for 10€.

## 4. Canal St Martin
## (and for Ménilmontant)

The closer you get to Parisian social culture the more you are aware of its impervious character. The city attracts almost 70 million visitors a year and yet influences on the inhabitants are superficial. They are inured to tourism and create their own social fashions without regard for Anglo-Saxon or other tastes and understanding. Popular tourist trails are often years (even decades) out-of-date because Parisians have long abandoned them. There are, for example, well-known restaurants where you will not hear a French accent, except from the staff. If the immediate vicinity of the Canal St Martin has become a fashionable place to live and socialise it is as a peculiarly French phenomenon. Nonetheless, even as an outsider you can appreciate that this is one of the most delightful parts of the city with the bonus of a disregarded hinterland to explore.

The canal was constructed in the early part of the 19th century and is still a going concern with fastidiously-decorated barges to be seen, most often when the Seine is in flood. The quaysides are now landscaped as part of the general improvement of a once poor area, while footbridges across the canal provide a privileged view of the operation of the locks – ideal for idlers.

The exposed section of the canal (it goes underground at the Bastille end) is almost five kilometres long and it is the southern part between the quai de Valmy and the quai de Jemmapes (and west of that) that is our focus. On a fine morning you should make your way to the iron footbridge spanning the canal which featured in Marcel Carné's 1938 film classic *Hôtel du Nord*, and see the locks and *croisières* about their business. Followed perhaps by breakfast at Chez Prune, very much of the moment, which overlooks it all.

The eastern side of the canal was the setting for the

*Barge on the Canal St Martin*

children's film, *Le Ballon Rouge*, in the once predominantly working-class district of Ménilmontant. Maurice Chevalier was proud of being born there and sang of it nostalgically as did Edith Piaf. A tiny museum with memorabilia of Piaf can be found at 5 rue Crespin du Gast (by appointment only, tel: 01 43 55 52 72) – strictly for the obsessive devotee. And if you have the energy it is worth traversing the district on foot up to the cemetery of Père Lachaise where she is buried along with other notables from the recent and distant past – Chopin, Oscar Wilde, Colette and, of course, Héloïse and Abélard, in an ornate Gothic tomb. Ménilmontant is popular with Parisians but for tourists it lacks decent hotels; you can make up your own mind about its other qualities.

## Principal sights

**Hôpital St-Louis**, entrance off the rue Bichet: originally established at the beginning of the 17th century to provide care for the victims of epidemics on a site outside the city walls. The public are admitted to the grounds of this working hospi-tal on the eastern side of the canal. The stone-framed brick buildings, the courtyards with lawns, benches and flower beds are typical of a Paris that has largely vanished.

**Porte St Martin and Porte St Denis** (17th century): at the south-ern end of the rue du Faubourg St Martin and the rue du Faubourg

St Denis, respectively, these two triumphal arches (for Louis XIV's forgotten victories) stand in startling contrast to their comparatively ordinary surroundings. Indeed, the world has changed around them, but surrounding buildings have always been on a much smaller scale so they look bigger than they are. Even the Porte St Denis (the larger) is less than half the height of the Arc de Triomphe, the Porte St Martin only a third.

As you stroll along the rue du Faubourg St Martin take a look at the grandiloquent turn-of-the-century **Mairie** for the 10th arrondissement (by Eugène Rouyer in Renaissance style); step inside to admire the opera-house foyer.

## Quiet hotels

### Hôtel Gilden Magenta

*35 rue Yves Toudic, 75010*
*Tel: 01 42 40 17 72*
*Fax: 01 42 02 59 66*
*E-mail: hotel.gilden.magenta*
*@multi-micro.com*
*www.gilden-magenta.com*
*Métro: République*
*32 rooms*
*Price: 85€ for a double room*
A modest hotel on a quiet street just north of the place de la République. Around half of the rooms give on to an interior courtyard garden. Outstanding value.

### Nord-Est Hôtel

*12 rue des Petits Hôtels, 75010*
*Tel: 01 47 70 07 18*
*Fax: 01 42 46 73 50*
*E-mail: hotel.nord.est*
*@wanadoo.fr*
*Métro: Poissonière*
*30 rooms*
*Price: 90€ for a double room.*
Between the rue La Fayette and the boulevard de Magenta, the hotel is set back from the street behind a garden. Quiet for the area and convenient for the Gare de l'Est and the Eurostar terminal at the Gare du Nord (you could walk there).

### Hôtel Aulivia Opéra

*4 rue des Petites Ecuries, 75010*
*Tel: 01 45 23 88 88*
*Fax: 01 45 23 88 89*
*E-mail: hotel.aulivia*
*@astotel.com*
*www.astotel.com*
*Métro: Château d'Eau/Strasbourg St Denis*
*32 rooms AIR CONDITIONED*
*Price: 145€ for a double room*
Part of the Best Western Group, this hotel is upmarket for an area where seedy hotels abound. In the low season (July/August) the room price drops by thirty euros which makes it good value then because the rooms are air conditioned and it has always had some specifically for non-smokers.

There is an excellent buffet breakfast for 11€ but it might be more fun (and cheaper) to go out to a café.

The surrounding area is interesting to explore and ethnically diverse but probably not one where a woman would want to be on her own. The famous Brasserie Flo is in the immediately adjacent cour des Petites Ecuries; and there is a range of Indian shops and restaurants in the passage Brady (see p. 85).

### Hôtel Mercure Paris Boulevard Magenta

*1-3 cour de la Ferme St-Lazare, 75010*
*Tel: 01 48 24 84 84*
*Fax: 01 48 00 91 03*
*Métro: Gare de l'Est*
*45 rooms AIR CONDITIONED*
*Price: 112-123€ for a twin/double room*

This used to be called the Hôtel Flora but has been taken over by the Mercure chain, hence the new name – a bit of a mouthful. Little has changed.

The hotel is on the corner of the busy boulevard de Magenta but is otherwise quietly situated. However, you would need to specify a room overlooking the side street (no traffic) which is its address. A possible choice for the summer because of the air conditioning, and when prices for a double room drop to 105€.

Breakfast is served in a windowless vaulted cellar: better to go to the immediately adjoining café Le Prévoyant (see below).

### Hôtel Regina Opéra

*11 bis, rue Mazagran, 75010*
*Tel: 01 47 70 93 05*
*Fax: 01 42 46 53 86*
*E-mail: hotel.regina@astotel.com*
*www.astotel.com/hotel-regina-opera-paris.plp*
*Métro: Bonne Nouvelle/ Strasbourg St Denis*
*48 rooms AIR CONDITIONED*

*Price: 135€ for a double room*

This hotel is good value because of its (for Paris) exceptionally large and light rooms – particularly on the upper floors. However, room prices (and availability) change during the periods of the salons (trade fairs); there is a surcharge at these times.

### Hôtel Jardins de Paris République

*30 rue Lucien Sampaix, 75010*
*Tel: 01 42 08 19 74*
*Fax: 01 42 08 27 28*
*E-mail: republique @hotelsjardinsdeparis.com*
*www.parisrepublique.com*
*Métro: Jacques Bonsergent*
*39 rooms*
*Price: 90€ for a double room (cheaper if booked online)*

Make no mistake about it, this is a very ordinary hotel but set back from what is an almost traffic-free street; and just a short walk from the lively quai de Valmy. You could conveniently breakfast at the celebrated café Chez Prune before it gets impossibly crowded. And some of the best bistrots are within easy walking distance. So it is included here for its situation; and as any estate agent will tell you, that's nine-tenths of the case.

## Breakfast

### Chez Prune

*36 rue Beaurepaire*
*Open: DAILY from 7.30 am (10.00 am Sunday)*

This place serves food all day (and until 1.45 am) but the cooking is unremarkable and the atmosphere unrestful. Morning is an exception and the view over the canal from an outdoor table (in good weather) is a constant pleasure.

Breakfast or not you should go to view part of a fashionable sub-culture. The style of the café is self-conscious scruff, with clients to match: definitely a place for poseurs. No, I was told, they don't have croissants (these tourists!) but I had a pain beurré and a café crème for 4,30€ which is quite cheap.

### Le Prévoyant
*Corner of the rue du Faubourg St Denis and the boulevard de Magenta*
*Open: DAILY from 7.00 am (8.00 am Saturday; 9.00 am Sunday)*
Notable for its good-value 6€ breakfast (orange juice, coffee, croissant, ficelle, butter and jam), this café is also well-placed for people-watching from the outside tables.

### La Marine
*55 bis quai de Valmy*
*Closed: Sunday*
*Open: 8.30 – 11.00 am for breakfast*
This is Maigret territory: quiet with just a few locals. There is a basket of croissants and pains au chocolat on the bar, and it's the sort of place where café crème would be an affectation. Try café allongé instead; with a croissant it will cost you 3,80€. And a window table will give you a good view of the canal.

## Public gardens

### Square Villemin
*Location: off rue des Récollets.*
This is by a long way the best park in the area and the largest, with many mature trees and grass you're allowed to sit on. But plenty of benches are provided as well.

There is a bandstand with occasional public concerts (a kind of glee club when I was there last, with audience participation). You will also find a screened children's area in the centre, good public lavatories and a *gardien* to make sure you behave yourselves.

### Square St Laurent
*Location: between the rue du Faubourg St Martin and the boulevard de Magenta.*
Not large but pleasantly laid out in a terraced fashion with a children's play area. Mature trees, flower-beds and shaded benches are all very welcome in this busy locality.

### Square Alban Satragne
*Location: on the western side of the rue du Faubourg St Denis near the junction with the boulevard Magenta.*
Although recently refurbished in a rather formal style with a fountain, play area and carefully regulated flower beds, this small park – for whatever reason – has been taken over by local undesirables and is shunned by others. By you also, I suggest.

### Place Franz Liszt
*Location: just in front of the church of St Vincent-de-Paul,*

*on the northern side of the*
*rue La Fayette.*
Not very big but interestingly elevated, it makes a pleasant and unusual place to rest your feet – in an area not well-served with gardens.

## Markets

### Marché St Quentin
*85 bis boulevard de Magenta,*
*75010*
*Tuesday to Saturday 8.00 am –*
*1.00 pm and 3.30 – 7.30 pm*
*(Sunday to 1.00 pm)*
Often missing from guidebook listings the Marché St Quentin, dating from the mid-19th century, is the most original remaining covered market in Paris. It certainly looks little different from how it did a hundred years ago. In the maze of alleys you will discover a great variety of specialist stall-holders, mainly selling foodstuffs. Everything you might need for a simple meal (or a more elaborate one) is here. Highly recommended.

### Rue du Faubourg St Denis, 75010 (market street)
*Tuesday to Saturday 7.30 am –*
*1.30 pm and 3.30 – 8.00 pm*
*(Sunday to 1.00 pm)*
*The opening hours here are only*
*approximate as some shops are*
*open later or take no lunch*
*break.*
This is the market street of the area and distinctive in its diversity, with a strong Turkish emphasis. There are many gourmet delights to be found but you need to be selective where and what you buy especially from the cooked meats/fast food outlets, because this is what Parisians call a *rue bactériolle* – no need to translate...

In case that sounds too negative, there are at least two very good grocers, particularly the one deceptively named **Fromager** which it is that but much more, and also **Ronalba** (see below for both, under Interesting Shops). In some of the smaller shops you find an amazing range of dates and sweetmeats as well as Turkish and Lebanese pastries. Fruit and vegetables also present an unusual range.

## Fromagers

As well as Fromager itself (see below, under Interesting Shops), there are two respectable fromagers in the Marché St Quentin:
– **Ferme St Quentin**
– **Le Marché aux Fromages**.

## Glacier

We haven't been able to find an actual ice-cream maker in this area but **Fromager** (below, under Interesting Shops) sells the ice-creams and sorbets of **Dagniaux** which are pretty good. They come in ½ litre cartons but also in small (130cl) cardboard cups in a number of interesting combinations, at 2,50€ for *un petit pot.*

## Neglected museum

### Musée de l'Eventail

*2 boulevard de Strasbourg, 75010*
*Métro: Strasbourg St Denis*
*Open: Monday, Tuesday and*
*Wednesday only, 2.00 – 6.00 pm*
*Entrance: 6€*

Quite difficult to spot: look for the blue door to the east of the junction with the boulevard St Denis. You have to ring the bell to gain entry.

Strasbourg St Denis was the quarter where fan makers flourished in the 19th century; the museum linked to a workshop where fans are still made and restored is a celebration of that era. The range of the fans on display is truly remarkable: from painted wood and paper to ivory, mother-of-pearl and tortoiseshell. Something we are hardly aware of is here shown in its central role in fashion through the ages and as a craft industry of major importance in its time.

There are three rooms on view including one where you can see a fan-maker at work. Fans are of every conceivable material including osprey feathers, and for respectable matrons as well as exotic dancers like Josephine Baker.

## Interesting shops

### Ronalba

*60 rue du Faubourg St Denis, 75010*
*Métro: Strasbourg St Denis*
*Open: usual market hours*

This multi-ethnic delicatessen is un-French in its diverse offerings which are European in the widest sense (Italian, Hungarian, Romanian, with a major specialism in Polish sausages, pickles, and the rest). They have an extensive range of olives, some unusual meat products, a limited choice of cheeses and innumerable delicacies. An excellent source for an outdoor lunch, or just a snack as you walk along.

### Fromager

*54 rue du Faubourg St Denis, 75010*
*Métro: Strasbourg St Denis*
*Closed: Monday, and Sunday*
*afternoon*
*Open: 8.00 am – 7.00 pm*
*(Sunday to 1.00 pm)*

The name is entirely deceptive because, although they have a good range of cheeses, this is but part of what they stock. In quality and variety they are grocers head-and-shoulders above anything else in the street (Ronalba comes near). You will find wines, breads, eggs (with feathers adhering), jams, oils, tinned cassoulet, rillettes, confits, etc.

Strongly recommended.

### Félix de Saint Quentin

*in the Marché St Quentin*
*85 bis boulevard de Magenta,*
*75010*
*Métro: Gare de l'Est*
*Open: usual market hours*

The sign reads: Antiquités – Brocante – Tous Débarras (junk) outside this stall with its extravagant clutter. No rarities here, but no high prices either, and M. Félix will be happy to talk to you (and even happier to sell you something). Not worth a special trip but not to be missed if you visit the market.

**Passage Brady**
*Between rue du Faubourg St Denis and boulevard de Strasbourg, 75010*
**Passage du Prado**
*Between the boulevard St Denis and the rue du Faubourg St Denis, 75010*
*Métro: Strasbourg St Denis*
We cannot ignore two of the historic *passages* of 19th century Paris: both close together, both sadly in need of restoration. One can, with attention, detect structural and decorative features dating from earlier in their history, if not original, like the art deco motifs on the upper part of the walls.

However, the passage du Prado smells strongly of disinfectant – presumably to mask odours that are worse; it contains an extraordinary number of hairdressers (busy) and restaurants (empty). There is also an hotel (the Prado) but I didn't inspect it.

The passage Brady is upmarket by comparison with a number of Indian restaurants including the well-regarded **Pooja**; in other respects it displays a similar degree of neglect.

# Bistrots

**Chez Arthur**
*25 rue du Faubourg St Martin, 75010*
*Tel: 01 42 08 34 33*
*Métro: Strasbourg St Denis*
*Closed: Sunday, Monday (Saturday lunchtime) and the whole of August*
*Open: noon – 2.30 pm and 7.00 – 11.30 pm*
This long-established bistrot is going through a bad patch. In the same family ownership, the restaurant offers traditional food which can be good. Certainly the prix fixe menus are a bargain: for example the 15€ lunch formule includes a main course, a glass of wine, and coffee. The all-day menu (which might include terrine de foie gras, magret de canard and charlotte maison) is 22€ for two courses, 28€ for three. But the cooking has become decidedly uneven – still better than most of the local alternatives, however.

**Chez Michel**
*10 rue de Belzunce, 75010*
*Tel: 01 44 53 06 20*
*Métro: Gare du Nord*
*Closed: Saturday, Sunday (Monday lunchtime) and three weeks in August*
*Open: noon – 2.00 pm and 7.00 pm – midnight*
Although a 'new' bistrot, the food at Thierry Breton's famous restaurant is essentially that of his native Brittany and so qualifies as 'traditional'. The wonderful value menu-carte at 30€ includes classic dishes such as the Breton version of pot-au-feu and that kind of rice pudding found in various forms in Brittany and Normandy. The only drawback is its popularity – you need to book well in advance. Broadly similar food is served at

Chez Casimir at no. 6 (tel: 01 48 78 28 80) with similar opening hours.

### Restaurant de Bourgogne: Chez Maurice
*26 rue des Vinaigriers, 75010*
*Métro: Jacques Bonsergent*
*Closed: Sunday, public holidays, last week in July and first three weeks in August*
*Open: noon – 3.00 pm and 7.00 – 11.00 pm*
This is a no-reservations, no-frills bistrot serving traditional food at amazing prices. There are in fact three menus costing 11€, 12€ and 16,50€ at dinner, and even cheaper at lunchtime. Wines en pichet cost 1,50-2,70€ for a ¼ litre and 3-5,40€ for a ½ litre; the wine list proper contains nothing over 15€.

Arrive by 8.00 pm for dinner or expect to queue.

### La Grille
*80 rue du Faubourg Poissonnière, 75010*
*Tel: 01 47 70 89 73*
*Métro: Poissonnière*
*Closed: Saturday, Sunday, public holidays and the last two weeks in August*
*Open: 12.30 – 2.30 pm and 7.30 – 10.30 pm*
A small bistrot in a rather unfashionable quarter but with a well-preserved décor and food that is entirely traditional, centred on meat and fish of high quality. They are particularly proud of their speciality of turbot (for two people).

No menus but a limited carte of good variety (about eight entrées and a similar number of plats and desserts) and three courses will set you back about 35€. Wines are available en pichet e.g. 6,80€ for a ½ litre of Côtes du Rhone.

Booking essential as there are only about nine tables crammed mainly into the back room. As you enter you may be startled by strange whistling and impenetrable remarks in French from a dark corner: that's the mynah bird.

### Chez Tante Alice
*31-33 rue du Château d'Eau, 75010*
*Tel: 01 42 40 62 34*
*Métro: Jacques Bonsergent/République*
*Closed: Sunday*
*Open: 11.30 am – 3.00 pm and 6.30 – 11.30 pm*
It is essential to book at this beautifully presented and well-run bistrot because it offers very good value in a pleasant setting: on balance, the best in the area.

There is a range of dishes (from bouillabaisse to côte de boeuf) with regional wines at modest prices; a 13€ formule at lunchtime and an 18€ menu of limited choice but three courses – for example:
  – rillettes maison
  – boeuf mode
  – tarte aux pommes chaudes.
Especially at dinner it is worth upgrading to the 30€ menu which could include:
  – foie gras
  – carré d'agneau
  – tarte tatin
or you can go à la carte for around 40€. Strongly recommended.

# Brasseries

**Brasserie Flo**
*7 cour des Petites Ecuries,*
*75010*
*Tel: 01 47 70 13 59*
*Métro: Strasbourg St Denis*
*Open: DAILY noon – 3.00 pm*
*and 7.00 pm – 1.00 am*
Located since time began in a shabby cul-de-sac off the rue du Faubourg St Denis, this Alsatian brasserie was the starting point for Jean-Paul Bucher's Flo chain which encompasses many other leading brasseries (Bofinger, Julien, for example) without, it has to be said, significantly impairing their character.

About all of them one can say that they are best at their central and straightforward classic dishes: seafood platters and choucroute (various pig-meat derivatives on a mound of pickled cabbage). Portions are huge but you should leave space for a pudding. Recommended as a *digestif* to finish the meal is the little-known marc d'Alsace, a fragrant, slightly herbal variant of the better known marc de Bourgogne.

There are menus at 22,90€ and 32,90€ but à la carte is not much dearer than the latter if you skip the entrée, which is itself like a main course.

**Julien**
*16 rue du Faubourg St Denis,*
*75010*
*Tel: 01 47 70 12 06*
*Métro: Strasbourg St Denis*
*Open: DAILY noon – 3.00 pm*
*and 7.00 pm – 1.00 am*
No more than five minutes' walk from the Brasserie Flo, Julien stands out in dramatic contrast to its seedy surroundings. Fish is the mainstay of the menu with predictable classics such as grilled sea bass and sole meunière. In general the cooking is more reliable than at its cousin in the cour des Petites Ecuries though the ambience of the latter is appealing in a different way. Here is one of the most elegant brasseries in Paris: the (much restored) interior is more open – and so appears larger-scale – than is usual. An exciting place to eat, enhanced by the swift professional service.

And for all this you can have a three-course meal for 30,50€ or two courses for 23,50€ with wines in ¼ litre and ½ litre pichets (about 13€ for the latter). Crêpes Suzette make for a good finale at 4,90€ extra. There is, in addition, an excellent carte at about twice the price. Specialities include cassoulet de Castelnaudary, choucroute de poissons (yes, with fish) and foie gras with asparagus (all at around 25€).

# 5. Nouvelle Athènes

A quarter of great contrasts but apparent uniformity. True it gets sleazier as you move up from the place St Georges to Pigalle where you have establishments aimed at the susceptible male; but even so they are intermingled with conventional small shops and cafés whose owners and clients accept their presence with equanimity.

The contrast between the comfortable bourgeoisie and those in straitened circumstances is found here in a way now less general than it once was and with a Parisian lack of ostentation in the distinction. In private roads and cul-de-sacs (the square d'Orléans off the rue Taitbout, the square Moncey off the rue Moncey) you can view the peaceful, protected residences of those who can pay for such privacy. Yet it is still mainly an area for those of modest means. 'Studios' often cost less than 150,000€ and even a two-bedroomed family flat little more than 300,000€ (but no lift). If you have a chance to visit the featureless modern outer suburbs of Paris you will see why areas like this have a strong appeal to young families.

There is history here but not of the kind that clamours for attention. If it is not an expensive area even now, until quite recently it was comparatively cheap. The bourgeois housing of the

nineteenth century, dignified though it is, did not strain budgets. Many impressionist painters chose to live here: most notably Renoir and Van Gogh. And earlier Chopin and George Sand lived at more than one address.

Don't expect dramatic sights, except for the picture-postcard views of Sacré-Coeur in the distance on north-trending streets like the rue des Martyrs. Yet there are minor gems such as the late 19th century Académie des Billards in the rue de Clichy – a private club but you can peer through the windows to glimpse the magnificent interior.

The district as a whole exemplifies the philosophy that it is well worth walking up every street. If you eat at the various bistrots we recommend you will come to regard the necessary journey (on foot) a secondary benefit, giving another chance to uncover the details that make the area both diverse and idiosyncratic. The dog photographed looking out of a shop doorway had, needless to say, an owner who was a dream analyst.

## Principal sights

None in the orthodox guidebook sense: what a relief!

## Quiet hotels

**Hôtel Résidence des 3 Poussins**
*15 rue Clauzel, 75009*
*Tel: 01 53 32 81 81*
*Fax: 01 53 32 81 82*
*E-mail: h3p@les3poussins.com*
*www.les3poussins.com*
*Métro: St Georges*
*40 rooms AIR CONDITIONED*
*Price:154€ for a mid-range double room (half of them equipped with 'cuisinette' at an extra cost of 15€)*
This hotel is well-suited to an extended stay, with good access to all quarters of the Right Bank. It is in the more upmarket part of the quarter and near some popular bistrots. There are some larger, more expensive rooms on the top floor (all with kitchette) with wonderful views south over the city; but all rooms are excellent.

Advance booking is essential, especially for peak periods.

**Hôtel Tour d'Auvergne Opéra**
*10 rue de la Tour d'Auvergne, 75009*
*Tel: 01 48 78 61 60*
*Fax: 01 49 95 99 00*
*E-mail: tourdauvergne @wanadoo.fr*
*www.hoteltourdauvergne.com*
*Métro: Cadet/Pigalle*
*24 rooms AIR CONDITIONED*
*Price: 130€ for a double room (but note that prices are higher during peak periods)*
There are cheaper (and smaller) rooms than the price listed; and a few that are larger and more expensive. But the price shown gives you a room of reasonable size, well-decorated, equipped and furnished with an excellent bathroom. The hotel has a non-smoking tradition and, unusually for a small hotel, offers good room service: cold main courses at 16€, sandwiches at 12€, cheese and desserts for 6€; and a ¼ litre of wine for 7€ – useful if you are arriving late, tired and hungry.

**Villa Van Gogh**
*2bis Cité Pigalle, 75009*
*Tel: 01 48 74 39 22*
*Fax: 01 45 96 04 09*
*E-mail: hotel-villavangogh*
*@yahoo.com*
*www.villavangogh.com*
*Métro: Pigalle*
*23 rooms (plus one apartment)*
*Price: 125€ for a double room*
*('chambre confort'); 145€ for a*
*room on the courtyard side*
*('chambre élégance')*
Situated in a private cul-de-sac off
the rue Pigalle, this is a charming
and quiet hotel. And Van Gogh
did live nearby with his brother
Théo.

**Hôtel Résidence Alba-Opéra**
*34 ter (=34b) rue de la Tour*
*d'Auvergne, 75009*
*Tel: 01 48 78 80 22*
*Fax: 01 42 85 23 13*
*www.parisby.com/alba-opera*
*Métro: Cadet/Pigalle*
*28 studios and apartments, all*
*with 'cuisinette'*
*Price: for studios with double or*
*twin beds: 109€ with shower,*
*125€ with bathroom*
Situated in a small cul-de-sac
(*impasse* in French) off the main
street this is a calm, well-run hotel.
Mme Alberola, the formidable
owner, is emphatic that she does
not just have rooms (chambres)
and she is right. The studios are
of a good size but there are also
larger apartments with separate
bedrooms for 237€. You will be
expected to admire the owner's cat
(stuffed) that sits on the reception
desk, having departed this life at
the age of 25 years.

The space and facilities enable

you to make good use of the excellent food shops in the nearby rue
des Martyrs market street.

**Monterosa**
*30 rue la Bruyère, 75009*
*Tel: 01 48 74 87 90*
*Fax: 01 42 81 01 12*
*E-mail: hotel.monterosa*
*@wanadoo.fr*
*Métro: St Georges/Trinité*
*36 rooms*
*Price: 119€ for a double room*
In the heart of the district this
moderately priced hotel offers
well-maintained no-frills accommodation. Twelve of the rooms
overlook an interior courtyard and
so are quieter though this is not a
very busy street.

**Hôtel le Cardinal**
*3 rue du Cardinal Mercier, 75009*
*Tel: 01 40 16 30 00*
*Fax: 01 40 16 30 30*
*www.lecardinal.fr*
*Métro: Place de Clichy*
*78 rooms AIR CONDITIONED*
*Price: 155-185€ for a double room*
Although at the upper end of our
price range (and beyond) this hotel
is exceptional value for what it
provides. Situated in a cul-de-sac
many of the rooms overlook the
two interior courtyards and so are
very quiet.

Unusually for hotels at this
price-level there is a very competent restaurant which serves a
range of good-value menus and
formules as well as à la carte. A
characterful (but unremarkable)
breakfast is available in the café
opposite: the octogenarian owner
is an entertainment in her own
right.

# Breakfast

## La Rotonde

*2 place Estienne d'Orves*
*Open: DAILY from 6.00 am*
If there is an unmissable breakfast experience in this area I haven't found it. But this café (no relation to the famous Montparnesse version) provides a decent breakfast (fresh orange juice, café crème and croissant) for about 9€. The bonus is that in summer you can sit at a shady pavement table overlooking the church of the Holy Trinity, as well as the hurly-burly of traffic and the passing scene of assorted pedestrians. The interior is altogether less appealing.

## Select Café

*37 rue des Martyrs*
*Open: DAILY from 7.30 am*
A good place for a bargain breakfast. For 5,90€ you get:
– orange juice
– boisson chaude (coffee, chocolate)
– tartine beurrée
– croissant or pain au chocolat
– two small pots of jam.
My only criticism is that the café au lait can be too milky (ask for it *fort* or *pas trop laiteux*).

# Public gardens

## Square d'Anvers

*Location: just south of Anvers Métro station between boulevard de Clichy and avenue Trudaine.*
Interestingly broken up into small gardens by hedges which give the illusion that the park is bigger than it is: there is even a bandstand. Two children's play areas but these are segregated within the design so it's easy to find a peaceful spot.

## Square Alex Biscarre

*Location: just off place St Georges (NW corner).*
Quite large and with a sense of privacy, surrounded as it is by the backs of the 'classical' houses of the quarter. An ideal place for a quiet read.

## Square Berlioz

*Location: at the crossroads of the rue de Bruxelles and the rue de Douai.*
A small oval-shaped garden presided over by a statue of Berlioz, which is almost entirely given over to a children's play area. Their mothers or carers sit on the surrounding seats shaded by trees. Spaces like this are scarce in the quarter so it is enormously popular. If you like children it is also restful in its way – and just a step from the frantic activity of the boulevard de Clichy.

## Place Gustave Toudouze

*Location: junction of the rue Henry Monnier and the rue Clauzel.*
Not a garden but a triangle of tarmac with trees and a few benches. I could sit here for ages (have done) absorbing the photogenic view of this delightful quarter. And it is 'Henry' not 'Henri'; Monnier must have had an anglophile mother.

## Square de Montholon

*Location: between the rue*

*de Montholon and the rue
Rochambeau.*

Surrounded on three sides by dignified apartment blocks this is a cool, shady garden (and you're allowed to sit on the grass except where it's *en repos*). Quite heavily used so a little worn but the mature trees and bird-song make up the predominant impression. True there is a lively play area but there are several corners where adults can seek peace.

### Square Estienne d'Orves

*Location: just in front of the church of La Sainte Trinité and to the west of the Trinité Métro station.*

The domineering façade of the church provides an impressive backdrop to this dignified oval garden with its well-maintained flower-beds and large, handsome trees. There is a defined play area but the tone is adult-oriented. Large enough to be restful despite the nearby traffic.

## Markets

### Place d'Anvers, 75009 (open-air market along two sides of the square d'Anvers)

*Friday afternoon 2.00 – 8.00 pm*
An innovation bordering on revolution: other open-air markets are morning-only affairs. This rather small market is setting out an identity for itself with an emphasis on organic products, particularly fruit and vegetables. Without doubt the best small food market in Paris, every stall a top class specialist with superb fish, meat, cheeses,

breads, charcuterie. The quality and freshness is remarkable with many uncommon items (black truffles at 10€ for five).

In fine weather you can eat your purchases in the immediately adjacent gardens.

### Rue des Martyrs, 75009 (market street)

*Most shops open early to late but usually with a long lunchtime closure: 1.00 – 4.00 pm and, like all such, closed on Sunday afternoon and all day Monday.*
It is the bottom half of the rue des Martyrs which is the market bit, a focus for local food shopping and so a wonderful opportunity for practising your French because the shopkeepers have little English. Altogether an excellent place to shop for a picnic lunch (the squares Montholon and Alex Biscarre are nearby).

## Fromagers

These two cheesemongers are to be found in the southern, market street end of the rue des Martyrs:
**Fromagerie Loty,** *26 rue des Martyrs*
**Fromagerie des Martyrs,** *5 rue des Martyrs*
Further up you find:
**J. Mollard,** *48 rue des Martyrs*, which specialises in goats' cheeses from small producers.

They all follow the normal market pattern of closing Sunday afternoon and all day Monday; otherwise open 8.00 am – 7.30 pm with the typical long lunch break.

# Glaciers

**Caramelo**
*47 rue des Martyrs, 75009*
*Closed: Monday*
*Open: Tuesday to Friday noon –*
*9.00 pm; Saturday and Sunday*
*11.00 am – 10.00 pm*
This small and very modern glacier opened as recently as October 2007 and is top-rated. Not a wide choice and caramel beurre salé is typical. You get one boule for 3€, two for 4€ and four for 6€ (in a big pot). They also sell excellent chocolat chaud for only 2,80€.

The famous ice-cream makers Baggi in the rue Chaptal closed some time ago after having been in business for 150 years; they have not been replaced.

# Neglected museums

**Musée de la Vie Romantique**
*Hôtel Scheffer-Renan, 16 rue Chaptal, 75009*
*Métro: Pigalle/St Georges*
*Closed: Monday and public holidays*
*Open: 10.00 am – 6.00 pm*
*Entrance: FREE to the permanent collection*
*www.vie-romantique.paris.fr*
The Romantic Movement celebrated here centres on George Sand and her circle with paintings, drawings and other memorabilia. The house belonged to the largely forgotten Dutch painter, Ary Scheffer, who had his studio here but, more importantly, hosted meetings of celebrated members of the Romantic Movement in the first half of the 19th century –

George Sand, Chopin and Liszt among them.

The narrow alley leading into the museum has a discreet charm of its own and brings you into a garden with trees and flowers and an excellent open-air café, much patronised by locals (open from 11.30 am).

Highly recommended.

**Musée Gustave Moreau**
*14 rue de la Rochefoucauld, 75009*
*Métro: Trinité*
*Closed: Tuesday*
*Open: 10.00 am – 12.45 pm and 2.00 – 5.15 pm (last admissions 4.30 pm)*
*Entrance: 4€*
*www.musee-moreau.fr*
Moreau's monument to himself, a lifetime's preoccupation with his legacy: a vast studio and exhibition space designed for him by the architect Albert Lafon with an ornate central staircase in the family house – of which there are a few rooms on display. Whatever you think of his paintings this is an intriguing place to visit.

# Interesting shops

**Detaille**
*10 rue St Lazare, 75009*
*Métro: Notre Dame de Lorette*
*Closed: Sunday, and Monday morning*
*Open: Monday 3.00 – 7.00 pm, Tuesday to Saturday, 10.00 am – 1.30 pm and 2.00 – 7.00 pm*
This is a shop literally with the perfume of the past. It was founded in 1905 by the Comtesse

de Presle, a pioneer motorist, who wanted a cream to stop her skin drying out under driving conditions. You can still buy her Baume d'Automobile. She named the shop after her husband, brother of the painter Edouard Detaille.

The simple interior of the shop with its tiled floor, wooden drawers and a single table as a counter, is soothing just to look at. There is a range of toilet waters at 59€ for men engaged in such activities as flying, yachting and fencing. Floral toilet waters for women cost 10€ more. Delightful.

## La Vaissellerie
*79 rue St. Lazare, 75009*
*Métro: Trinité*
*www.lavaissellerie.fr*
*Closed: Sunday*
*Open: 10.00 am – 7.00 pm*
Although there is much kitsch (for those who like it) the predominant theme here is stylish and plain white table and kitchenware at rock bottom prices. As an example a coffee cup and saucer costs 1,50€.

There are branches at 85 rue de Rennes (6th) and 92 rue St Antoine (4th).

## Champagne et Collections
*6 place Estienne d'Orves, 75009*
*Métro: Trinité*
*Closed: Sunday and Monday*
*Open: 10.00 am – 8.00 pm*
This is the place to find rare and obscure brands of champagne – they stock 300 different makes. They also deal in the capsules from the tops of champagne corks (a collecting craze in France). Apart from champagne they have a range

of excellent modestly priced table wines (under 10€) from the likes of Louis Jadot.

## Brocantes
*1 rue Henry Monnier, 75009*
*Métro: St Georges*
*Closed: Sunday and Monday*
*Open: erratically Tuesday to Saturday*
This chaotic shop which verges on dealing in antiques is run by a charming Irish woman who trained as a nurse in London; so you won't need your French. Her stock is a wild assortment but the prices are modest and she is perfectly happy for you to poke around.

## Antiquités
*27 rue Clauzel, 75009*
*Métro: St Georges*
*Closed: Sunday and Monday*
*Open: 10.00 am – 6.00 pm (closed for lunch usually 1.00 – 3.30 pm)*
The owner is a specialist in old glass of which she has a huge quantity, mainly 19th to early 20th century. Her prices are much lower than elsewhere in the city with a wonderful range of old champagne flutes (from the time before the saucer-shaped bowl became predominant in the 1900s). She has these from singletons up to sets of six.

There are also hundreds of decanter stoppers (often missing from decanters you might have or buy elsewhere). But you have to take your decanter with you to ensure finding one that fits and is in the right style. Cost: about 8€. Or she'll sell you a complete decanter.

# Bistrots

## Le Charlain

*23 rue Clauzel, 75009*
*Tel: 01 48 78 74 40*
*www.lecharlain.fr*
*Métro: St Georges*
*Closed: Sunday (Saturday and Monday lunchtimes)*
*Open: Tuesday to Friday noon – 2.30 pm and 7.00 – 11.00 pm (Saturday and Monday 7.00 – 11.00 pm)*

This large and very successful bistrot de quartier is just the kind of traditional establishment this guide is about, with sound food and careful service.

There is a 30€ three-course menu with a choice from 5 entrées, 6 plats and 3 desserts (or cheese – camembert, livarot and munster) and for that you might get soupe de poissons, confit de canard and crème brûlée. However, for 49€ you have the run of the carte plus a half-bottle of wine, e.g. quails' eggs with foie gras, magret de canard with confit of shallots, and crème de mûre and gaufre Normande with apple sorbet and Calvados.

Tables are of a good size and well-spaced, the atmosphere calm and pleasant. It is essential to book as the restaurant is full from 8.00 pm.

## Casa Olympe

*48 rue St Georges, 75009*
*Tel: 01 42 85 26 01*
*Métro: St Georges*
*Closed: Saturday and Sunday, first two weeks in May, three weeks in August, Christmas and New Year*
*Open: noon–2.00 pm and 8.00–11.00 pm*

A restaurant with that rarity in France a female chef, Dominique Versini, who produces both traditional dishes (with some influence from her native Corsica) and those more 'inventive': I have sometimes found the latter too strongly flavoured and the restaurant is here for its more traditional fare. With a menu-carte at 38€ this is remarkable quality for price and there are some excellent wines in the range 25-50€ a bottle with some half-bottles from 14€; wines are also available by the glass.

Reservations are not accepted more than a week in advance and it is essential to book. Mme Versini doesn't make it too easy for you: those without reservations are turned away even if there are empty tables (there usually aren't). Worth the effort.

## Côté 9ème

*5 rue Henry Monnier, 75009*
*Tel: 01 45 26 26 30*
*www.cote9eme.com*
*Métro: St Georges*
*Closed: Sunday (Saturday lunchtime) and two weeks in August*
*Open: noon – 2.30 pm and 7.30 – 11.30 pm*

This used to be a favourite bourgeois bistrot called La Table de la Fontaine. Its name and character is now bang up-to-date but the food has its roots firmly in tradition. Entrées are 6-8€ (e.g. saumon mariné aux épices et asperges verts); plats 17-18€ (e.g. gigot

d'agneau à la sangria et chorizo –
it works!) with desserts at 6-7,50€
(e.g. crème brûlée au jasmine).
Drink the table waters from Alsace
(4€ a half litre). It is essential to
book; ask for a window table.

### Relais Beaujolais

*3 rue Milton, 75009*
*Tel: 01 48 78 77 91*
*Métro: Notre Dame de Lorette*
*Closed: Saturday, Sunday, public*
*holidays and the whole of August*
*Open: noon – 2.15 pm and*
*7.30 – 10.00 pm*
With an uncompromisingly
French cuisine (and many variants
of beaujolais) this is a local restaurant with an informal family
atmosphere and a faithful clientèle. The food is entirely
unpretentious if not tourist-
oriented (fricassée of pigs' ears, for
example) which may explain why
I have never heard other than
French accents here. Altogether it
is a million miles from a contemporary bistrot of the kind managed
by a chef of great name (but at
some distance). Sound cuisine and
an immensely likeable atmosphere.

There is a three course 'sugges-
tion du jour' at 28€ but à la carte
costs little more than that. They
bring a bottle of wine to the table
and you only pay for what you
drink.

### Pétrelle

*34 rue Pétrelle, 75009*
*Tel: 01 42 82 11 02*
*Métro: Poissonière*
*Closed: Sunday (Saturday and*
*Monday lunchtime), the whole of*
*August and a week at Christmas*
*Open: noon – 1.30 pm and*
*8.00 – 9.30 pm*
I am in two minds about this
restaurant. It is nowhere near a
'bistrot de quartier' (although I
have seen it described as such). It
has a contrived, over-controlled
atmosphere that some may find
irritating. Elaborate chandeliers
scarcely pierce the gloom. Your
table will likely have a few books
carefully scattered with rose
petals... and so on. But the food is
superb, not as fancy as the setting,
and the clientèle fashionable (as
you might expect in a street that is
of the anonymous, out-of-the-way
variety).

There is a three course no-
choice menu at 29€, otherwise
main courses are about that price.
Reckon on 45€ for two courses,
60€ for three. No wines under 22€;
half-bottles start at 16€. Cheeses
are brought entire to your table
and you help yourself; with a free
meringue at the end.

The delicious food won me
round, in particular the casseroled
duck and a lavender-flavoured
cream dessert. There are only eight
tables so booking is essential. If
you're in favour the black and
white cat will share your table.

### Velly

*52 rue Lamartine, 75009*
*Tel: 01 48 78 60 05*
*Métro: Cadet*
*Closed: Saturday, Sunday and*
*three weeks in August*
*Open: noon – 2.00 pm and*
*7.30–10.45 pm*
A small restaurant, even if it is on
two floors. Food is traditional and

varies according to what's available at the market. Wines are good value and are also served by the glass. The three-course menu at 31€ is the recommended choice. Essential to book but don't go too early as no one seems to arrive before 8.30 pm.

## Brasseries

### Charlot (Roi de Cocquillages)
*12 place de Clichy, 75009*
*Tel: 01 53 20 48 00*
*Métro: Clichy*
*Open: DAILY noon – 3.00 pm*
*and 7.00 pm – midnight (to 1.00*
*am Thursday, Friday, Saturday)*
One comes for the seafood to this art deco extravaganza in one of the busiest parts of Paris: the fish soup, the seafood platters, the fish of the day. Animated with a diverse clientèle it has an ambience to lift your heart; and it lives up to its name, a king in its own domain.

Lunch is served on the light and spacious first floor level and the 30€ menu (typically: amuse-bouche, fish soup, whole grilled sea bream, soufflé Grand Marnier, a glass of wine and a half-bottle of mineral water) is arguably Paris' best value. You can have two courses for 25€, but why? Dinner is served on the ground floor as well. There is no menu in the evening: à la carte costs around 60€ and above, but is still worth it. The sea-bass, baked in a salt-crust,

and expertly prepared and served is memorable.

One to save for a Sunday when other restaurants are mainly closed and most of those that stay open are to be avoided.

### Mollard
*115 rue St Lazare, 75008*
*Tel: 01 43 87 50 22*
*Fax: 01 43 87 84 17*
*E-mail: espace.clients@mollard.fr*
*www.mollard.fr*
*Métro: St Lazare*
*Open: DAILY from noon to*
*1.00 am*
Situated opposite St Lazare station (and just into the 8th arrondissement) for some reason this fantastic (literally) late 19th century brasserie is missing from most guidebooks. The exotic oriental-art nouveau interior beats anything in Paris. Designed by Edouard Niermanns, in its present form it opened in 1895.

Another establishment dedicated mainly to seafood, especially oysters, plateaux des fruits de mer (for two) are priced at 68,95€ or 96,85€ including lobster – good value.

In addition there is a sound three-course menu of traditional dishes at 42,65€ including a half-bottle of wine or mineral water. The reasonably-priced wine list has bottles from 18-90€.

Strongly recommended but it is essential to book.

# 6. Faubourg Montmartre

This is a fascinating part of Paris – provided that you look beneath the surface. It is extraordinarily compact: so much so that some of its more intriguing sights are concealed. Take Chartier for instance, the late 19th century *bouillon-brasserie* on the main street where the entrance is so narrow you would miss it if you didn't know it was there. It is well-known, of course, but on a first visit nothing prepares you for the business-like bustle of the vast interior which has seen nothing of the restorer's hand. The continuity here is real: *bouillon* (beef broth) has been served every Monday since 1896.

But what marks out this area (lacking guidebook sights as it does) are the early 19th century *passages* (shopping arcades) which, whilst they have changed their character somewhat, have not been heavily restored like the galeries Vivienne and Colbert in the 2nd arrondissement, or denatured like the passage des Princes near the boulevard des Italiens.

This is the place for 'unsmart' shopping; and much of it is to be found in the passages des Panoramas, Jouffroy and Verdeau. The passage Jouffroy also contains the Hôtel Chopin with its remarkable (interior) façade: it's been there as an hotel since the passage was built in 1846. Two other passages, close by, were closed or demolished in 1927 – Bergère and Richer: you can still see the sign for the latter over what was the entrance on the rue du Faubourg Montmartre. There has been little change since then.

Yet at the back of one's consciousness is the suspicion that a time will come when the area (very central) is seen as ripe for 'improvement'. You are urged to go there before that happens. One surprising feature of the district (possibly part of its compactness) is that there are no green spaces. Surely there must be but if so they've eluded me so far; perhaps some narrow alley I've walked by leads into something of that kind – well hidden, which would certainly be in character.

## Principal sights

This is the great area of the 19th century *passages* and one where many have survived – see the section for Interesting shops. And there is the occasional gem of 19th century public architecture like the 'Greek revival' façade of Corroyer's (1881) extravaganza in the rue Bergère, with its allegorical statues of Prudence, Commerce and Industry (now the Banque Nationale de Paris).

## Quiet hotels

### Hôtel Chopin
*46 passage Jouffroy, 75009*
*(entrance to the arcade at 10 boulevard Montmartre)*
*Tel: 01 47 70 58 10*
*Fax: 01 42 47 00 70*
*Métro: Grands Boulevards*
*36 rooms*
*Price: 88€ for a double room on the upper floor (single occupancy)*
Although the décor is a little faded this hotel is remarkable for its position, being at the end of one of the famous passages, and for its long history: it has always been an hotel. The best (and lightest) rooms are on the top floor overlooking the Musée Grévin next door – the latter not recommended because of its exorbitant charges (17,50€ adults, 10,50€ children) to see indifferent waxworks.

Booking is essential as the hotel is well-known for its value and character. Send a fax and then ring up to check they've received it.

The arcade closes at 10.00 pm so you have to ring the night bell on the iron grille to get in, there being no other access to the hotel.

### Hotels in the Cité Bergère:
This L-shaped, traffic-free street is like an arcade without a roof – and no shops, but full of hotels. Built at the same time as the shopping passages it is too scruffy to be charming. The bigger hotels (like the Victoria at 2bis-4) seem always to be full of adolescents on package holidays and who are presumably responsible for the monotonous graffiti that cover all accessible surfaces. The hotels, in the main, have the well-worn quality of relentless exposure to the demands of undiscriminating tourism.

Some of them are at the upper end of our price-range: these are well-equipped and maintained but you can get better value and a more appealing setting elsewhere. The two hotels identified below represent the best value.

### Hôtel des Arts
*7 Cité Bergère, 75009*
*Tel: 01 42 46 73 30*
*Fax: 01 48 00 94 42*
*E-mail: hda9@free.fr*
*www.arts-hotel-paris.com*
*Métro: Grands Boulevards*
*25 rooms*
*Price: 81-128€ for a double room (cheaper in winter)*
A small and privately owned hotel which is altogether in a better state than most of the competition in this price range.

### Hôtel d'Espagne
*9 Cité Bergère, 75009*
*Tel: 01 55 33 50 90*
*Fax: 01 55 33 50 99*
*E-mail: he@hotels-emeraude.com*
*www.hotels-emeraude.com*
*Métro: Grands Boulevards*
*45 rooms*
*Price: 96€ for a double room*
Round the corner which runs into the rue Bergère this is the best choice of the cheaper hotels in the Cité Bergère: basic but efficient and well-maintained with an attractive façade.

### Villa Fénélon
*23 rue Buffault, 75009*
*Tel: 01 48 78 32 18*
*Fax: 01 48 78 38 15*
*E-mail:*
*villa.fenelon@wanadoo.fr*
*www.hotelvillafenelon.com*
*Métro: Cadet/Notre Dame*
*de Lorette*
*38 rooms*
*Price: 118€ for a double room*
Most of the rooms at this well-placed hotel overlook an interior courtyard garden, where you can take breakfast which is included in the price. So it has a lot in its favour, but at the time of my last visit I felt that maintenance was not as good as it might be.

### Hôtel Touring
*21 rue Buffault, 75009*
*Tel: 01 48 78 09 16*
*Fax: 01 48 78 27 74*
*E-mail: infos@hotel-touring.fr*
*www.hotel-touring.com*
*Métro: Cadet/Notre Dame*
*de Lorette*
*54 rooms*

*Price: 105€ for a double room*
Next door (to the Villa Fénélon) this well-maintained but very busy hotel probably has the edge over its competitor. The rue Buffault is a comparatively quiet street.

## Breakfast

### La Tour des Délices (Valentin)
*32 passage Jouffroy*
*Open: DAILY from 9.30 am*
*(10.00 am Sunday)*
Just a step away from the Hôtel Chopin this is a delightful confiserie-café especially in the colder months of the year when the view of the arcade gives you a sense of being protected but not isolated.

Serving a range of specialised teas and good value lunches, Valentin's café is included here for the breakfast formules. *Le Parisien* which offers tea or *café allongé* (a diluted version of the standard espresso) together with a croissant or pain au chocolat for 4,40€ or, for 9,40€, *Le Détente* comprising orange juice, tea or café crème, pain grillé (toast), croissant, jam and butter.

Altogether a pleasant way to start the day.

### Royal Cadet
*11 rue Cadet*
*Open: DAILY from 7.30 am*
*(8.30 am at weekends)*
This is a very large café in a busy market street, with a formule for 7€:

    – orange juice
    – boisson chaude
    – croissant or tartine

Well patronised by locals and welcoming to tourists.

### Au Général La Fayette
*52 rue La Fayette*
*Open: DAILY from 10.00 am*
This busy café/brasserie (see p. 106) is an excellent place to have breakfast provided you don't want it before ten in the morning (they stay open until 4.00 am). For 5,60€ you get a large café crème and three mini-viennoiseries which you can consume while you watch the staff getting ready for a long day.

## Public gardens?

Well, there aren't any... The nearest – at the top end of the rue Cadet, on the northeastern perimeter – is the **square de Montholon** (see p. 91-2).

## Markets

### Rue Cadet, 75009 (market street)
Mostly closed Monday and Sunday pm, this is a short and very busy market street running north-east from the rue du Faubourg Montmartre. With many specialist food shops, including fruiterers and a small supermarket, it can meet almost all your needs. There is an excellent baker **Maison Dupuy** at no. 13 *(Tous nos pains sont façonnés à la main)* and their prune bread at 85 centimes is the best eat-as-you-go snack imaginable.

**Produits d'Auvergne** at no. 17 is good for charcuterie and other delicacies – ideal with Dupuy's *pain de campagne.*

## Fromager

### Autour d'un Fromage
*20 rue Cadet, 75009*
*Closed: Sunday afternoon and Monday*
*Open: 8.30 am – 1.00 pm and 2.30 pm – 7.00 pm*
A very new shop with a modest range of cheeses in fine condition.

## Glacier

### L'Artisan La Fayette Zagori
*6 rue La Fayette, 75009*
*Closed: Sunday*
*Open: 8.00 am – 8.00 pm*
With 34 superb flavours on offer this is not to be missed (if you like ice-cream). Picking three almost at random: *myrtille* (bilberry), *miel nougat* (honey nougat), *citron vert* (lime). Prices are cheaper than some of the competition at 2,50€, 3,70€ and 4,50€ for one, two or three *boules.* Cheerful, friendly service from young women who demanded of me: why was I asking all these questions?

There is also a range of superb chocolates and quite beautiful marzipan fruits.

### Neglected museums

### Musée de la Parfumerie Fragonard
*9 rue Scribe, 75009*
*39 boulevard des Capucines, 75002*
*Métro: Opéra*

*Métro: Opéra*
*Closed: Sunday and public*
*holidays*
*Open: 9.00 am – 6.00 pm*
*Entrance: FREE (guided tour)*
Housed in a 19th century town house and the former Théatre des Capucines, these collections are slightly out of our area but worth the extra walking distance; they're free but an adjunct to the boutiques selling Fragonard perfumes.

A chance to see rare and beautiful objects, going back five thousand years, connected with the making, storing and use of perfume; the scent bottles appear as works of art in their own right.

### Musée du Grand-Orient de France

*16 rue Cadet, 75009*
*Métro: Cadet*
*Closed until 2009. Check on*
*websites for new entrance hours*
*Group visits may be possible in*
*interim: ring 01.45.23.43.97*
*www.godf.org/foreign/uk/musee*
*_uk.html or www.godf.org/*
*musee.asp for more up to date*
*information*
The broad, modern and rather anonymous building in the rue Cadet is in marked contrast to the bustle of the surrounding shops. It does have a rather closed, secret look about it.

Without giving away any secrets, the museum has a comprehensive display of objects, documents and pictures relating to freemasonry, including portraits of distinguished masons of the past (Lamartine, Diderot).

## Interesting shops

It is in the 19th century passages that this district offers the greatest interest for the curious shopper; and the three best are close together – more or less in a line from south to north (Métro: Grands Boulevards). We begin with the most southerly (and the oldest): the **passage des Panoramas**, 75002 *(open DAILY 6.00 am – midnight)*.

The original arcade built in 1800 runs from 11 boulevard Montmartre to 10 rue St Marc; but interlinked arcades were subsequently added running from 38 rue Vivienne to 151 rue Montmartre. In its day it was a major attraction of the Right Bank and one of the first public places to be lit by gas (in 1816). Something of the original character remains, not least in the premises of the stationer and engraver **Stern** at no. 41 with its original shop front. One of the arches over the arcade bears the legend: Stern Graveur: Cartes de Visite. Nowadays the character of most of the shops is more mundane (unless you are a stamp collector) but there is an excellent café which also serves meals, **L'Arbre à Cannelle**, calm and spacious but with some tables out in the passage itself (closed Sunday but otherwise open from midday to 6.00 pm).

On the northern side of the boulevard (and directly opposite) we come to the **passage Jouffroy**, 75009 *(open DAILY 7.00 am – 10.00 pm)*.

Built 1845-46 it is in remarkably original condition and runs, in
two stages, from 10-12 boulevard
Montmartre to 9 rue de la Grange
Batelière. The adjoining waxwork
museum (**Grévin**, built in 1882)
has an entrance within the passage
itself. A dealer in traditional canes
and umbrellas is long-established.
One of the most appealing toy
shops in Paris – **Pain d'Epices** is at
no. 31, specialising in dolls, dolls'
houses and furniture (closed
Sunday, open 9.00 am – 7.30 pm
Monday to Friday, from 10.00 am
Saturday). In the more northerly
section is to be found **Olivier** at no.
63, one of the few dealers in Paris
specialising in antique silver – high
quality and fair prices (open
Monday to Friday, 10.00 am – 7.00
pm). And there are bookstores, a
dealer in film memorabilia and
another dealing in old postcards,
meticulously catalogued. Altogether a good way to spend much
of an afternoon – with tea at
Valentin's.

After which you can stroll
across to the **passage Verdeau**,
75009 on the other side of the rue
de la Grange-Batelière *(open
Monday to Friday, 7.30 – 9.00 pm;
Saturday and Sunday to 8.30 pm)*.
The entrance is at no. 6, for the
record, because you can't miss it.

This arcade was constructed at
the same time and as part of the
same project as the one you have
just left, and the character is much
the same even today. One shop
stands out and that is **Amicorum**
at no. 19 which sells watercolours
and drawings (unmounted) from
the 16th-20th century. Usually

unsigned and unattributed there
are thousands to browse through
at prices often less than 100€, some
less than 50€.

As you re-enter the rue du
Faubourg Montmartre you are
immediately adjacent to the
confectioners:

### A la Mère de Famille

*35 rue du Faubourg Montmartre,
75009*
*www.lameredefamille.com*
*Métro: Le Peletier*
*Open: Monday to Saturday, 9.30
am – 8.30 pm; Sunday 10.00 –
1.00 pm*

Founded in 1761 and still with its
later 19th century shop-front, this
is the most seductive confectioners
in Paris. A bold claim – go and
see.

They make their own chocolates (delicious, and if you are a
good customer they may give you
one to try). But their great strength
is the range of sweetmeats from
all over France. Everything you've
ever heard of is here and they make
up baskets of assorted goodies
which make attractive presents.
It's difficult to pick things out but
particularly recommended are the
stuffed Agen prunes (pruneaux
d'Agen fourrés).

Not recommended are their
ice-creams (summer only) which
are disappointing. There are
branches elsewhere in the city in
the 6th, 7th and 17th arrondissements selling the same things but
without the ambience.

One other arcade has to be
mentioned: the **passage des
Princes**, 75002 *(open Monday to*

Saturday, 8.00 am – 8.00 pm) which runs from 5 boulevard des Italiens to 97 rue de Richelieu. Originally constructed in 1860 it has recently been restored and somewhat denatured in the process: now given over entirely to modern shops for children.

## Bistrots

### Pré Cadet

*10 rue Saulnier, 75009*
*Tel: 01 48 24 99 64*
*Métro: Cadet*
*Closed: Sunday (Saturday lunchtime), the first week in May, three weeks in August, Christmas to New Year*
*Open: noon – 2.00 pm and 7.30 – 10.00 pm*

An unremarkable exterior in an unremarkable side-street near the Folies Bergère; but here you'll find first-rate traditional food. Meat is a speciality (tête de veau, onglet, carré d'agneau) but there are a few fish dishes. There is an exceptional value menu at 30€ which includes a kir aperitif with three courses (a choice of six entrées and eight plats, then cheese or dessert). A la carte will set you back about 45€. There is a good range of wines from 21€.

This is a restaurant with a strong following so it is essential to book.

### Bistrot Papillon

*6 rue Papillon, 75009*
*Tel: 01 47 70 90 03*
*Métro: Cadet*
*Closed: Sunday (Saturday lunchtime), public holidays, the first week in May, three weeks in August*
*Open: noon – 2.00 pm and 7.00 – 10.00 pm*

You will find this provincial-style restaurant in a street directly opposite the square de Montholon. Classic dishes are its hallmark and there are daily specialities on the three-course menu at 29€. A la carte costs around 45€ and the good quality wines are in the range 16-30€ a bottle.

### Aux Lyonnais

*32 rue St Marc, 75002*
*Tel: 01 42 96 65 04*
*Métro: Bourse/Grands Boule-vards/Richelieu Drouot*
*Closed: Sunday, Monday (Satur-day lunchtime), the last week in July and first three weeks in August, Christmas Eve to New Year*
*Open: noon – 2.00 pm and 7.30 – 11.00 pm*

Forty years ago, under M. Viollet, this was the most famous Lyonnais restaurant in Paris; with his departure there was a protracted period of decline. When I dined there in the late 1990s it was a sad relic of its former self, even if the original tiled interior looked as fresh as ever. Then, at the beginning of the new millennium the star chef Alain Ducasse took control of its fortunes, if not its kitchen.

Almost aggressively re-invented as an institution, the food is nonetheless traditional with an added flair; only the memory of forty years ago gives me pause.

Very popular, booking is essential. There is a good-value but restricted choice menu at 30€; à la carte costs 40-45€.

## Le Gavroche

*19 rue St Marc, 75002*
*Métro: Bourse/Grands Boule-*
*vards/Richelieu Drouot*
*Closed: Sunday and the whole of*
*August*
*Open: 7.00 am through to 2.00 am*
*(this is a wine bar cum bistrot)*
Wines are primary here and much of what is offered is bottled especially for them: fine quality in the price-range 14-22€ a bottle. The food, as befits a wine-bar, is both traditional and straightforward and can be as basic as *steack-frites*, for example. Even à la carte is not a high-price option and three courses is likely to be no more than 25€. No reservations and the value means it is often crowded, but the atmosphere (psychological) is attractive.

## A la Grange Batelière

*16 rue de la Grange Batelière,*
*75009*
*Tel/Fax: 01 47 70 85 15*
*E-mail: lagrangebateliere*
*@wanadoo.fr*
*Métro: Richelieu Drouot/Grands*
*Boulevards*
*Closed: Saturday, Sunday and*
*evenings (except for private*
*parties)*
*Open: lunch only Monday to*
*Friday, noon – 3.30 pm*
It is sometimes true to say that the more successful a restaurant is in Paris, the less often it is open. That is certainly the case here as they no longer open for dinner on a regular basis. If you go for lunch you'll see why – they don't need to.

We have normally excluded lunch-only restaurants but this is an honourable exception. Excellent traditional food from chef Benoist Gérard is featured on menus at 25€ and 30€ with wines to match.

Highly recommended but make sure you book well in advance.

## Le Vieux Pressoir

*30 boulevard Poissonière, 75009*
*Métro: Grands Boulevards*
*Closed: Sunday*
*Open: noon – 2.00 pm and 7.00 –*
*10.00 pm (to midnight Friday*
*and Saturday)*
In a stretch of tacky establishments this main boulevard bistrot stands out with its well spaced tables and handsome interior. There is a restricted three-course menu (no drinks) for 18,90€, but the real value is in the 31€ menu which includes a kir apéritif, three courses, a half-litre pichet of wine and coffee.

The food couldn't be more traditional with entrées like soupe à l'oignon gratinée and œuf mayo; plats such as saucisse de Toulouse with frites or jarret de porc aux lentilles vertes; and desserts of crème caramel and tarte aux pommes.

Exceptional value but the idiosyncratic owner may decide he doesn't like the look of you...

# Brasseries

## Au Petit Riche
*25 rue Le Peletier, 75009*
*Tel: 01 48 24 10 79*
*Métro: Le Peletier*
*Closed: Sunday, also Saturday*
*from mid-July and three weeks*
*in August*
*Open: noon – 2.15 pm and 7.00*
*pm – 12.15 am*
A classic belle époque brasserie
made up of dining rooms of varying sizes with some more open
than others. The service is attentive
and professional, the style of the
food unchanging from one decade
to another. There is a good value
lunch menu at 25,50€ and one for
28,50€ at dinner; à la carte costs 35-
55€. Wines are available in a
variety of formats from a single
glass upwards.

## Au Général La Fayette
*52 rue La Fayette, 75009*
*Metro: Le Peletier/Cadet*
*Open: DAILY 10.00 am through*
*to 4.00 am*
This is the kind of café-brasserie
where booking would be an affectation. I stepped inside one day to
avoid the rain, and over a vin chaud
watched a continuous stream of
French families coming in for
lunch.

Food here is of the substantial
snack variety, if 'snack' is the right
word for their *grandes assiettes
Auvergnates* of cheeses, charcuterie etc. for 13€. They do excellent
omelettes (e.g. espagnole at 9,50€):
these come with a salad but you
can ask for frites.

A good place to come if you're
not sure what you want to eat, or
want to eat quickly.

## Chartier
*7 rue du Faubourg Montmartre,*
*75009*
*Métro: Grands Boulevards*
*Open: DAILY 11.30 am – 3.00*
*pm and 6.00 – 10.00 pm*
Taking the narrow alley leading in
from the street you come to an
unprepossessing entrance: which
opens on to a vast, glass-roofed
dining room where little of importance has changed in over a
hundred years. Chartier is a great
institution for locals and tourists
alike because no guidebook,
including this one, would dream of
omitting it. A couple of points: we
don't give a telephone number
because reservations are not
accepted (you'll understand when
you get there); and the 10.00 pm
deadline is for last orders.

The overwhelming impression
is of professionalism: no-one
wastes time here while you ponder
the 'carte'. The waiter writes your
order on the paper tablecloth, and
adds up the bill in the same way.
You share tables (four to a table)
and you exercise reserve. The food
is unremarkable at best except for
its regular incursion into the culi-
nary past. Although not as
absurdly cheap as it once was, you
would be pushing the boat out to
exceed 25€ on your bill. The quality of the food is variable as is the
service: sometimes it can be down-
right sloppy. Nonetheless an
experience not to be missed.

# 7. Palais-Royal
# (and for Les Halles and the Louvre)

The most distinguished quarter of the Right Bank is to be found here with the conservative style of not drawing attention to itself. The survival of the area is remarkable, close as it is to the *grands boulevards* so beloved of Baron Haussmann and his bourgeois sponsor and master, Louis Napoléon (III). If you compare the discretion and lack of ostentatious display of the Palais-Royal with the over-dressed Opéra Garnier (a centre-point of Haussmann's grandiose plan) less than a kilometre away, the contrast is dramatic.

Both handsome and rewarding, here is classic Paris at its best: and with so much to discover even if the area we have delimited is a fairly narrow one. For those who see shopping and dining as the most civilised of urban activities, the appeal is infinite. Within the Palais itself with its garden and the arcaded shops (all specialists of one kind or another) there are good restaurants including the most illustrious: Le Grand Véfour in the rue de Beaujolais.

It is not immediately apparent that this is a great area for shopping: there is nothing of the raucous consumerism of the rue de Rivoli a few hundred metres to the south. Apart from the shops of the Palais there are the 19th century shopping arcades, here mainly called *galeries*: Vivienne, Colbert and Véro-Dodat – restored but not ruined in the process – the last named being particularly beautiful. And there is the interestingly shabby passage Choiseul, often overlooked: see the relevant entries (pp. 111-13).

Outside our main area (and our main emphasis) the Palais du Louvre is vast and unmissable, with easy access to the Jardin des Tuileries, with its perspective up to the distant Arc de Triomphe and old-fashioned amusements like carousels for children. The place des Victoires to the northeast is one of the less well-known squares of Paris but, like its more famous cousin the place Vendôme, now a chosen focus for high fashion. Despite 19th century depredations it retains much of its original atmosphere.

To the north of the area, and another defining influence, lies the Bourse (Stock Exchange). The concentration of dealers in rare coins and medals (not for the casual shopper) in the upper reaches of the rue de Richelieu reflects a proper appreciation of its central concerns, as does the high density of prosperous restaurants.

## Principal sights

**The Palais-Royal** (17th-18th century): beginning with Richelieu's palace the site was redeveloped in the late 18th century into its present form. A day is not too much to explore the many facets of this extraordinary group of buildings – all in harmony and offset by the black and white columns of the contemporary sculptor, Daniel Buren.

**Bibliothèque Nationale de France** (17th-19th century), 58 rue de Richelieu: library, museum and exhibition space, in particular the Galeries Mansart and Mazarine; but the main library is now transferred to Bercy.

**Place des Victoires** (late 17th century): originally a tribute to Louis XIV whose statue, a 19th century replacement, is in the centre. From some perspectives you can get an idea of how the square was intended to look.

**Musée du Louvre** (mainly 12th-19th century): the greatest treasure-house of the arts in the western world which has evolved under different kings, emperors

and republics. It has been a museum for two hundred years, with each century adding to (or subtracting from) the total. Pei's famous glass pyramid (1989) is the most recent major construction. The collection is overpowering in scale and has to be viewed selectively; studying the *Guide Michelin* is an essential preliminary.

And in Les Halles:

**Centre Georges Pompidou**: the 'inside out' cultural centre in explicitly controversial late 20th century style. Its piazza-like open space is host to mime artists, fire-eaters (and pickpockets) amongst the crowds of visitors.

**Musée National d'Art Moderne** (within the Centre): an extraordinary permanent collection of 20th century art and design.

## Quiet hotels

**Hôtel des Victoires**
*19 rue Hérold, 75001*
*Tel: 01 42 36 04 02*
*Fax: 01 45 08 14 09*
*Métro: Louvre-Rivoli*
*29 rooms*

*Price: 140€ for a double room*
A relative bargain for quality and location in a quiet street that runs into the place des Victoires, which still retains something of its 17th century elegance.

**Hôtel Molière**
*21 rue Molière, 75001*
*Tel: 01 42 96 22 01*
*Fax: 01 42 60 48 68*
*E-mail: info@hotel-moliere.fr*
*www.hotel-moliere.fr*
*Métro: Palais-Royal-Louvre*
*29 rooms (and 3 suites) AIR CONDITIONED*
*Price: 165-185€ for a double room*
The price goes just above our target range but this delightful hotel is so well-situated, and so quiet in a street which traffic appears to avoid, that it had to be included. The rooms on the sixth floor with a balcony are particularly recommended. Although the breakfast room is not particularly exciting, the buffet breakfast is very good and worth the 12€ charge.

**Hôtel Thérèse**
*5-7 rue Thérèse, 75001*
*Tel: 01 42 96 10 01*
*Fax: 01 42 96 15 22*
*E-mail: hoteltherese@wanadoo.fr*
*www.hoteltherese.com*
*Métro: Pyramides/Palais-Royal-Louvre*
*40 rooms (and 3 suites) AIR CONDITIONED*
*Price: 150-170€ for a double room with shower*
There are larger (and more expensive) rooms than the price quoted above, but those at the price given are of a reasonable size and this is a very good quality hotel: beautifully decorated and maintained, set in a quiet street in an expensive area.

**Vivienne**
*40 rue Vivienne, 75002*
*Tel: 01 42 33 13 26*
*Fax: 01 40 41 98 19*
*E-mail: paris@hotel-vivienne.com*
*www.hotel-vivienne.com*
*Métro: Grands Boulevards*
*45 rooms*
*Price: 90€ for a double room*
In the upper reaches of our area this is an hotel with larger than average rooms on a fairly quiet street. Pleasant, well-maintained and exceptional value. *And* you can take breakfast in the Vaudeville (see below).

# Breakfast

**Vaudeville**
*29 rue Vivienne (see main entry p. 116)*
*Open: DAILY 7.00 – 11.30 am for breakfast*
The splendid situation immediately facing the Bourse adds a dimension to breakfast here: a bargain at 7€ for which you get orange juice, café crème or an alternative, tartine beurrée, croissant and pain au chocolat.

There are tables under an awning outside. Inside, the breakfast area is to the right but you still get a good view. The elegant (and much larger) dining room is to the left. Service is swift and friendly.

**Paul**
*61 rue Montorgueil*
*Open: DAILY from 7.30 am*
A few outside tables where you can take breakfast. There are two formules: *Express* offers coffee and croissant for 2,20€, or *Parisien* for 3,30€, comprising a large café crème, and croissant or pain au chocolat.

## Public gardens

### Jardin du Palais-Royal
Within the Palais-Royal this garden, like the Palace itself, was originally the creation of, and for Cardinal Richelieu who lived there until his death in 1642. In its essentials it is still as it was at the end of the 18th century: its formal character the epitome of that 'classical' era. Beyond the double colonnade the garden is sheltered (by the surrounding buildings and supremely elegant arcades) and yet open to the sun. To the east and west are rows of immaculately pollarded trees with benches underneath; to the north and south two fine central lawns with, at each end, small enclosed gardens, complete with diminutive sand-pits. The cafés in the arcades at the north-west corner may let you take a tray of drinks into the garden if you ask nicely.

The splendid central fountain is surrounded by free-standing metal chairs so you can sit with your feet up on the edge of the bassin and watch the spray: very cooling on hot days.

Children will also enjoy scram-bling over Buren's truncated columns at the south end: a suitable fate for an art-work?

(There are more attractions for children in the nearby Tuileries.)

### Square Louvois
*Location: on the western side of the rue de Richelieu and facing the Bibliothèque Nationale.*
A rather formal small garden which occupies the site of the old Paris Opéra (demolished in 1820). It is in peaceful contrast to the much-visited gardens of the Palais-Royal.

## Markets

### Rue Montorgueil, 75001 (market street)
*Tuesday to Saturday 8.00 am – 7.00 pm (Sunday to midday)*
Opening hours vary a little from shop to shop in this famous market street just outside our area to the northeast. You could happily spend a morning exploring it. The street runs from the rue de Turbigo to the rue Réaumur, with the main concentration of food shops in the lower half; including the long-established pâtisserie, **Stohrer** at No.51, with a magnificently decorated 19th century interior.

### Bourse, 75002
*Tuesday and Friday afternoons 12.30 – 8.00 pm*
One of the new breed of afternoon markets, this one occupies the open space adjacent to the Bourse, useful for those who work locally. Very small, most stalls are for food,

many of them of the snack variety, the best being a couple of Lebanese caterers. Although there is a good fishmonger it is not a market for comprehensive shopping, more a place to buy for an open-air picnic.

## Fromagers

### Chez Tachon
*38 rue de Richelieu, 75001*
*Closed: Sunday, Monday, and the whole of July and August*
*Open: 9.30 am – 2.00 pm and 4.00 – 8.00 pm*
It is an education to visit this fromagerie. There are small notices telling you about the many different varieties of cheese so it's a place where customers can learn and experiment: don't just stick to what you know!

### La Fromagerie
*8 rue Montorgeuil, 75001*
*Closed: Monday, and Sunday afternoon*
*Open: 8.00 am – 7.00 pm*
There is an excellent range of cheese here, pain Poilâne to eat with it, and decent wines to wash it down if your budget runs to that. A variety of other high quality groceries gives you further choice.

## Glaciers

### Amorino
*82 rue Montorgeuil, 75001*
*Open: DAILY noon to midnight*
Another branch of this excellent Italian glacier (see p. 137).

Alternatively, **Dammann** has a kiosk near the octagonal pond in the Tuileries.

## Neglected museum

**Cabinet des Monnaies, Médailles et Antiques (Bibliothèque Nationale de France)**
*58 rue de Richelieu, 75002*
*Métro: Bourse*
*Closed: Sunday*
*Open: afternoons only, 1.00 – 5.45 pm (to 4.45 pm Saturday)*
*Entrance: 5€*
The National Library has (mainly) moved to the Mitterrand building on the quai François Mauriac in the 13th arrondissement.

Here is now housed one of the most interesting museums in Paris, principally of coins and medals – about half a million of them – but many other objets d'art and historical items (like the coronation throne of the Kings of France). It is possible to suffer from mental indigestion if you are too conscientious – but fascinating if you follow your inclinations. Much under-visited.

This museum should not be confused with the Musée de la Monnaie de Paris (the Paris Mint) on the quai de Conti (see p. 170).

## Interesting shops

If you feel that serious shopping – which is not just about buying – is one of life's more civilized pleasures you are in for a treat. But it requires the persistence of those who see shopping as a dedicated form of research: necessary here because the most interesting shops are tucked away, many of them in galeries and passages. We'll start with the most important.

**Galeries du Palais-Royal, 75001**
These are not like the other (mostly 19th century) shopping arcades in Paris. In the main they turn their backs to the surrounding streets but are open on the interior side, sheltered by the arcades. They are largely shops for specialist collectors (stamps, coins, toy soldiers), and when they are not you are likely excluded by price; but the window shopping is a pleasure in itself.

You need to get a clear grasp of their layout. To the north of the Palais is the rue de Beaujolais: so the interior arcade is called the **galerie de Beaujolais**. To the west the **galerie de Montpensier** parallels the street of the same name; and to the east the **galerie de Valois** runs alongside the rue de Valois. The latter has a wonderful restaurant with a terrace overlooking the garden, **Le Palais-Royal** at no. 110. It is here too that you find the most exclusive shop imaginable for gardening clothes and tools (**Le Prince Jardinier**). Other shops are of dealers in tapestries, porcelain, autographs and manuscripts, engravings, heraldry – and so it goes on.

On the other side of the garden at 22-24 galerie Montpensier you can find the shop of **Didier Ludot** (Open: 11.00 am – 7.00 pm Monday

to Saturday, and 1.00 pm – 7.00 pm Sunday). This is the place to find vintage big-name luggage and handbags, all expensive of course but beautifully renovated and with the patina that makes the new look vulgar. There are also some relatively inexpensive restaurants/cafés here, with tables outside in good weather; a possibility for breakfast.

To the north in the galerie de Beaujolais (entrance at no. 17 rue de Beaujolais), you have perhaps the most distinguished and certainly the oldest restaurant in Paris: **Le Grand Véfour** with its two Michelin stars.

The various entrances into the arcades are themselves called 'passages' and it is in one of these, very near the restaurant that you find the intriguing shop of **Anna Joliet**, passage de Perron, 9 rue de Beaujolais (closed Sunday, otherwise open 10.00 am – 7.00 pm). She specialises in musical boxes. Prices may seem high but there are some well-made examples for under fifty euros.

**Other galleries and arcades:**

All of these shopping arcades date from the third decade of the 19th century but they couldn't be more different.

**Galerie Véro-Dodat**, 75001 runs from 19 rue Jean-Jacques Rousseau to 2 rue du Bouloi (Métro: Palais-Royal-Louvre). This is the most authentic-looking arcade: even the light globes have the diffuse quality of gas lamps. The shops are variable but there is an interesting mix of art dealers and dealers in contemporary furniture. (Closed Sunday and public holidays, otherwise open 7.00 am – 10.00 pm.)

The elegant **galerie Vivienne**, 75002 runs from 4 rue des Petits Champs to 5 rue de la Banque and 6 rue Vivienne (Métro: Bourse), open DAILY 8.30 am – 8.30 pm. You will find the unusual children's shop **Si Tu Veux** at no. 68, selling beautifully made fancy-dress outfits as well as quality craft and cookery sets for children. A good place for a special birthday present (open Tuesday to Saturday, 10.30 am – 7.00 pm).

Running in parallel from 6 rue des Petits Champs to 4 rue Vivienne, is the **galerie Colbert** (Métro: Bourse) which has now been taken over by the University of Paris. You can go in (past security guards) but the only things you can see – apart from the arcade itself – are lecture and seminar rooms. True, the brasserie **Le Grand Colbert** (p. 116) backs on to part of it but its entrance is in the rue Vivienne.

**Passage Choiseul**, 75002 runs from 40 rue des Petits Champs to 23 rue Augustin with a small spur into the rue St Anne (opens DAILY 7.00 am – 9.00 pm; Sunday from 8.00 am). In terms of condition it is the poor relation (even the street sign is broken) but there are characterful compensations. The shops are a very mixed bunch at the lower end, just clothes retailers and fast-food outlets; however, the level is coming up with some interesting

art galleries. At no. 74 is the toyshop **Un Jeu d'Enfant** which specialises in traditional metal pedal cars – at a price.

**Duthilleul et Minart**
*14 rue de Turbigo, 75001*
*Métro: Etienne Marcel*
*Closed: Sunday*
*Open: 9.30 am – 6.30 pm*
If you've ever wondered where brasserie waiters get their long white aprons, the answer is here. The catering trade is the main emphasis but all the craft professionals' garb is available. Their biggest selling items are the work clothes (*bleus de travail*) which are fashionable amongst those who reject formal fashion. All strongly made and 'les bleus' will wear and wash to fade to the desired shade....

**E. Dehillerin**
*18-20 rue Coquillière, 75001*
*Métro: Les Halles*
*Closed: Sunday (and Monday lunchtime)*
*Open: 8.00 am – 6.00 pm*
This is the utensils complement to Duthilleul et Minart. There is everything here for the professional cook, all of durable quality and a million miles from the conventional trendy 'kitchenware' shop. Their copper (but nickel-lined) saucepans are the real thing and will last a lifetime in a domestic kitchen. Bearing in mind the quality, prices are not high.

**Elvis: My Happiness**
*9 rue Notre Dame des Victoires, 75002*

*Métro: Bourse*
*Closed: Sunday*
*Open: 10.30 am – 7.00 pm, but with
a long lunch hour: 1.00-2.30 pm*
A shop entirely given over to Elvis
Presley souvenirs and memorabilia. Even if you're not a fan you
should pop in to wonder at the
preoccupations of those who are.

### G. Detou

*58 rue Tiquetonne, 75002*
*Métro: Etienne Marcel*
*Closed: Sunday*
*Open: 8.30 am – 6.30 pm*
This unpretentious family grocers
with its amazing range, impossible
to list (oils, olives, dragées, sardines
millesimées and so on) is here for
two reasons. First it is one of the
best places to buy marron glacés:
you can even get 'morceaux'
(broken pieces) at 19,30€ for a kilo
box; and secondly for its tinned
and bottled dishes from the South-
West (garbure, cassoulet, etc).

## Bistrots

### Chez Pauline

*5 rue Villédo, 75001*
*Tel: 01 42 96 20 70*
*Métro: Pyramides*
*Closed: Sunday (and Saturday
lunchtime)*
*Open: 12.30 – 2.30 pm and
7.30 – 11.00 pm*
Some hesitation in including this
classic bourgeois bistrot even
though it has long been a personal
favourite. The truth is that it has
been in a steady decline, a process
difficult to halt. The food can be

good but it is not always reliable.
You come here for boeuf bourguignon (burgundy is a strong
influence elsewhere on the menu),
roast poulet de Bresse and the like.
Wines are heavily weighted in the
direction of the region and there is
an excellent house beaujolais:
plenty to choose from at under
45€ a bottle.

The 52€ three-course *menu
classique* provides a good choice,
and if you go without a pudding it
will work out about 43€. The
menu is in any case a safer bet than
the carte. Give it a chance; it's
worth the experience.

### Chez Georges

*1 rue du Mail, 75002*
*Tel: 01 42 60 07 11*
*Métro: Bourse*
*Closed: Sunday, the whole of
August, Christmas and New Year*
*Open: noon – 2.00 pm and
7.00 – 9.30 pm*
Another example of the truly classic bistrot – not cheap, unchanging
in standards and the dishes it
serves. The middle-aged waitresses
(motherly or bossy depending on
your taste) are part of the reassuring, no-nonsense ambience. The
early closing hour (for last orders)
typifies the style: this is not a place
for *les branchés* (the 'switched-on'
younger generation).

Booking is required: it's always
full. And there is no prix fixe to
tempt you in: they don't need it. A
la carte is at the top of our price
range but you can't practise
moderation all the time.

## Chez la Vieille

*1 rue Bailleul, 75001*
*Tel: 01 42 60 15 78*
*Métro: Louvre-Rivoli*
*Closed: Saturday, Sunday and*
*three weeks in August*
*Open: noon – 2.00 pm and*
*7.30 – 9.30 pm*

This famous old bistrot was taken over by Marie-José Cervoni in 1994 and while some offerings reflect his Corsican origins, the traditional character of the food remains with such dishes as calves liver with shallots, whole roasted veal kidneys and so on. There is a generous lunch menu at 27€; à la carte costs around 50€. Famous for the laden trolleys of entrées and desserts from which you receive generous portions, this is a restaurant where (a) it is essential to book and (b) you need to starve yourself beforehand, i.e. skip breakfast or lunch; or both.

## L'Epi d'Or

*25 rue Jean-Jacques Rousseau,*
*75001*
*Tel: 01 42 36 38 12*
*Métro: Louvre-Rivoli*
*Closed: Sunday (and Saturday*
*lunchtime)*
*Open: noon – 2.30 pm and*
*7.45 – 10.30 pm*

A bistrot with a history dating back to the 19th century when it served workers from the nearby Les Halles. It is now more upmarket but otherwise resolutely traditional with an appearance to match – large zinc bar, striking wall clock, and a hundred and one details that bespeak care and attention. This is a highly successful bistrot in classic style where it is essential to book.

There is a formule available until 1.30 pm at lunch and until 9.00 pm at dinner: two courses at 18€, three for 22€. A la carte is around twice that. Plenty of wines by the bottle in the range 20-30€ with some half-bottles. But they offer a sauvignon and a claret for 3€ a glass.

## L'Incroyable

*26 rue de Richelieu, 75001*
*Tel: 01 42 96 24 64*
*Métro: Palais-Royal-Louvre*
*Closed: Saturday and Sunday*
*(and Monday evening)*
*Open: noon – 2.00 pm and*
*7.00 – 9.00 pm*

Serving very respectable traditional meals at 'incroyable' prices, this little bistrot has nothing to do with fashion or haute cuisine: here you eat as in the family. There is a 'menu du jour' at 16,50€ for two courses, 21,50€ for three. A la carte is correspondingly inexpensive. Wines are 2,90€ a glass, 3,50-4,40€ for a ¼ litre, and pro rata. There are other restaurants as cheap but not as good for the price.

You need to look out for the sign as it is tucked away in a narrow passage.

# Brasseries

## Gallopin

*40 rue Notre-Dame des Victoires,*
*75002*
*Tel: 01 42 36 45 38*

*Métro: Bourse*
*Closed: Sunday, and also*
*Saturday during August*
*Open: noon to midnight*
The streets surrounding the Bourse
are well provided with brasseries,
as one might expect; and the late
19th century Gallopin has the
charisma of long-established
professionalism. The food here is
a good deal better than at the
Grand Colbert but otherwise the
experience is similar: exciting, stimulating. There is a lunchtime
formule express at 19,50€ comprising an 'assiette gourmande' plus
dessert plus wine/beer/water and
coffee.

There are three day-long
menus: e + pl or pl + dess at 23€;
e + pl + dess at 28€; and with added
wine for 33,50€. A la carte will cost
in the region of 40€.

### Le Grand Colbert

*2 rue Vivienne, 75002*
*Tel: 01 42 86 87 88*
*Métro: Bourse*
*Open: DAILY noon – 1.00 am*
This much restored 19th century
restaurant (part of the galerie
Colbert) has the frantic bustle that
is the essence of such places. It is
popular with Parisians but the food
is decidedly uneven. There is a
lunch menu at 17,50€ and a dinner
menu at 26€; à la carte will cost

about fifty per cent more, but as
portions are enormous you may
save by not having a first course. In
any case, prices are modest for such
a setting.

### Vaudeville

*29 rue Vivienne, 75002*
*Tel: 01 40 20 04 62*
*Métro: Bourse*
*Open: DAILY 7.00 – 11.30 am*
*(for breakfast – see p.00), noon –*
*3.00 pm and 7.00 pm to half past*
*midnight*
In style similar to La Coupole
(but smaller) it is, perhaps
inevitably, a member of the Flo
group, yet it has its own distinctive buzz: it is a characterful place
to take breakfast (with a similar
formule) but somehow here you
feel you're more at the heart of
things. This is an exciting place
to be at any time of day. The self-
assured professionalism of the
food and service is another kind of
comfort.

There is an excellent two-
course (e + pl) 'menu du garçon' at
21€ and this can include oysters
or foie gras canard as the entrée,
and magret de canard or quenelles
de brochet for the plat – very good
value. The three-course 'menu
brasserie' is 31€ with three choices
for each course. A la carte from
45€.

# 8. Batignolles-Monceau

The composite title reflects the inclusion of the parc Monceau which is its own justification: one of the city's most beautiful open spaces set within a district of fine private houses and public buildings. But the character of the quarter lies in the still predominantly working-class Batignolles, and this has none of the conventional imperatives of tourism. Not only are there no guidebook sights, the buildings and streets are, in general, on a smaller scale than elsewhere in Paris. In one sense it is an unremarkable area.

Blockaded to the north by vast railway marshalling yards there is no route for traffic through Batignolles, and this is part of its isolation: you don't come to this part of the city unless you choose to. The boulevard Malesherbes to the west demarcates the fashionable sector of the 17th arrondissement whose inhabitants may shop in the adjacent market street of the rue de Lévis (p. 120) but rarely penetrate beyond that. Yet the further east you go, crossing the rather dreary main road, the rue de Rome, the more you are into the heart of the district. The principal streets – the rue des Dames, the rue des Moines and the rue des Batignolles – contain a range of small shops that will appeal to the systematic idler (no conscious purpose but you explore thoroughly). People are friendly in an almost provincial way. Coming out of  the square des Batignolles on to the place du Docteur Lobligeois with the handsome backdrop of the church of Sainte Marie des Batignolles, I encountered an impromptu concert (to no particular audience) given by a colourfully dressed group of black women in their role as *gardiennes d'enfants* with their inevitable white charges. I applauded and they did a reprise. At one level not typical, but yet of the relaxed style of the area. You need to experience it for yourself.

## Principal sights

The **parc Monceau** (18th century in origin) certainly qualifies: see the separate entry under Public gardens.

**Cathédrale St-Alexandre-Nevsky** (mid-19th century), rue Daru: a five-minute walk from the park, the Russian Orthodox Church of Paris is built in exotic Byzantine style on a Greek cross plan, and famed for its magnificent sung Mass. The visitor can admire the gilded domes of the exterior and the golden richness of the interior (but note that admission is limited: 3.00 – 5.00 pm Tuesday, Friday, Sunday).

## Quiet hotels

### Hôtel des Batignolles
*26-28 rue des Batignolles, 75017*
*Tel: 01 43 87 70 40*
*Fax: 01 44 70 01 04*
*E-mail: hotel@batignolles.com*
*www.batignolles.com*
*Métro: Rome*
*50 rooms*
*Price: 74-88€ for a double room*
Although on the busy main street of the district, this well-maintained hotel is set back and all rooms overlook a courtyard. The price given is for the renovated rooms – worth the modest extra cost.

### Hôtel du Roi René
*72 place Docteur Félix-Lobligeois, 75017*
*Tel: 01 42 26 72 73*
*Fax: 01 42 63 74 99*
*Métro: Rome*
*28 rooms*

*Price: 85-90€ for a double room*
For some reason the place du Docteur Félix-Lobligeois is sometimes not marked on maps but it is just south of the square des Batignolles so very attractively situated. Not a noisy area and, in any case, half of the rooms give on to an interior courtyard.

### Hôtel Excelsior
*16 rue Caroline, 75017*
*Tel: 01 45 22 50 95*
*Fax: 01 45 22 59 88*
*E-mail: excelsior-caroline @wanadoo.fr*
*www.excelsior-paris-hotel.com*
*Métro: Place de Clichy/Rome*
*22 rooms*
*Price: 100€ for a double room; 120€ for a 'supérieure'*
Right in the heart of the Batignolles quarter this is a relatively smart hotel – hence the higher prices. Large well-equipped rooms, many with magnificent marble fireplaces. Note that breakfast is included in the room price.

### Hôtel Jardin de Villiers
*18 rue Claude Pouillet, 75017*
*Tel: 01 42 67 15 60*
*E-mail: hoteljdv@wanadoo.fr*
*www.paris-hotel-villiers.com*
*Métro: Villiers*
*26 rooms AIR CONDITIONED*
*Price: 104-160€ for a superior double room*
The best hotel in the area, behind the famous market street of the rue de Lévis which attracts Parisians from all over the city. Very well-equipped and situated on a quiet street with little traffic; half of the rooms overlook the interior garden so are even quieter.

The buffet-breakfast is included in the price and can be taken in the garden.

## Breakfast

### Le Sauret
*54 rue de Lévis*
*Open: DAILY from 7.30 am*
This largish corner brasserie, bustling and busy, is at the heart of things. The men crowded at the bar look like extras for a French movie. A diverting place for breakfast and good value at 6,80€, for which you get:
– fresh juice
– coffee, chocolate etc.
– croissant
– baguette
– butter and jam
– and, if you feel up to it, three fried eggs for 2,60€.

### Paul
*24 rue de Lévis*
*Open: DAILY from 7.30 am*
This branch has a small number of tables (down one side of the shop) where you can choose from the usual range of breakfast formules.

## Public gardens

### Parc de Monceau
*Location: between the boulevard de Courcelles and the rue de Monceau.*
This is one of the finest parks in Paris, essentially laid out in the 18th century, much modified later and opened as a public park in 1861 complete with specimen trees and statuary.

The adjective 'elegant' is irresistible: the classical design, the well-dressed promenaders with their typically Parisian diminutive dogs, all contribute to the ambience. Even the natural functions are catered for with taste: public lavatories are to be found in a kind of Greek temple (the Rotunda) at the boulevard de Courcelles entrance.

Quite different from the eastern side of the 17th arrondissement yet it is no more than ten minutes' walk from the market street, the rue de Lévis. In fine weather a picnic overlooking the lake with its 'ruined' colonnade is the stuff of memories.

### Square des Batignolles
*Location: between the church of Ste Marie des Batignolles and the rue Cardinal.*
This is very much the green space of the Batignolles quarter and something of a community centre (courts for boules, etc). Laid out in the mid-19th century in the French conception of an English garden, it has an artfully constructed 'naturalism' including brooks and waterfalls. The small (but splendid) lake is colonised by ducks but graced by the addition of black swans; small humans are well catered for in the play areas with roundabouts, go-kart tracks and table-tennis.

## Markets

### Batignolles, 75017
*Saturday only 8.00 am – 2.00 pm*
This open-air market is to be

found in the boulevard de Batignolles between the rue des
Batignolles and the rue Puteaux.
A relative newcomer to the market
scene it is hugely popular and has
a speciality of organic produce,
with many stall-holders growing
what they sell. Smaller than the
better known *marché biologique*
in the boulevard Raspail but of
an equal standard with many
specialists.

### Rue de Lévis, 75017 (market street)

*Open variably Tuesday to Satur-
day 7.30 am – 1.00 pm and 3.30 –
7.30 pm (Sunday to 1.00 pm)*
By common consent the best
market street in Paris after the rue
Mouffetard – and less touristy; it's
also one of the most lively with
stall-holders calling out to passers-
by and hectoring anyone who
shows signs of stopping. Individual shops have their own opening
hours but most close for lunch.
The branch of **Paul** (p. 119) is
recommended for its excellent
range of sandwiches (3-4€) which
can also be part of a formule
including a drink and a dessert for
only a couple of euros more.
**Monoprix** also has two large stores
here (one for clothes, one for
food): their fresh fruit is particularly cheap.

## Fromagers

### Alain Dubois
*79 rue de Courcelles and 80 rue
de Tocqueville, 75017
Closed: Monday
Open: Tuesday to Friday, 9.00*

*am – 1.00 pm and 4.00 – 8.00 pm;
Saturday 8.30 am – 7.30 pm;
Sunday 9.00 am – 1.00 pm*
This highly regarded fromagerie
stocks cheeses hard to find elsewhere and specialises in goats'
cheese in many varieties.

### Alléosse
*13 rue Poncelet, 75017
Closed: Monday
Open: Tuesday to Thursday, 9.00
am – 1.00 pm and 4.00 – 7.00 pm;
Friday and Saturday 9.00 am –
1.00 pm and 3.30 – 7.00 pm;
Sunday 9.00 am – 1.00 pm*
Just outside our area but too
important to be omitted. Regarded
by many as the most distinguished
fromager in Paris, Alléosse supplies
many of the top restaurants. An
extraordinary range of unusual
cheeses from all over France.

### Androuet
*23 rue de la Terrasse, 75017
Closed: Monday, and Sunday
afternoon
Open: Tuesday to Friday, 9.30
am – 1.00 pm and 4.30 – 7.30 pm;
Saturday 9.30 am – 7.30 pm;
Sunday 9.30 am – 1.30 pm*
Part of a reliable chain of cheese
shops, this branch is conveniently
placed in the market-street area –
but take note of the long lunch
break.

### G. Gautier
*43 rue de Lévis, 75017
Closed: Sunday
Open: 9.00 am – 1.30 pm and
3.30 – 7.00 pm*
Gautier is now the fromagerie of
the rue de Lévis; the long established firm of Jean Carmes et fils at

No. 24 is no more, being replaced by a branch of Paul. But this is an entirely satisfactory alternative and note that, exceptionally, it is open on Monday.

## Glacier

**Mister Ice**
*6 rue Descourbes, 75017*
*Closed: Sunday and Monday*
*(and every morning)*
*Open: 2.00 – 7.30 pm*
Out of our area (and out of the way) this is an address for aficionados. Fabien Foenix, like Thomas Dammann, is in a different tradition from the creamy Italian ice-creams that dominate the scene. His style is more ascetic. Most of his trade is with top-ranking restaurateurs; however, the quality justifies the trek across the boulevard Pereire. Unusual flavours include vanilla with olive oil, fromage blanc cheese-cake and melon.

The scale of production and its usual city-wide destinations mean that what you buy is very frozen. But if you take your purchases to the parc Monceau, by the time you get there they will be ready to eat.

## Neglected museums

**Musée Jean-Jacques Henner**
*43 avenue de Villiers, 75017*
*Métro: Malesherbes/Wagram*
*Closed: Monday*
*Open: 10.00 am – 12.30 pm and 2.00 – 5.00 pm*
*Entrance: 4€*
Henner's house and studio display

the work of an artist (like Hébert) highly regarded in his day but overtaken by the new generation of painters who emerged in the late 19th century. That said, the house and its contents are a powerful evocation of its time. (NB Closed for renovation at the time of going to press.)

**Musée Cernuschi**
*7 avenue Velasquez, 75017*
*Métro: Villiers*
*Closed: Monday and public holidays*
*Open: 10.00 am – 5.30 pm*
*Entrance: FREE to the permanent collection*
The house and collection of Henri Cernuschi was donated to the city in the late 19th century at a time when it was de rigueur for a banker to be a patron of the arts. Cernuschi devoted his life and ample resources to collecting Oriental art. Even to the uninitiated this is a stunning collection, notably Chinese bronzes and jade.

**Musée de la Grande Loge de France**
*8 rue Puteaux, 75017*
*Métro: Rome*
*Closed: Saturday, Sunday and public holidays*
*Open: 10.00 am – 5.30 pm*
*Entrance: FREE*
An insight into the history of freemasonry in France, with an extraordinary assembly of ceramics, banners, ceremonial aprons, medals and documents.

**Musée Nissim de Camondo**
*63 rue de Monceau, 75017*
*Métro: Villiers*

*Closed: Monday, Tuesday and*
*public holidays*
*Open: 10.00 am – 5.00 pm*
*Entrance: 4,60€ (FREE to*
*under 18s)*
One of the most memorable and
moving museums in Paris, this
turn-of-the-century *hôtel partic-*
*ulier* and its contents was donated
to the city by Count Moïse de
Camondo in memory of his aviator son, killed in action in 1917.
The house, built in 18th century
style at the beginning of the 20th
century, has a superlative collection of 18th century art and
furniture. But it is a house rather
than a museum, and evokes the
poignancy of a man who had
everything but lost what was most
important to him.

# Interesting shops

### Produits Régionaux
*40 rue des Batignolles, 75017*
*Métro: Rome*
*Closed: Sunday*
*Open: 7.30 am – 8.30 pm*
This shop, the title of which speaks
for itself, is unusual in the range of
foodstuffs it sells - including the
more popular cheeses such as
Cantal and Beaufort. But its real
strength is in hams, pâtés, dried
sausage and a wide selection of
prepared dishes. An excellent
source of food for a simple, or
more elaborate meal. The non-stop
opening hours are an added conve-
nience.

### La Fourmée d'Augustin
*31 rue des Batignolles, 75017*
*Métro: Rome*

*Closed: Sunday*
*Open: 7.30 am – 8.00 pm*
Winner of the best baguette in
Paris award in 2004 this boulangerie is included for the superb
sandwiches it sells – in the prize-
winning baguette. Wonderful.

### Jean-François Bavat
*34 rue des Batignolles, 75017*
*Métro: Rome*
We don't give the opening hours
because that is irrelevant. This
portrait photographer is here
for the beautiful traditional shop
front and the amazing display. Go
and see.

### A la Mère de Famille
*30 rue Legendre, 75017*
*www.lameredefamille.com*
*Métro: Villiers*
*Closed: Sunday*
*Open: 9.00 am – 7.30 pm (from*
*10.00 am Monday and Saturday)*
A branch of the famous confectioners in the 9th arrondissement
which offers the same range, lacking only the atmosphere of the
original (see p. 103).

### Aux Douceurs d'Alys
*18 rue de la Terrasse, 75017*
*Métro: Villiers*
*Closed: Sunday*
*Open: 9.00 am – 1.00 pm and*
*3.00 – 7.00 pm*
An old-fashioned sweet shop of
great appeal to children (of all ages)
selling a variety of traditional
boiled sweets, lollipops and the
like; and superb pâtes de fruits.

### Antiquités
*10 rue des Batignolles, 75017*
*Métro: Rome*

Opening hours variable (better to check first – tel: 01 45 22 30 41)
A large shop with an eclectic choice at fair prices – porcelain, silver, bronzes, furniture, carpets, coins, medals and jewellery. Fascinating variety and much better value than the dealers in the flea markets.

## Bistrots

### Chez Léon
*32 rue Legendre, 75017*
*Tel: 01 42 27 06 82*
*Métro: Villiers*
*Closed: Saturday, Sunday, public holidays, the whole of August, a week at Christmas*
*Open: noon – 2.00 pm and 7.30 – 10.00 pm*
The finest bistrot in the area and one of the best in Paris. On my last visit I had lamb confit (preserved in its own fat) and served en casserole: delicious.

The understated professional service backs up the uncomplicated, French, clean-tasting food. The lunch menu of two courses for 24€ and three for 32€ is splendid value and there is a range of good quality wines by the glass at 3-5€. Prices are only a little higher for the dinner menu.

If you stay in the area you'll want to go there every night!

### Bistrot de Théo
*90 rue des Dames, 75017*
*Tel: 01 43 87 08 08*
*Métro: Rome*
*Closed: Sunday, public holidays, three weeks in August, Christmas to New Year*

*Open: noon – 2.30 pm and 7.30 – 11.00 pm*
This is quite an elegant 'bistrot de quartier' specialising in foie gras and dishes from the South-West. The 14€ lunchtime formule (two courses) is a great bargain; and there is a three course menu at 25€, with à la carte costing around 30€. The food here is of a very high standard midway between traditional and inventive, e.g. brochettes de veau et d'agneau, salade aux herbes et tomates confites.

### Le Petit Villiers
*75 avenue de Villiers, 75017*
*Tel: 01 48 88 96 59*
*Métro: Villiers*
*Open: DAILY noon – 11.00 pm*
The avenue de Villiers is a fine, broad street with some interesting 19th century buildings (like the neo-medieval Banque de France) but it is hardly lively so Le Petit Villiers comes as something of a surprise: and without doubt the best value in this part of Paris. The whole thing is organised to a formula (15 entrées, 15 plats and 15 fromages/desserts). There is a three-course all-day menu at 21€; a lunch-time formule at 13€ (two courses) or 16€ (three courses). All dishes are mainstream, traditional in character.

Wines cost 2,50€ a glass or you can get a ¼ litre pichet for 3,50€, ½ litre for 5,50€. Wines by the bottle cost 8,50-32,50€.

The nearest thing to a **brasserie** as we have nothing under that section. It is advisable to book for dinner, however.

# 9. Montmartre

Like the Batignolles quarter Montmartre has a strong village identity: to be a Montmartrois is a matter of local pride. But
Batignolles does not contain some of the most-visited sites in the
city so the sense of local community here may appear hard to
explain. Until you go and see for yourself: because there is
almost a kind of apartheid, though how it is regulated is something of a mystery. One moment you are in the midst of jostling
crowds, surrounded by strident appeals for attention from tourist
shops, cafés and self-styled artists; the next you pass through an
invisible curtain to find yourself virtually alone. For example, if
you follow the north-trending section of the rue Lepic from the
rue des Abbesses, after a couple of hundred metres the clamour
has faded and a different atmosphere prevails. Here you will find
the bistrot Au Virage Lepic, which discourages vegetarians and
those in search of *cuisine inventive*.

It is only the area immediately around the place du Tertre
and Sacré-Coeur (they are in line) that concentrates the visitors.
And this focus is very marked because moving down towards the
boulevards de Clichy and Rochechouart, increasingly you find
shops, cafés and restaurants that serve a different, essentially
local clientèle. This is most apparent in the southern, market-street
section of the rue Lepic which emerges at the place Blanche: next
to that sad relic, the Moulin Rouge.

Behind Sacré-Coeur tourism does not run at all. The rue
Lamarck which curls round its northern side is a better place to
find a café or restaurant, including the best bistrot in the area –
Le Bistrot Poulbot (p. 130).

Day visitors definitely get the worst of it (true of all popular tourist destinations). Early morning is the time to stand on
the steps below Sacré-Coeur, taking in the distant panorama, to
stroll along the cobbled streets and up and down the connect-
ing steps, each with its own vista. Montmartre is an enchanting
part of Paris: but you have to stay there to find it.

# Principal sights

**Sacré-Coeur** (late 19th-early 20th century): the basilica, like many famous landmarks, remains controversial yet appears always to have been there. Much less impressive close to than at a distance, where it can be seen from all over Paris framed by busy streets that contrast with the glittering white domes; and conversely, offers the visitor the best view of the city, seen from the high external gallery.

**Eglise St-Pierre-de-Montmartre** (12th-18th century), rue du Mont-Cénis: one of the oldest churches in the city and all that remains of the Benedictine Abbey of Montmartre. Much modified over the centuries but harmonious nonetheless.

**Eglise St-Jean-l'Evangeliste** (late 19th-early 20th century), rue des Abbesses: in contrast, the first church in Paris to be built of reinforced concrete, with a mixture of art nouveau and neo-Gothic styles. Its aesthetic qualities are widely disputed: I like it.

# Quiet hotels

**Damrémont**
*110 rue Damrémont, 75018*
*Tel: 01 42 64 25 75*
*Fax: 01 46 06 74 64*
*E-mail: hotel.damremont*
*@wanadoo.fr*
*www.damremont-paris-hotel.com*
*Métro: Jules Joffrin*
*35 rooms*
*Price: 95€ for a double room*

*with shower, 110€ with bath*
Located in a part of Montmartre that sees few tourists, this is a well-maintained hotel with those rooms overlooking the courtyard being especially quiet. Note that the rates given can be reduced by frequent promotions.

**Roma Sacré-Coeur**
*101 rue Caulaincourt, 75018*
*Tel: 01 42 62 02 02*
*Fax: 01 42 54 34 92*
*E-mail: hotel.roma@wanadoo.fr*
*www.hotelroma.fr*
*Métro: Lamarck-Caulaincourt*
*57 rooms*
*Price: 100€ for a superior double room*
Situated close to the cemetery of Montmartre and with good views of Sacré-Coeur it is nonetheless far enough away from the tourist hub to be fairly peaceful. There is a narrow interior courtyard but the rooms on this side are small and not recommended; in any case there is a garden at the front and the street is not busy.

A long-established favourite and an excellent base for getting to know the district.

**Hôtel Prima Lepic**
*29 rue Lepic, 75018*
*Tel: 01 46 06 44 64*
*Fax: 01 46 06 66 11*
*E-mail: reservations@hotel-prima-lepic.com*
*www.hotel-prima-lepic.com*
*Métro: Blanche/Abbesses*
*35 rooms (and 3 apartments)*
*Price: 130€ for a double room on the courtyard side; 160€ overlooking the street*

Built around a maze of courtyards this is an hotel where the rooms vary considerably – in size and also in quietness. Ask for one of the larger, courtyard rooms on an upper floor, but don't accept the lower ones because they are gloomy and sometimes small. Otherwise, street-side is better.

### Hôtel Regyn's Montmartre
*18 place des Abbesses, 75018*
*Tel: 01 42 54 45 21*
*Fax: 01 42 23 76 69*
*E-mail: hotel@regynsmont-martre.com*
*www.regynsmontmartre.com*
*Métro: Abbesses*
*22 rooms*
*Price: 80-115€ for the best double rooms; 65-99€ for the others (seasonal variations)*
Right in the heart of Montmartre, the hotel is run by M. Cardin who is a fanatical proponent of the village character of the quarter; and he is equally fanatical about the standards of his good-value hotel.

Most of the rooms overlook the lively place des Abbesses, which boasts a Guimard Métropolitain entrance with glass canopy. The rooms on the upper floors have a panoramic view of Paris. Rooms at the rear are a good deal quieter, and those at the top also have excellent views.

It is essential to book well in advance.

### Ermitage Hôtel
*24 rue Lamarck, 75018*
*Tel: 01 42 64 79 22*
*Fax: 01 42 64 10 33*

*www.ermitagesacrecoeur.fr*
*Métro: Lamarck-Caulaincourt*
*12 rooms*
*Price: 94€ for a double room*
Nothing about this Second Empire hôtel particulier says 'hotel' in the contemporary sense except two discreet gold stars under the small name-plaque.

An extremely well-maintained hotel in family ownership for a generation, the great attraction lies in the splendid view over Paris from the back rooms (seven in number). Exceptional value because the room price includes breakfast.

## Breakfast

### Le Gastelier
*1 bis rue André Tardieu*
*Closed: Monday*
*Open: from 9.00 am*
This is by a long way the best place for breakfast and amazingly quiet despite being close to the rampant tourist spots. For 7,10€ you get:
  – café crème, chocolate or tea
  – croissant and brioche and pain grillé
  – fruit juice
  – butter and jam.
It's also a popular venue for ice-cream (see p. 129). In summer they open the folding doors so you can people-watch. A bit of a walk but some of our recommended hotels are quite near.

### Au Relais
(see main entry p. 130)
*48 rue Lamarck*
*Open: DAILY from 8.00 am*

Further up the butte is this popular café-bistrot. No formule for breakfast, but fruit juice, coffee, croissant and tartine will cost 10-12€ and you can eat it at the tables set out under the trees in the adjacent square.

# Public gardens

## Square Nadar and Square Willette
*Location: either side of the small funicular railway up to Sacré-Coeur*
Nadar provides a panoramic view to the west. The much bigger Willette has a children's play area and merry-go-round.

A better place to rest your feet than to have a quiet lunch because, inevitably, there are hordes of eager visitors following the well-marked route to the top.

## Parc de la Turlure
*Location: behind Sacré-Coeur, and therefore quieter*
This park with its multiple terraces and a extensive view of the east of Paris is the most attractive in the vicinity. Not much grass but what there is you can sit on; otherwise plenty of seats, shrubs and trees, and shady pergolas.

It caters for all ages: the older men playing boules and vigorous youngsters on the climbing frames; and there's also a sandpit, much patronised. Another feature is the waterfall/weir that children play under in hot weather.

## Square Jehan Rictus
*Location: off the passage des Abbesses, north of the place des Abbesses.*
Small and shady; no grass but pleasant walks and flowerbeds. Quiet in comparison with the nearby activity.

## Place Constantin Pecqueur
*Location: adjacent to the St Vincent cemetery.*
A small garden, with no grass, but delightfully shaded by large trees.

## Place Emile Goudeau
*Location: roughly between the rue Garreau and the rue Berthe.*
Not a garden but an elevated, traffic-free cobbled square with plenty of benches and trees – and even more tourists. Charming nonetheless.

## Jardin sauvage St Vincent
*Location: south of the rue St Vincent, next to the vineyard (established in 1933)*
It is worth taking the trouble to visit this small wild garden (complete with nettles) opposite the cemetery. Only open on Saturdays and Sundays from the beginning of April to the end of October, 10.00 am – 12.30 pm and 1.30 – 6.30 pm (to 5.30 pm in October), it is a garden to see and appreciate rather than a place to picnic. Recommended.

## Square Carpeaux
*Location: off the rue Carpeaux, near the crossroads of the place Jean Froment (a pleasant café terrace there)*

Not much grass and largely given over to children's play areas. But plenty of seats set back and shaded by mature trees; an elderly bandstand in the centre.

### Square Suzanne Buisson

*Location: between the avenue Junot and the rue Simon/place Casadesus: entered through the allée des Brouillards.*

This is a distinctive terraced garden, ascending from the avenue and much used by locals of all ages, with a children's play area. An excellent place to sit and watch a game of boules in progress. It is small and there is no grass, but there is an air of calm restraint about it; even the trees are pollarded.

## Markets

### Rue Lepic, 75018 (market street)

*Tuesday to Saturday 7.30 am – 1.00 pm and 3.00 – 8.00 pm (Sunday to 1.00 pm)*

It is the southern half of the rue Lepic, between the rue des Abbesses and the place Blanche, which makes up the famous market street, always busy particularly at weekends.

Apart from the usual range there is a pâtisserie artisanale (**Les Petits Mitrons**) at no. 26 which sells superlative caramelised tarts. And the épicerie next door has a tempting range of nougat (sliced, cake style) and an unusually wide range of soups in jars (au pistou; de lentilles vertes).

## Fromagers

### Chez Virginie

*54 rue Damrémont, 75018*
*Closed: Monday*
*Open: Tuesday to Saturday, 9.15 am – 1.00 pm and 4.00 – 8.00 pm; Sunday 10.00 am – 1.00 pm*

Owned and run by the daughter of the original owner and the shop reflects that background. Many of the leading cheese specialists are women and Virginie is expert – take her advice.

### Fromagerie Lepic

*20 rue Lepic, 75018*
*Closed: Monday*
*Open: Tuesday to Thursday, 7.30 am – 1.00 pm and 3.30 – 8.00 pm; Friday and Saturday, 7.30 am – 8.00 pm non-stop; Sunday 9.30 am – 1.00 pm*

Located in the market street and the most comprehensive fromagerie in the area. A range of cheeses in fine condition and you can buy sliced pain Poilâne (just as in London) to eat with it. They also have a range of wines to go with the cheese: primarily robust reds.

## Glaciers

### La Butte Glacée

*14 rue Norvins, 75018*
*Open: DAILY 9.30 am – midnight (Monday 10.30 am – 7.00 pm)*

A busy Italian ice-cream parlour on the main street leading in to the place du Tertre. There is a permanent queue and brisk service so you need to be sure what you want. Almost 40 different flavours including *soupe à l'anglaise* (cinnamon-flavoured vanilla) which used to be a speciality of the now-defunct Calabrese in the rue d'Odessa. Prices are from 3-5,20€. You get a generous portion for 3€ though a bit sweet for my taste.

## Le Gastelier
*1 bis rue André Tardieu, 75018*
*Closed: Monday*
*Open: 9.00 am – 6.00 pm*
Possessing a quiet charm, that cannot be said of La Butte Glacée, you can also sit down here to enjoy your ice-cream, which you can sample in a variety of combinations. It is cheaper than the competition (2€ for one boule, 3,60€ for two, 4,50€ for three). There is an outlet for Häagen-Dazs a few doors down where prices are 25 per cent higher and the quality inferior.

# Neglected museum

## Musée de Montmartre
*12 rue Cortot, 75018*
*Métro: Lamarck-Caulaincourt*
*Closed: Monday*
*Open: 10.00 am – 12.30 pm and 1.30 – 6.00 pm*
*Entrance: 7,50€*
This is the collection of la Société du Vieux Montmartre and amazingly comprehensive it is with eight rooms of exhibits including a reconstruction of Utrillo's *Café de l'Abreuvoir*. Paintings, porcelain, documents, the range is fascinating. The house itself is 17th century – at that time very much a country house.

Highly recommended.

# Interesting shops

## Belle de Jour
*7 rue André Tardieu, 75018*
*Métro: Abbesses*
*Closed: Sunday*
*Open: 10.30 am – 1.00 pm and 2.00 – 7.00 pm*
In the midst of retailers selling tourist tat is this sophisticated shop run by the enthusiastic Yan Schalburg, dealing in scent bottles primarily 20th century and including many classic designs from the art deco period. Beautifully presented this is a place to admire even if you don't buy. But you might do just that because some of them (not all expensive) are desirable and evocative design objects.

## Ebène
*1 rue des Abbesses, 75018*
*Métro: Abbesses*
*Closed: Sunday to Wednesday*
*Open: Thursday to Saturday, 2.00 – 7.30 pm*
Marie-Pierre Vallet, who has been here for thirty years, specialises in 1930s-70s small furniture, glass, jewellery and the like, with prices from under a hundred euros to much larger sums. But don't be shy to go in or ask the prices: you will be welcomed in any case.

# Bistrots

### Le Bistrot Poulbot
*39 rue Lamarck, 75018*
*Tel: 01 46 06 86 00*
*Métro: Lamarck-Caulaincourt*
*Closed: Sunday and Monday*
*lunchtime*
*Open: noon – 1.30 pm and 7.30 –*
*10.00 pm*
Under the previous chef-owner, Jean-Paul Langevin (when it was known as Au Poulbot Gourmet) this was one of the best bistrots in Paris. Now we have a female chef-owner in charge (Véronique) who has put her own stamp on the place: very much a family restaurant; her sister works here and some of the recipes come from her grandmother, Mamie Louise. It exudes good-hearted charm, and you will be charmed by it.

The menus are on the daily-changing *ardoise*: a good value lunch menu at 17€ for three courses (two choices for each) or two courses for 14€. The dinner menu is 34€ or two courses for 14€. There is a limited carte *(Les Plats de Mamie Louise)* which will set you back about 40€. The food is highly traditional and there is a basic choice of wine at the same level of cost.

### Au Relais
*48 rue Lamarck, 75018*
*Tel: 01 46 06 68 32*
*www.lecafe1904.com*
*Métro: Lamarck-Caulaincourt*
*Open: DAILY and continuously*
*for meals noon – 10.30 pm and*
*from 8.00 am for breakfast*
This popular place has been a

bistrot for over a hundred years and is very proud of the fact (check their website). They should be even more proud of the bargain lunch (two courses and coffee) at 11€ (but not at weekends). No dinner menu: the heady heights of the à la carte will take you up to 35€.

There are tables outside on the pavement and in the small square. Book for dinner, but it's not necessary at lunchtime.

### La Galère des Rois
*8 rue Cavallotti, 75018*
*Tel: 01 42 93 34 58*
*Métro: Place de Clichy*
*Closed: Sunday (Saturday*
*lunchtime), the whole of August*
*and Christmas week*
*Open: noon – 2.30 pm and*
*7.30 – 11.00 pm*
Serving traditional food which does not aim to be haute cuisine, this bistrot is situated in a street running along the south side of the Montmartre cemetery. There are bargain lunch menus at 12,50€ and 15€; à la carte will cost at least twice that.

### Le Petit Caboulet
*6 place Jacques Froment, 75018*
*Tel: 01 46 27 19 00*
*Métro: Guy Moquet*
*Closed: Monday (Sunday*
*evening), and two weeks in*
*August*
*Open: 10.00 am through to*
*midnight*
Outstanding value for the quality. There is a lunch menu for 10€; à la carte will be nearer 30€. In each case you will get traditional food,

well-prepared. Of all the bistrots on our list this is one where you will feel you'd like to be a regular (it has plenty of those from the neighbourhood). In good weather tables on the pavement are to be preferred.

### Au Virage Lepic
*61 rue Lepic, 75018*
*Tel: 01 42 52 46 79*
*Métro: Abbesses*
*Closed: Tuesday, a week in*
*August and a week at Christmas*
*Open: for dinner only 7.00 –*
*11.30 pm*

Largely hostile to vegetarians, this small bistrot with a traditional carte is exceptional value for money. Entrées such as bone marrow, and duck gizzard salad cost 7-9€; plats which include veal kidneys, duck confit (and one miserable salad for vegetarians) cost 14-20€; cheese is 7€ and desserts 6,50€. Wines by the glass cost 2,80-3,00€; a ¼ litre pichet 5,50€ and 10-11€ for a ½ litre; bottles 15-45€. Booking is essential if you are to be sure of a table. Incidentally, they have a speciality of traditional aperitifs such as Salers and Pineau des Charentes. Strongly recommended: provided you're not vegetarian.

## Brasserie

### Brasserie Wepler
*14 place de Clichy, 75018*
*Tel: 01 45 22 53 24*
*Métro: Place de Clichy*
*Open: DAILY noon – 1.00 am*
This splendid brasserie almost opposite Charlot (p. 97) is in marked contrast to much of the surrounding area. One comes here primarily for seafood: you can get a plateau des fruits de mer for 28€ or 38,50€ for one person; more generous versions for two cost 94€ or 130€ with lobster.

If the elegant interior doesn't suit you then there is a terrace which is good for lunch, particularly the midi-express at 16€ for the familiar two-from-three courses. But it is dinner that sets the character of the place: and here you can get a bargain three-course menu for 26€ (20€ for two courses). Wines are from 10,50€ for a half-bottle, from 17,50€ for a bottle. Highly professional service; essential to book for dinner – or you can queue.

# 10. Montparnasse

A first impression of the main boulevard may be one of mild disappointment: the name conjures up an ill-defined vision of raffish eccentricity even if we recognise that its intellectual and artistic heyday is long past. In which case the business-like appearance of this, the main thoroughfare, suggests that nothing much remains. But as you penetrate the area, work the side-streets and appreciate it at different times of day, increasing familiarity gradually shifts your perception.

Take the Tour Montparnasse, for example; at almost 700 feet high it dominates the skyline, a symbol of 1960s' urban styling, fiercely controversial (a recurring theme in Paris) and an object of public anger – an attitude I once shared. And yet, more recently, seen in the distance from the Luxembourg Gardens and softened by the morning haze, it looked graceful despite its size – almost unearthly.

No re-assessment is warranted of the extensive rebuilding that has taken place in the southernmost reaches of Montparnasse (you get something similar on the east side of the place d'Italie in the 13th arrondissement). But there is plenty to discover in the established streets just south of the boulevard that separates the 6th from the 14th. This north/south divide is an economic and social one: prices are higher, the atmosphere a bit snootier in the 6th. Hotels are consistently cheaper in the 14th – and that includes the Istria where many of the great names of the 1920s once stayed, among them Man Ray, the American photographer, the sculptor Constantin Brancusi and the poet André Breton who coined the language of surrealism. Brancusi and Man Ray are buried in the nearby Montparnasse cemetery along with Maupassant, Baudelaire and, together, Sartre and Simone de Beauvoir, presided over by a bronze angel, Daillion's *Eternal Sleep* in the centre. Brancusi's contrasting cubist sculpture *The Kiss* can be found at the north-east corner.

So with some persistence, and a little imagination, you will pick up the threads of the past; starting perhaps with the musées Zadkine and Cartier-Bresson.

## Principal sights

**La Tour Montparnasse** (1973), entrance in the rue de l'Arrivée: built as part of the commercial redevelopment of the area, and as far as tourists are concerned notable for the extraordinary panoramic view of the city from the top (59th) floor. The best time is in clear weather (obviously) but especially at night. The high speed lift gets you there in forty seconds; your stomach follows a little later.

**L'Observatoire** (17th century), avenue de l'Observatoire: the French equivalent of the Greenwich Observatory in England which enjoys a similar range of functions and a distinguished history of discoveries up to the present day. The distinctive dome is a later 19th century addition. The Observatory gardens (p. 136) are one of the hidden pleasures of Paris.

**Les Catacombes,** place Denfert-Rochereau: these 18th-century ossuaries contain the orderly remains (skulls neatly stacked) of several million skeletons removed from other sites and placed in former quarry excavations. Interesting but sobering.

## Quiet hotels

### Hôtel Jardin le Bréa
*14 rue Bréa, 75006*
*Tel: 01 43 25 44 41*
*Fax: 01 44 07 19 25*
*E-mail: brea.hotel@wanadoo.fr*
*www.jardinlebrea-paris-hotel.com*
*Métro: Vavin*

*23 rooms AIR CONDITIONED*
*Price: from 132€ for a double room; 162€ for a 'supérieure'*
This is an extremely comfortable and well-maintained hotel in a quiet street opposite where the famous Russian restaurant Dominique stood until its closure in 2007 – after almost 80 years. Note that rates are higher during the period of the salons; but lower during July/August. The buffet-breakfast at 12€ is excellent.

### Hôtel Istria
*29 rue Campagne Première, 75014*
*Tel: 01 43 20 91 82*
*Fax: 01 43 22 48 45*
*www.istria-paris-hotel.com*
*Métro: Raspail*
*30 rooms*
*Price: 110-150€ for a double room*
In a quiet street just south of the boulevard, the Istria has a famously avant-garde past in the 1920s and 1930s when the likes of Man Ray, Rilke and Marcel Duchamp stayed there. The present-day clientèle, as might be inferred from its appearance in this guide, are a good deal more restrained.

### Hôtel Delambre
*35 rue Delambre, 75014*
*Tel: 01 43 20 66 31*
*Fax: 01 45 38 91 76*
*E-mail: delambre*
*@club-internet.fr*
*www.hoteldelambre.com*
*Métro: Vavin*
*30 rooms AIR CONDITIONED*
*Price: 95€ for a double room;*
*115€ for a 'supérieure'*
This is by a long way the best value hotel in the area: I almost didn't

include it in the guide but altruism triumphed. A handsome building with its original tiled façade, the hotel is located in the quieter upper part of the street and some rooms give on to the interior courtyard.

### Hôtel Apollinaire
*39 rue Delambre, 75014*
*Tel: 01 43 35 18 40*
*Fax: 01 43 35 30 71*
*E-mail: info@hotel-apollinaire*
*www.apollinaire-paris-hotel.com*
*Métro: Vavin*
*36 rooms AIR CONDITIONED*
*Price: 140€ for a street-side*
*double room; 150€ for one on the*
*courtyard side (called 'chambres*
*privilèges')*
A very well-maintained hotel with decent-sized rooms and baths rather than showers – again because of size.

## Breakfast

### Christian Constant
*37 rue d'Assas*
*Open: DAILY from 8.00 am*
This is an 'haute couture' pâtis-serie, if that makes sense: everything beautifully presented and of superb quality. But we are here for breakfast; the rather plain little café is immediately adjacent round the corner at 18 rue de Fleu-rus. Café crème and a croissant cost 5€, and you can buy an ice-cream on the way out.

### La Coupole
*102 boulevard du Montparnasse*
*Open: DAILY 8.00 – 10.00 am*
*for breakfast*

Appreciate the low-key morning-after atmosphere sitting on the banquettes of this vast brasserie, with the friendly, expert waiters – just slightly impertinent – who will bring you the ample breakfast (described on p. 30). A great bargain at 9,50€ and far more than you should eat.

### La Rotonde
*105 boulevard du Montparnasse*
*Open: DAILY from 8.00 am*
I would only choose this in pref-erence to La Coupole on a sunny morning because of its south-facing terrace. Being on the corner round into the boulevard Raspail you can adjust for sun/shade to suit, looking out over the place Pablo Picasso.

There is an *express formule* for 5€ (coffee, orange juice, tartine beurrée) but the recommended option is the 9€ version (orange pressée, boisson chaud, tartine, croissant and jam).

## Public gardens

### Square et place Ozanam
*Location: junction of rue*
*Stanislas and rue de Cicé at the*
*boulevard du Montparnasse.*
Next to the church of Notre-Dame-des-Champs you'll find a long narrow garden with chestnut trees and a children's playground: a delightful oasis close to the busy boulevard and central to our area.

### Jardin Marco Polo
*Location: junction of the avenue*
*de l'Observatoire (northern*

*section) and the boulevard du Montparnasse.*
Overlooked by opulent apartment blocks and public buildings on either side, this is a very formal-looking garden with its much photographed magnificent fountain where bronze horses and dolphins are cavorting in the spray, and giant turtles projecting water from their mouths. The severely regimented trees offer a striking perspective up to the Palais du Luxembourg. A place to sit and ponder and, despite the formality, there is an appealing children's play area.

Further north you come to the **Jardin Cavalier de la Salle**, which brings you to the Luxembourg Gardens themselves (p. 145).

**Square Nicolas Ledoux**
*Location: adjacent to the place Denfert-Rochereau (with the Lion de Belfort in the centre).*
There are in fact three small gardens here (one just for children). The square Nicolas Ledoux is the central one and the best for adults with seats set round an attractive lawn, the whole well-screened from the traffic by trees and shrubs.

**Jardin de l'Observatoire**
*Location: between the avenue Denfert-Rochereau and the rue du Faubourg St Jacques; entrance in the boulevard Arago.*
A more natural 'English' garden than most, and secluded. Public access is limited to afternoons in the summer months: 1.00 – 7.00 pm April to August, and until 6.00 pm

September and October.
Quite different from any other, this is one of the most pleasurable gardens to stroll round; the local cats have the same idea for this is prime hunting territory for them.

## Markets

**Rue Daguerre, 75014 (market street)**
*Tuesday to Saturday 8.00 am – 1.30 pm and 3.00 – 7.00 pm (Sunday to 1.30 pm)*
Perhaps for tourists a less well-known market street, yet one of the best. It occupies the eastern pedestrianised section between the avenue de Général Leclerc and the rue Boulard and a lot is crowded into this space. You can find familiar names here (like Amorino and Fromage Rouge) as well as resolutely local establishments.

**Edgar Quinet, 75014**
*Wednesday 7.00 am – 2.30 pm and Saturday 7.00 am – 3.00 pm*
One of the oldest street markets in Paris, running in a double bank along the central reservation of the boulevard Edgar Quinet (beginning at the rue de Départ) just to the north of the Montparnasse cemetery. It is thronged with locals on a Saturday morning when there are more stalls: a wide range but especially vegetables, fruit and salad stuffs.

## Fromagers

### Pascal Beillevaire
*8 rue Delambre, 75014*
*Closed: Monday and Sunday*
*afternoon*
*Open: Tuesday to Saturday 8.30*
*am – 1.00 pm and 4.00 – 8.00 pm;*
*Sunday 9.00 am – 1.00 pm*
This new fromagerie opened in
October 2006 (previously it was
Fromage Rouge and, before that,
Androuet). Let us hope the new
incarnation survives because its
young owner is a great enthusiast.
A fine range of cheeses plus jams,
honeys and so on.

### Fromage Rouge
*19 rue Daguerre, 75014*
*Closed: Monday, and Sunday*
*afternoon*
*Open: 9.30 am – 1.00 pm and*
*4.00 – 7.30 pm, and all day*
*Saturday*
This small chain (there is another
in the rue St Dominique) offers
cheeses in fine condition – not an
enormous range – and carefully
chosen wines to go with them
(hence the name). Very good
service: they will prepare cheese
platters for your dinner party.
This branch has tables set out in
the street where you can take
lunch (salad, a selection of five
cheeses, a glass of wine, coffee)
for 12,50€.

### Vacroux et fils
*5 rue Daguerre, 75014*
*Closed: Monday, and Sunday*
*afternoon*
*Open: 8.00 am – 7.00 pm*
*(Sunday to 1.00 pm)*

An excellent fromagerie with a
wide range but a particular
specialism in cheeses from the
midi-Pyrénées.

## Glaciers

### Christian Constant
*37 rue d'Assas, 75006*
*Open: DAILY from 8.00 am*
Ice-cream is dispensed in the little
café next door to the main shop –
round the corner in the rue de
Fleurus: you can sit in or take
away. He has a speciality of
unusual chocolate combinations
(with whisky, for example). Only
a small number of flavours, about
ten, is on display at any one time;
my vote goes for the superb fruit
sorbets – blackcurrant *(cassis)* in
particular. One large scoop costs
3€.

### Amorino
*17 rue Daguerre, 75014*
*Open: DAILY noon to*
*midnight*
In this market street you find the
original (and main) branch of the
leading Italian ice-cream makers
in Paris. There are always at least
twenty flavours *(parfums)* on offer
with occasional innovations like
lemon-orange-carrot – a surprisingly successful combination.

Also at
*4 rue Vavin, 75006*
Across the road from the western
edge of the Luxembourg Gardens
– a good place to eat your ice
cream.

# Neglected museums

### Fondation Henri Cartier-Bresson
*2 impasse Lebouis, 75014*
*Métro: Gaîté*
*Closed: Sunday and Monday*
*Open: Tuesday to Friday, 1.00 –*
*6.30 pm; Saturday 11.00 am –*
*6.45 pm*
*Entrance: 6€*

Although mainly devoted to the work of France's most famous photographer, there are also other temporary exhibitions related to photography. Cartier-Bresson's work is international in character, but includes some of the most powerful images of Paris: see www.henricartierbresson.org

### Musée du Montparnasse
*21 avenue du Maine, 75015*
*Métro: Montparnasse*
*Closed: Monday*
*Open: 12.30 – 7.00 pm*
*Entrance: 5€*
*www.museedumontparnasse.net*

There is no permanent exhibition here and the museum is closed in between the temporary exhibitions which are loosely related to the social and cultural history of the quarter.

### Musée de la Poste
*34 boulevard de Vaugirard,*
*75015*
*Métro: Montparnasse*
*Closed: Sunday and public*
*holidays*
*Open: 10.00 am – 6.00 pm*
*Entrance: 5€ to the permanent*
*collection or temporary exhibi-*
*tions; 7€ to both*

*www.museedelaposte.fr*

A must for stamp collectors but there is much of general appeal. Of particular historical interest is the collection of *ballons montés*: letters flown out of Paris by balloon during the Franco-Prussian war of 1870-71. But it's not just about letters and stamps: the whole nature and organisation of the postal service is covered.

### Musée (et atelier) Zadkine
*100 bis rue d'Assas, 75006*
*Métro: Notre-Dame-des-Champs*
*Closed: Monday*
*Open: 10.00 am – 6.00 pm*
*Entrance: FREE*
*www.zadkine.paris.fr*

Drawings and sculptures by the artist displayed in the studios and garden of the house where the Russian-born Ossip Zadkine lived from 1928-1967. Whatever one's view of the artist's work, which is of the tormented variety, this is a most appealing setting. He was laid to rest, if that's the right term, in Montparnasse Cemetery.

### Musée Bourdelle
*16 rue Antoine Bourdelle, 75015*
*Métro: Falguière*
*Closed: Monday and public*
*holidays*
*Open: 10-00 am – 6.00 pm*
*Entrance: 5€*
*www.bourdelle.paris.fr*

Antoine Bourdelle (1861-1929) was Rodin's most famous pupil but is now little known to the general public. The garden and studios where he worked all his life house the permanent collection. His work is on a (literally) monumental scale and his output was enormous.

## Interesting shops

### Artisinat Monastique
*68 bis avenue Denfert-Rochereau, 75014*
*Métro: Denfert-Rochereau*
*Closed: Sunday*
*Open: Monday to Friday, noon – 6.30 pm; Saturday 2.00 – 7.00 pm*
If you didn't know it was there you would never find it: no window display, just a blue-painted door and a small poster. Yet in the vaults of the convent you can find craftwork produced by religious houses all over France. The range includes table-linen, scent, embroidery, handmade paper and children's clothes; if not high fashion they are nonetheless delightful.

### Bistrots d'Autrefois
*135 boulevard Montparnasse, 75006*
*Métro: Vavin*
*Closed: Sunday (and every morning)*
*Open: 2.00 – 6.00 pm*
Selling old to antique bistrot furnishings, including magnificent zinc bars, this is a fascinating place. It is here that those renovating (or re-creating) a traditional bistrot come for the authentic touch. For private buyers the chairs and tables would add something distinctive to a contemporary conservatory, kitchen or dining room. Everything is in fine condition: and expensive. The numerous

desirable objects (jugs, glasses, ashtrays) that complement the furniture and fittings are sadly not for sale. Better than a museum.

### L'Art du Papier
*48 rue Vavin, 75006*
*Métro: Vavin*
*Closed: Sunday*
*Open: 10.30 am – 7.00 pm (Monday from 2.00 pm)*
Apart from many fine papers this thoughtfully assembled shop sells a range of paper-craft materials: delicate stickers to make patterns, hand-stamps, deckle-edged scissors, ribbons, pens in great variety, stencils – the list is endless. An excellent place to buy for children and adults.

## Bistrots

### Aux Produits du Sud-Ouest
*21-23 rue d'Odessa, 75014*
*Métro: Montparnasse/Edgar Quinet*
*Closed: Sunday, Monday, public holidays, last week in July, the whole of August*
*Open: noon – 2.00 pm and 7.00 – 11.00 pm*
Without question the best value in the area, an entirely straightforward place with no pretensions towards style. It is a shop as well as a restaurant selling a range of tinned terrines, cassoulets and the like (from the family establishment in Beaumont de Lomagne). The lunch formule at 7€ comprises the plat du jour and either coffee or a glass of wine – a bargain by any standard. There are several variations

but the two-course menu at 11,50€ offers, typically, a choice that might include a terrine (entrée), cassoulet or poulet basquaise (plat), apple tart with armagnac (dessert): or all three for 16€. The 22€ menu is exceptional value and includes main courses like cassoulet au confit d'oie, salmis de pigeon, confit de canard aux pommes sarladaises, and coq au vin.

A ¼ litre of wine costs 2,60€ and recommended is the aperitif Floc de Gascon (similar to Pineau des Charentes, i.e. a blend of brandy and unfermented grape juice).

This is a bistrot enormously popular with local people (like Le Languedoc, pp. 156) and whilst they take block bookings for large parties, otherwise you just take your chance on getting a table.

### Wadja
*10 rue de la Grande Chaumière, 75006*
*Tel: 01 46 33 02 02*
*Métro: Vavin*
*Closed: Sunday (Monday lunchtime) and the whole of August*
*Open: noon – 2.00 pm and 7.30 – 10.00 pm*
An art deco classic with a long history, Wadja suffered a period of slow decline until it passed into new ownership in the 1990s. Food is a mixture of the traditional (sea bass baked in a salt crust) and the mildly innovative (chicken sautéed with ginger and lemon). There is a two-course value lunch menu at 14€; dinner is à la carte only and will cost around 50€ – more than

that if you choose the prized Utah Beach oysters for your entrée.

Booking essential for dinner and, though not cheap, strongly recommended.

### Monsieur Lapin
*11 rue Raymond Losserand, 75014*
*Tel: 01 43 20 21 39*
*Métro: Gaîté*
*Closed: Monday (Saturday lunchtime) and the whole of August*
*Open: noon – 2.00 pm and 7.30 – 11.00 pm*
In many ways an excellent restaurant, and one where rabbit figures largely, both on the menu and in the hundreds of models scattered around. There is a comfortable, calm atmosphere to the place and service is efficient and unflustered.

Prices for food are reasonable: 25€ for a two-course lunch menu, 35€ for the three-course dinner. The straightforward dishes are best; as at Casa Olympe (p. 95) the more inventive ones tend to be over-flavoured and lacking in substance.

There is a strong wine list with strong prices – nothing under 29€, a few half-bottles from 15€. You can ask for a glass of wine but it will cost 6€. Even if you take the dinner menu it would be difficult to have a complete meal for much less than 60€.

### Chez Marcel
*7 rue Stanislas, 75006*
*Tel: 01 45 48 29 94*
*Métro: Vavin*
*Closed: Saturday, Sunday and*

*the whole of August*
*Open: noon – 2.00 pm and*
*7.30 – 10.00 pm*
Established in 1919 this classic bistrot has the well-worn or 'patinated' charm that is hard to find and impossible to fabricate. The wallpaper (from its style and condition) looks original and the same appears to be true of the paintwork. This is a small narrow restaurant serving good value traditional food (e.g. artichaud vinaigrette followed by coq au vin, and nougat glacé). Entrées are around 7€, plats around 15€ and dessert/fromage around 6€.

It is essential to book. One small item of information: to get to the lavatory you have to go through the (very small) kitchen at the back.

## Brasseries

Montparnasse is home to the most famous brasseries in Paris and, since they are a distinctively Parisian phenomenon, in the world. And with the exception of La Closerie des Lilas which is in a different league, they are all clustered together, adjacent to the Vavin Métro station. It has to be emphasised that you do not come to them just for the food. Brasseries are not, and never have been, about fine cooking: their size and pace is against them. But they constitute an exciting experience and are good value in most respects.

A recommended first port of call is:

### La Coupole
*102 boulevard du Montparnasse,*
*75014*
*www.coupoleparis.com*
*Métro: Vavin*
*Open: DAILY from 8.00 am*
*through to 1.00 am (to 1.30 am*
*Friday and Saturday)*
This is a vast brasserie seating around 450 people so the entertainment is watching the scene in which the waiters are star turns. In the evening the activity is nothing short of frenetic and you can't book for dinner: if there aren't any tables you get a numbered ticket and wait at the American bar, which is a pleasure in its own right.

It is impossible not to be stimulated by the buzz of the place: when you are tired of La Coupole you are tired of life. The cooking is sound, unremarkable but excellent value. The recommended *menu découverte* (e + pl + dess + ½ bottle of wine or water) at 34,50€ is certainly worth it; but you can eat more economically with the menu at 24,50€ which also includes wine or water.

The 9,50€ breakfast has already been mentioned, and you can get 'afternoon tea' (coffee, tea or chocolate with a pastry or crêpes or a parfait) for 7,50€.

### Le Dôme
*108 boulevard du Montparnasse,*
*75014*
*Tel: 01 43 35 25 81*
*Métro: Vavin*
*Closed: Sunday and Monday*
*in August*
*Open: (with above exception)*

*DAILY noon – 3.00 pm and
7.00 pm – 12.30 am*
This is quite different from the
other brasseries: privately owned,
relatively expensive (at the upper
end of our price range and a bit
beyond), and specialist – you come
here for fish. No menus or other
money-saving conventions. If the
spectre of cost (around 65-85€ for
a meal) puts you off you should try
their annexe, the **Bistrot du Dôme**
just round the corner at 1 rue
Delambre (Tel: 01 43 35 32 00) –
same opening hours as the parent
institution – where you can eat
well for little more than half the
price.

**Le Sélect**
*99 boulevard du Montparnasse,
75006
Tel: 01 42 22 65 27
Métro: Vavin
Open: DAILY 7.00 am through
to 2.00 am (to 4.30 am Friday
and Saturday)*
More café than restaurant, though
there is a bargain formule for 16€
served from noon to 6.00 pm
Monday to Friday: the plat du
jour, and either an entreé or a
dessert, plus a ¼ litre of Côtes du
Rhône (or beer or water).

The Sélect probably has more

of the 1920s' atmosphere than any
of the competition but the carte is
hardly good value.

**La Closerie des Lilas**
*171 boulevard du Montparnasse,
75006
Tel: 01 40 51 34 50
Métro: Vavin
Open: DAILY noon through
to 11.00 pm*
Here the brasserie (to the left) is
separate from the restaurant (to
the right). General opinion favours
the brasserie – its carte is certainly
cheaper – but the restaurant gets an
entry in our *Special Restaurants*
section because it offers a not-too-
dear luncheon menu and a splendid
carte in a conservatory-style
setting.

The brasserie is evocative of
times long gone and, if there are no
longer any lilacs, the terrace tables
are well-screened by greenery from
the busy boulevard intersection.
No menus in the brasserie and a
full meal à la carte costs around
50€ (compared with 80€ plus in
the restaurant). You can reduce
the cost by taking fewer courses
but in any case it's not cheap. You
have to reckon on paying something for the company of the
ghosts of the past.

# 11. Luxembourg

This quarter is not difficult to define in physical terms: to the north it is bounded by the Palais de Luxembourg, to the west by the famous gardens, to the east by the Panthéon – home to the mortal remains of France's great – and to the south by the former abbey of Val-de-Grâce (now the Army Medical School) with its 'Roman' dome. Further to the east the rue Mouffetard and its tributaries constitute a boundary of a quite different character.

However, the ethos of the area has many elements, and here the institutions of higher education play a major part. In France the Grands Ecoles are the pinnacle of the educational system, being at a level above universities. And it is in these institutions that the future academic, commercial and political élites are formed. To this day French politicians are more conspicuously intellectual than their English or American counterparts. The presence of some of the most prestigious schools, including what has been the hotbed of French intellectualism, the Ecole Normale Supérieure, is a defining influence and one that can be sensed in the streets, the cafés, the bookshops. Can there be anywhere else in the world with so many erudite and specialised shops selling books that reflect the knowledge and taste of their owners? – and who form an element in the academic community.

In all dimensions the civilised character of the district is apparent, especially perhaps in the numerous cafés. Watching the people who inhabit this world is one of the pleasures of outsiders like ourselves.

It is not an area heavy with tourists. Perhaps for that reason locating places to stay is less easy than in other parts of Paris; but worth the effort if it enables you to discover for yourself some of the elusive qualities of French social culture.

## Principal sights

Le Panthéon (18th century), place du Panthéon: one of the dominant landmarks of the city and designed by Soufflot after whom the approaching street is named. Intended as a church, post-Revolution it became the Temple of Fame in which the bodies of the great are interred – often long after their death (the writer Alexandre Dumas being a recent example).

Val-de-Grâce (17th century), place Albert Laveran: recently beautifully cleaned and restored, this former abbey was designed by François Mansart. Since the mid-19th century it has been the Army Medical School. (See p. 146 for museum details.)

Théâtre de l'Odéon (18th century), place de l'Odéon (to the north of the Palais du Luxembourg): in recent years somewhat over-restored and rechristened the Odéon-Théâtre de l'Europe, it now specialises in performing classic plays from other European countries in their own language. The symmetrical façade is best appreciated from the semi-circular place de l' Odéon.

## Quiet hotels

### Hôtel Pierre Nicole
*39 rue Pierre Nicole, 75005*
*Tel: 01 43 54 76 86*
*Fax: 01 43 54 22 45*
*E-mail: hotelpierre-nicole@voila.fr*
*Métro: Vavin*
*33 rooms*

*Price: 95€ for a double room; 110€ for a 'suite'*
This is a plain, quite basic hotel; if you take a 'suite' on the top floor – still relatively cheap – you also get a small sitting area with a desk and a couch.

The whole place has an unobtrusive charm. In a quiet street and well-situated, except that there is no Métro nearby (Port Royal and Luxembourg are RER stations).

### Les Jardins du Luxembourg
*5 impasse Royer-Collard, 75005*
*Tel: 01 40 46 08 88*
*Fax: 01 40 46 02 28*
*E-mail: jardinslux@wanadoo.fr*
*www.les-jardins-du-luxembourg.com*
*Métro: Odéon*
*27 rooms AIR CONDITIONED*
*Price: 142-152€ for a double room*
Situated in a cul-de-sac near the Luxembourg Gardens, this discreet and elegant hotel is exceptionally quiet.

### Hôtel de Senlis
*7-9 rue Malebranche, 75005*
*Tel: 01 43 29 93 10*
*Fax: 01 43 29 00 24*
*E-mail: hoteldesenlis@wanadoo.fr*
*www.paris-hotel-senlis.com*
*Métro: Odéon*
*30 rooms*
*Price: 88-103€ for a double/twin room*
A bargain for such a central and well-maintained hotel in a quiet street. Eight of the rooms overlook a narrow interior courtyard and are therefore a bit gloomy on

the lower floors. However, the street-side rooms are quiet enough although the nearby Aussie Bar (sic) generates some noise in the evening.

## Breakfast

### Le Soufflot
*16 rue Soufflot*
*Open: DAILY from 7.00 am*
A smart modern café with an excellent covered terrace and outside tables for a summer breakfast with, depending on where you sit, views of the Panthéon nearby, or the Eiffel Tower and the Tour Montparnasse in the distance.

The 7,80€ breakfast formule gives you orange juice, a boisson chaude (coffee/tea/chocolate), croissant or pain au chocolat and a tartine beurrée.

### Dalloyau
*2 place Edmond-Rostand*
*Open: DAILY from 9.00 am*
If you want to cosset yourself this classy tea salon (on the first floor above the pâtisserie) opposite the Luxembourg Gardens is a recommended treatment. A wide range of teas, but café crème is what you'll probably need. Taking a window table you can order the 10€ formule which includes fresh fruit juice, coffee etc. and two or three viennoiseries. For where it is and what it is this is not an expensive place for breakfast.

### Le Rostand
*6 place Edmond-Rostand*
*Open: DAILY from 8.00 am*

A very smart place with a splendid view of the Luxembourg Gardens from the large terrace (heated in winter). The breakfast formule at 10€ is close competition for Dalloyau: fresh fruit juice, coffee, a tartine, croissant and jam.

## Public gardens

### Jardin du Luxembourg
You don't need to be told the location of this, without question the best public garden in Paris, and unmissable from any of the surrounding quarters. The jardin des Tuileries is bigger but its perspective-dominated design makes it a rather bleak place to explore. The greater attraction of Luxembourg is in its variety.

There are formal and informal parts; curiosities like the Marionettes Theatre and its attractive café; the round pond for sailing yachts; an English-style garden and plenty of French formalism; the set-piece of the Italianate fountain of the Medici, and a multiplicity of statues. It attracts the inhabitants of the district like a magnet: some to stroll, some to play boules or basketball, some to sit and wonder at those on their daily run along the perimeter path. 'Le jogging' was popular here long before the energetic Nicolas Sarkozy became President.

### Place de l'Estrapade
*Location: from the rue des Fossés St Jacques it is sandwiched between the rue de l'Estrapade and the rue Llomond.*

A triangle of tarmac so no grass, but trees and benches within a frame of flowerbeds surrounding a fountain: you couldn't be anywhere but Paris.

## Market

**Port Royal, 75005**
*Tuesday and Thursday 7.00 am – 2.30 pm; Saturday 7.00 am – 3.00 pm*
This street market is to be found on the boulevard de Port Royal where it backs on to Val-de-Grâce. Smaller than most it nonetheless has some interesting specialists (in teas, for example).

It is at the weekend that you see it at its best, with the beautifully restored lead and gilt dome in the background.

## Fromagers

Those in the rue Mouffetard are not far away, but there is a good one in the Port Royal street market: **A la Petite Fermière**.

## Glacier

**Summerbird Chocolatier**
*62 rue Monsieur le Prince, 75005*
*Closed: Wednesday*
*Open: 10.00 am – 7.00 pm*
This classy chocolatier has a highly original line in ice-cream, chocolate-related in interesting combinations: mandarine truffle noir, cassis chocolat blanc, mangues fêves de cacao. Buy a *petit pot* for 3€. It is also a source of the best chocolat chaud in Paris (yes, I know about the others). Variously and subtly flavoured they are fuel against cold weather.

## Neglected museums

**Musée du Service de Santé des Armées**
*Place Albert Laveran (by the rue St-Jacques, 75014)*
*Métro: Les Gobelins*
*Closed: Monday, Thursday, Friday*
*Open: afternoons only, Tuesday, Wednesday, Saturday, Sunday, 2.00 – 5.00 pm*
*Entrance: 5€*
There is a two-fold appeal to this museum. First it allows entry to the old convent buildings. Secondly, it evokes the concern of the French nation for their warwounded. The practical character of the exhibits and videos, particularly of the First World War, shows how central this concern has been. If you want a perspective on the horrors of war that is not just rhetorical, this will give it to you.

The museum is, in fact, something of a mixture and includes a collection of old pharmaceutical implements (including the humble pestle and mortar); and of the achievements of eminent practitioners in the Army Medical Services.

**Musée Curie**
*11 rue Pierre et Marie Curie, 75005*
*Métro: Odéon/Cluny-La Sorbonne*

Closed: Saturday, Sunday and Monday
Open: Tuesday to Friday, 10.00 am – 6.00 pm
Entrance: FREE

This small museum of the work-rooms and laboratories of Marie Curie, her daughter and son-in-law is on the ground floor of the Institute she founded – and which is still a centre for research.

The carefully collected and presented memorabilia, including the equipment involved in their discoveries of radioactivity, are viewed as part of a guided tour (in French) lasting 45 minutes, at regular intervals from the opening time.

### Musée de Minéralogie
60 boulevard St Michel, 75006
Métro: Odéon/Cluny-La Sorbonne
Closed: Sunday, Monday and public holidays
Open: Tuesday to Friday, 1.30 – 6.00 pm; Saturday 10.00 am – 12.30 pm and 2.00 – 5.00 pm
Entrance: 5€ (children half-price)

The museum is located within the fine 18th century building occupied by The Ecole Nationale Supérieure des Mines. Precious and semi-precious stones, beautiful crystals and meteorites are all presented in an appealing fashion with ample explanation: but it's enough just to look.

### Centre de la Mer et des Eaux
195 rue St Jacques, 75005
Métro: Cluny-La Sorbonne
Closed: Monday, the first two weeks in September (and weekends in August)
Open: Tuesday to Friday, 10.00 am – 12.30 pm and 1.30 – 5.30 pm; Saturday and Sunday, 10.00 am – 5.30 pm
Entrance: 4,60€ adults, 2€ children

Situated in the Institut Océangraphique this is much more than a 'museum' being contemporary and multi-faceted – aquaria, exhibitions, hi-tech activities (and an excellent shop). Of interest to all ages – in fact anyone concerned about the conservation of sea-life and exploration of the oceans.

Popular with Parisian families it is little visited by tourists.

## Interesting shops

### Jadis et Gourmande
88 boulevard de Port Royal, 75005
Métro: Vavin
Closed: Sunday
Open: 9.30 am – 7.00 pm (Monday from 1.00 pm)

This is a serious chocolatier, less well-known than some. They source their ingredients from various cocoa-producing countries and specialise in unusual shapes and designs. Best of all, perhaps, is their chocolate birthday card. For the quality and flair the prices are very reasonable.

### Les Herbes du Luxembourg
3 rue des Médicis, 75006
Métro: Odéon
Closed: Sunday, and one week in August
Open: 10.00 am – 7.30 pm (from 11.00 am in July and August)

You come here for the old-fashioned toilet waters (rose and lavender) which they sell amazingly cheaply in equally old-fashioned blue bottles: just one possibility in an enormously varied stock – soaps, oils, herbs (of course), honey, vanilla – it's a long list. All a bit chaotic, but charming.

### J. P. Cosinier

*8 rue Gay Lussac, 75005*
*Métro: Cluny-La Sorbonne*
*Closed: Sunday*
*Open: Monday to Thursday,*
*7.15 am – 8.15 pm; Friday*
*7.15 am – 8.00 pm; Saturday*
*8.00 am – 7.45 pm*
This boulanger/pâtissier has a speciality of marshmallow (*guimauve*) even better than that sold by Millet in the rue St Dominique. It bears no relation to the lumps of pink and white sugared cottonwool sold under that name in the UK. Here it comes in strips for 1,30€ (coffee, raspberry, vanilla and lime flavour) or you can buy mixed cubes in packets. They also make their own *nougat tendre*.

### La Route du Tibet

*198 rue St Jacques, 75005*
*Métro: Cluny-La Sorbonne*
*Closed: Sunday*
*Open: 10.30 am – 7.30 pm*
A shop name like this normally signals a bogus assembly of vaguely ethnic tat but this is a different enterprise altogether. The quality of what they sell is a revelation: jewellery, clothes, bronzes, small furniture, and especially the most beautiful hand-embroidered bedcovers (from Northern India) executed with great skill, taste and colour sense. At 169€ they seem absurdly inexpensive for what they are.

There is an associated restaurant **Tashi Delek** at 4 rue des Fossés St Jacques and a bookshop in the same street at no. 3. For further information you can consult their website: www.tibet-planet.com.

## Bistrots

### Perraudin

*157 rue St Jacques, 75005*
*Tel: 01 46 33 15 75*
*Métro: Cluny-La Sorbonne*
*Closed: Sunday, the whole of*
*August and first week in*
*November*
*Open: noon – 2.15 pm and*
*7.00 – 10.00 pm*
This is a well-known, long-established, relatively cheap and entirely traditional Parisian bistrot. The cuisine is not 'haute' and they do the straightforward classic dishes best. The three-course lunch menu is 18€, the dinner menu 29,90€. Wines are available by the glass or en pichet at 5€ for a ¼ litre, 9,50€ for a ½ litre. A full bottle costs around 18€.

Booking not essential but you may have to queue.

### Restaurant Les Fontaines

*9 rue Soufflot, 75005*
*Tel: 01 43 26 42 80*
*Métro: Odéon*
*Closed: Sunday*

*Open: noon – 3.00 pm and 7.00 – 11.00 pm*

This very successful bistrot is a short distance from the Panthéon. It doesn't have menus: it doesn't need them because it's always packed out with those who appreciate the reasonably-priced, severely traditional carte. Entrées mostly cost around 6-10€, plats 13-25€, desserts 6-8€ and an assorted plate of cheeses is 6,90€.

Wines are available by the glass from 2,50-4,60€. You could skip the first course because portions are large. In any case reckon on a very satisfactory meal for under 45€. Booking essential.

### Polidor

*41 rue Monsieur le Prince, 75006*
*Métro: Odéon*
*Open: DAILY noon – 2.30 pm and 7.00 pm – 12.30 am (to 11.00 pm Sunday)*

We don't give a telephone number because you don't book: just turn up – though if you're not there by 7.30 pm be prepared to queue. This is the best-known bargain bistrot in Paris and it's in every guide book as well, not least because of the 12€ lunch menu. There are more 'expensive' prix fixes in the evening (20€ and 30€) but you probably won't need the latter. Wines rarely go above 15€ a bottle; in any case wine is available en pichet – ½ litre at 2,50€, ¼ litre at 1,50€.

This is the place to bear in mind the (unchanging) daily specials:

Sunday: gigot d'agneau, haricot blancs géants

Monday: petit salé aux lentilles
Tuesday: hachis parmentier
Wednesday: poulet basquaise
Thursday: saucisse d'Auvergne aux lentilles
Friday: calmars à l'armoricaine
Saturday: langue de boeuf, sauce piquante

As in many of the small, traditional bistrots the place is run by women who know their own mind, including here the patronne who looks as if she could cope with anything, and anyone, and I'm sure she does.

## Brasserie

### Bouillon Racine

*3 rue Racine, 75006*
*Tel: 01 44 32 15 60*
*Métro: Odéon/Cluny-La Sorbonne*
*Closed: two weeks in August*
*Open: DAILY noon – 3.00 pm and 7.00 – 11.00 pm*

Originally founded in 1906 by Camille Chartier (of Chartier fame), this version has had an uneven history and continues to do so. It has to be said that the (restored) art nouveau interior is a greater attraction than the food which features Northern French/ Belgian specialities like carbonnade. It's not expensive (14,90€ for a two-course lunchtime formule, 16,50€ for Sunday brunch and a 29€ three-course dinner menu) but it is variable (both food and service). On balance we've included it but its admission is not unqualified.

# 12. Mouffetard

The main identity of this quarter is defined by the most photo-genic market street in Paris, leading down to the small church of St Médard. But the appeal is more than visual because it is also the best, which is why it is crowded with locals and others from across the city. True, the upper part of the street is heav-ily weighted in the direction of the tourist and, along with the rue du Pot de Fer, full of restaurants to be avoided.

Yet nothing detracts from the light-hearted ambience of the place de la Contrescarpe at the top end, which looks like a 1950s' film set for a Gene Kelly dance routine.

Away from this focus of activity, moving east towards the Jardin des Plantes you find streets that are almost deserted and where good restaurants can struggle to survive, particularly in the evening. At lunchtime it is a different story as those who work and study at the University of Paris Jussieu campus spill out into the surrounding area in search of their midday formule.

The presence of major institutions of the Arab world is part of the diversity: given visual expression in the distinctive archi-tecture, traditional and contemporary, of the Grande Mosquée and the Institut du Monde Arabe. To the north there is the Musée de la Sculpture en Plein Air in the Jardin Tino Rossi on the banks of the Seine. Who but the French would give such prominence to a popular singer, and see the whole as compatible?

And in contrast to everything, here is one of the major sites of the Roman occupation of Northern Europe, the Arènes de Lutèce, where you can wander with scarcely a tourist in sight (apart from yourselves, of course).

## Principal sights

**La Mosquée de Paris** (1920s), entrance place du Puits de-l'Ermite: the focus of the Muslim community; the dignity of this religious institution is a palpable force requiring respect. The style of the architecture, the gardens reminiscent of the Alhambra, the interiors, the superb carpets in the prayer-room, all communicate a sense of calm and well-being.

Architecture apart, there is a *hammam*, a traditional steam bath (separate days for men and women); and you can recuperate in the adjacent all-day tea salon and restaurant offering the usual North African specialities (entrance in the rue Daubenton).

**Institut du Monde Arabe** (late 20th century), entrance rue des Fossés St Bernard: one of the most striking modern buildings in Paris (architect: Jean Nouvel) with much to offer the visitor. There are not only exhibitions (from carpets to calligraphy) but a scientific museum (especially for mathematics and astronomy), a library, a shop (p. 155) and a café serving mint-tea and rich pastries. The top floor has a terrace with a fine view and a restaurant, Ziryab where the food is not quite up to the setting (p. 210).

**Jardin des Plantes** (17th century in origin), quai St Bernard, entrance place Valhubert: first established as a botanical garden by royal decree, it includes alpine, tropical and rose gardens – all free. Also a menagerie, rather ill-housed by modern standards, but appealing for young children, and some important museum galleries (not free) most notably the Grande galerie de l'Evolution with its life-size displays of the animal kingdom.

Older children may prefer the zoological park at Vincennes where hundreds of different species of animals and birds are shown in something like their natural habitat (see p. 227).

**Arènes de Lutèce** (2nd century AD), entrance rue des Arènes: a Roman amphitheatre rediscovered in the course of building excavations in the second half of the 19th century. Quite large, and in a reasonable state of preservation bearing in mind its history of neglect. Men play boules; children operate in greater variety. At other times, early in the day for example, it can present a slightly ghostly aspect.

## Quiet hotels

**Saint Christophe**
*17 rue Lacépède, 75005*
*Tel: 01 43 31 81 54*
*Fax: 01 43 31 12 54*
*E-mail: saintchristophe*
*@wanadoo.fr*
*www.charm-hotel-paris.com*
*Métro: Place Monge*
*31 rooms*
*Price: 115-125€ for a double room, depending on season*
On the corner of the rue de la Clef and the rue Lacépède, the hotel is charming and quiet, and exceptionally well-maintained.

**Libertel Maxim**
*28 rue Censier, 75005*
*Tel: 01 43 31 16 15*
*Fax: 01 43 31 93 87*
*E-mail: H2810-GM*
*@accor.hotels.com*
*Métro: Censier-Daubenton*
*36 rooms*
*Price: 108-118€ for a double room*
Situated in a quiet side-street, with
a third of the rooms on the side
overlooking a small courtyard; the
upper rooms here are lighter.

**Hôtel de l'Espérance**
*15 rue Pascal, 75005*
*Tel: 01 47 07 10 99*
*Fax: 01 43 37 56 19*
*E-mail: hotel.esperance*
*@wanadoo.fr*
*www.hoteldelesperance.fr*
*Métro: Censier-Daubenton*
*38 rooms*
*Price: 79€ for a double room*
*with shower, 87€ with bath*
The rue Pascal has very little
through traffic but, in any case,
some rooms overlook the interior
patio where you can take breakfast
in fine weather – a good-value
option at 6€ reflecting the general
good value of this hotel in an overlooked part of Paris.

# Breakfast

### Gérard Beaufort
*6 rue Linné*
*Closed: Sunday, and the whole*
*of August*
*Open: from 7.30 am*
The croissants at this well-known
boulangerie/pâtisserie are among
the best in Paris even if high in
calories; but then what are you
here for? There is a row of chairs
and tables inside, a few outside. A
large café crème and a delicious
croissant cost just 2,90€.

### Café Mouffetard
*116 rue Mouffetard*
*Open: DAILY from 7.00 am*
Some tables outside but there is a
relaxed, pub-like interior where
you can take a comprehensive
breakfast, excellent value at 5,80€:
coffee/tea/chocolate, orange juice,
croissant or two tartines and jam.

# Public gardens

### Square Ortolan
*Location: on the north side of*
*the rue Ortolan (across the rue*
*Mouffetard from the rue du*
*Pot de Fer).*
Like so many of these small
gardens it is very quiet in marked
contrast to the hectic activity of
the market street itself.

### Square St Médard
*Location: along the side of*
*the church which lies between*
*the rue Censier and the rue*
*Daubenton.*
Small and detached from the
surrounding hubbub; but you still
feel a part of it.

### Square Scipion
*Location: the corner of the rue*
*Scipion and rue du Fer à Moulin.*
This square of reasonable size is
focused on a children's play area
but is well-treed and provided with
plenty of seats for adults.

### Arènes de Lutèce/Square Capitan

*Location: between the rue des Arènes and the rue des Boulangers.*

Situated at the northern end of the quarter, and a most interesting place to sit and absorb the atmosphere. It is also a favourite playground for local children; depending on your temperament you will be either charmed or irritated by this.

See also the **Jardin des Plantes** (p. 151).

# Markets

### Rue Mouffetard, 75005 (market street)

*Tuesday to Saturday 7.30 am – 7.00 pm, with some lunchtime closures (Sunday to 1.00 pm)*

The pedestrianised market section of the street actually begins halfway down from the place de la Contrescarpe (with its shades of Hemingway). We have sufficiently eulogised the atmosphere of the market and described its constituent parts elsewhere: much here in a small space, and there are even gardens nearby where you can consume what you've bought.

### Place Monge, 75005

*Open: Wednesday and Friday 7.30 am – 2.30 pm; Sunday 7.00 am – 3.00 pm*

This street market, which alternates with the market in the place Maubert (p. 161), has a high preponderance of non-food stalls – cheap clothing and the like –

presumably because of the proximity of the rue Mouffetard.

# Fromagers

At the lower end of the market street, near Eglise St Médard, there are no fewer than four cheesemongers within a short distance of each other (all keep market hours):

**Androuet,** 134 rue Mouffetard: part of a chain with branches in the 7th, 12th, 15th, 16th, 17th arrondissements

**La Fromagerie,** 131 rue Mouffetard: highly recommended – and it doesn't close at lunchtime

**Fromagerie Quatrehomme,** 118 rue Mouffetard

**Fromager C. Baudonin,** 105 rue Mouffetard

– not a great deal to choose between them but La Fromagerie has the most comprehensive range.

At the top end of our area:

### La Ferme des Arènes

*60 rue Monge, 75005*
*Closed: Monday, and Sunday afternoon*
*Open: 8.30 am – 12.45 pm and 3.30 – 7.45 pm*

This is a superb fromagerie, also selling a range of other groceries. It is owned by Christian LeLann who also owns La Ferme St Aubin in the rue St Louis-en-l'Ile (p. 64) as well as another branch in the 20th arrondissement. His website: lelann-sell.com gives further details.

## Glaciers

### Gelati d'Alberto
*45 rue Mouffetard, 75005*
*Open: DAILY noon-midnight*
*April to November*
Towards the top end of the street
and on the left as you descend is
this shrine to the glacier's art. You
might even see the serveuse
instructing a junior on how to
make the famous cornet where the
layers of ice-cream are formed like
flower petals.

Prices from 3€ – but that is
ample, believe me, and you could
always go back for more. The
range is considerable, with regular
innovations like date-with-
cinnamon (it works).

Also at
*12 rue des Lombards, 75004*
*Open: all year round*

## Neglected museums

### Collection de Minéraux
### Université Pierre-et-Marie-Curie
*34 rue Jussieu, 75005*
*Métro: Jussieu*
*Closed: Tuesday and public*
*holidays*
*Open: afternoons only, 1.00 –*
*6.00 pm*
*Entrance: 4,50€ adults, 2€ children*
Don't be inhibited by the address:
this is a welcoming museum of
great attraction to children and
adults alike, and constructed with
imagination. Even the entrance is
made up to look like a mine and
the exhibition area has a dazzling
display of minerals.

### Musée de la Sculpture en Plein Air
*Square Tino Rossi, quai St*
*Bernard, 75005*
*Métro: Jussieu*
*Open: DAILY*
*Entrance: FREE*
Along the banks of the Seine in a
garden dedicated to one of France's
most popular singers (*J'attend-
rai... Paris, voici Paris*, etc.) is a
remarkable assembly of large
sculptures by the likes of Brancusi
and Zadkine; you can sit there to
admire the exhibits – and to rest
your feet.

## Interesting shops

### Paris Jazz Corner
*5-7 rue de Navarre, 75005*
*Métro: Place Monge*
*Closed: Sunday*
*Open: 11.30 am – 8.00 pm*
For serious jazz enthusiasts this is
an important source of rare and
unusual LPs, jazz memorabilia and
CDs. Everything is in good condition but it requires time to unearth
what interests you.

### La Luminaire de l'Oeil
*4 rue Flatters, off the boulevard*
*de Port Royal, 75005*
*Métro: Censier-Daubenton*
*Closed: Sunday and Monday*
*Open: Tuesday to Friday, 2.00 –*
*7.00 pm; Saturday 11.00 am –*
*5.00 pm*
This small shop specialises in gas,
oil and electric light fittings from
the period 1850-1925, all in superb
original condition and working
order. Prices may seem high but

assembling this kind of stock is no easy matter. If you're looking for period light fittings that are the real thing, not reproduction, you'll find nowhere else like it.

### Craft shop: Institut du Monde Arabe

*Rue des Fossés St Bernard, 75005*
*Métro: Cardinal Lemoine*
*Closed: Monday*
*Open: 10.00 am – 6.00 pm*
The craft shop is now housed in a large marquee opposite the main building. The quality and price of what they offer make it an excellent place to buy presents and cards – for yourself and others. The ceramics are outstanding if often too large or too fragile to transport. However, the soft furnishings, the wood and metalwork, jewellery and silverware give you plenty of choice.

An essential part of a visit to the Institut even if you don't actually buy anything.

### Pierre Champion

*110 rue Mouffetard, 75005*
*Métro: Censier-Daubenton*
*Closed: Monday, and Sunday afternoon*
*Open: 8.00 am – 7.00 pm*
*(Sunday to 1.30 pm)*
The only Paris branch of a company based in the Périgord that specialises in food products of the South-West, particularly goose and duck foie gras. There is not space to expiate on this profound subject but, briefly, you can buy this *cru*, i.e. fresh (and not always available); *mi-cuit*, i.e. pasteurised which retains the

flavour but has to be kept refrigerated; and *cuit*, i.e. sterilised, like most of the stuff available worldwide, which can be kept for years – and isn't worth the money.

Foie gras apart, the great thing here is the range of plats cuisinés: cooked dishes in tins or jars. If you want to recreate a French meal you could choose from: chou farci, 6,40€ for a 400g tin; petit salé aux lentilles, 420g at 3,70€; coq au vin de Bergerac, 750g for 8,10€; even blanquette de veau aux girolles, 400g for 11,25€ (you're paying for the mushrooms). A splendid place to stock up.

## Bistrots

### Le Buisson Ardent

*25 rue Jussieu, 75005*
*Tel: 01 43 54 93 02*
*Fax: 01 46 33 34 77*
*Métro: Jussieu*
*Closed: Saturday, Sunday, the whole of August and Christmas week*
*Open: noon – 2.00 pm and 7.30 – 10.30 pm*
With original décor dating from the 1920s, this is a favourite haunt of academics from the nearby university campus, particularly at lunchtime, when there is a 17€ menu.

Booking is essential for the evening when the 32€ menu represents good quality for price with a choice from six entrées (e. g. asperges blanches vinaigrette; terrine de lapin), seven plats (e. g. haricot de cochon; chicken casseroled with turnips, artichokes and potatoes) followed by cheese or a choice of six desserts of the traditional with a twist variety. There is a careful selection of wines, intelligently described, in the range 25-36€ a bottle; also wines by the glass at 4,70-5,70€, ¼ pichet at 6,80-8,50€, ½ pichet at 11,50-14,50€.

Pleasant and efficient service. My only criticism is that the tables are a bit close together, otherwise this restaurant is strongly recommended.

## L'Equitable

*1 rue des Fossés St Marcel, 75005*
*Tel: 01 43 31 69 20*
*Métro: Censier-Daubenton*
*Closed: Monday (and Tuesday lunchtime)*
*Open: noon – 2.30 pm and 7.30 – 10.30 pm*

An excellent example of a good-value modern bistrot (like Casa Olympe in the 9th) where the food is essentially traditional but with inventive touches. It offers menu-cartes (which can be combined or selected from) according to a mathematical exactness that would make you dizzy if an explanation were attempted: basically at 33€ (35€ on a Sunday).

The greatest bargain is the weekday lunchtime menu with its own complex pattern, but where the most simple variant offers a main course, dessert and coffee for 16€. Dishes like roasted cod, gigot d'agneau, tête de veau ravigote, rognons de veau à la moutarde are typical. Wine is available by the glass for 3,00-6.30€, and on the wine list proper there are half-

bottles for between 13,10 and 23,90€.

## Au Petit Marguery

*9 boulevard de Port Royal, 75013*
*Tel: 01 43 31 58 59*
*Métro: Gobelins*
*Closed: Sunday, Monday and the whole of August*
*Open: noon – 2.15 pm and 7.30 – 10.15 pm*

Booking is essential at this *cuisine bourgeoise* restaurant, with comfort to match, noted for its game dishes in the season when great classics like lièvre à la royale (something like our jugged hare) are on the menu.

For what is offered value is exceptional with a formule (e + pl + dess) for 35€. For this you might get rabbit terrine, roasted sea bass and Grand Marnier soufflé. There is a similar menu with a more restricted range at lunchtime for 25€ for three courses. Wines are from 24€ a bottle or 16€ a half; by the glass from 5€.

## Le Languedoc

*64 boulevard de Port Royal, 75005*
*Métro: Gobelins*
*Closed: Tuesday and Wednesday*
*Open: noon – 2.00 pm and 7.00 – 10.00 pm*

Make no mistake about it, this is a perfectly ordinary bistrot where the customers are almost all local regulars eating the 20€ menu (three courses plus a half-bottle of wine, beer or mineral water). Your main dish comes as a matter of course with a salad sprinkled with diced cantal cheese.

Run by M. et Mme Dubois

since 1974, the atmosphere will delight your heart. The food is too predictable to list but entirely sound. Don't bother to book at first – then do so for the next day, or whatever.

**Le Refuge du Passé**
*32 rue du Fer à Moulin, 75005*
*Tel: 01 47 07 29 91*
*Métro: Censier-Daubenton*
*Open: DAILY noon – 2.30 pm and 7.30 – 10.30 pm*
With a name like this it could hardly be anything else but the ultimate in traditional bistrots. In a rather out-of-the-way street, and despite good cooking and reasonable prices it is struggling to survive. At the time of my last visit mine was one of only two tables occupied – usually a bad sign – but here not justified.

There is a good menu-carte of three courses for 34€, two for 27€ (the latter not available Friday evening, public holidays and weekends). The lunchtime formule at 18€ for a main course and coffee is not particularly competitive except that the daily speciality might include veau Marengo, lapin à la moutarde or coq au vin – which all figure here. Quality is good and

portions are generous. Wines are relatively expensive: nothing under 28€, and a few half-bottles.

A lot of thought and care has gone into this place: I hope it survives.

# Brasseries

**Marty**
*20 avenue des Gobelins, 75005*
*Tel: 01 43 91 39 51*
*Métro: Gobelins*
*Open: DAILY noon to midnight*
Just around the corner from the boulevard de Port Royal, this is not the kind of brasserie that has one large dining room. On the ground floor (to be preferred) it is sectionalised into alcoves at different levels. The art deco interior and furniture, if rather repro-looking, is beautifully maintained.

There is a 23€ lunch menu and a 30€ menu of three courses, and wine by the glass at around 5-6€. Cooking of exceptional quality for price; game figures largely in season. Cocktails (expensive) and plateaux des fruits de mer (ditto) are worth it if your budget allows.

Very comfortable with a sophisticated but friendly ambience.

# 13. Maubert

If it lacks the conspicuous sights of adjoining areas there is, in fact, more of the ancient city to be found in this quarter than any other. Here is much of what remains of medieval Paris. Though most of the architecture is later, the many small side-streets spreading northwards to the Seine from the place Maubert retain something of the feel of those distant times: the occasional façade or doorway, the inner core of many buildings and the configuration of the streets themselves.

Later centuries have superimposed their own identity down to modern times. For example, the early 1930s' Maison de la Mutualité, in cinema art deco style, was built on the site of a 17th century seminary. An intriguing building, it is the centre for a federation of mutual welfare organisations, which reflect one dimension of French idealism and sense of social responsibility (that can co-exist with other less admirable qualities).

Add to this the long academic tradition which saw the  foundation of colleges in the 13th and 14th centuries. Today the colleges and their ancillary institutions set the tone in an atmosphere a good deal calmer than the more obvious studenty ethos of St Michel. By comparison, Maubert has a kind of gravitas, typified by the solitary young woman reading beside the bust of Ronsard in a garden on the rue des Ecoles.

François Mitterrand lived in the nearby rue de Bièvre, a street of old houses with the unplanned look of natural growth, in contrast to his own elaborately planned grand schemes. No incongruity here, because he represented a bold sense of innovation alongside a profound appreciation of the past, only occasionally in conflict and characteristic of the city.

On your first visit to this quarter you will become a Francophile or you will be lost: the different facets of Maubert constitute multiple patterns of appeal. You will find them in the narrow winding streets, the unusual shops, the gardens and the quais with spectacular views of the Seine and the islands. Above all in the life of the cafés and restaurants, for here are some of the great classic bistrots: Au Moulin à Vent, Moissonnier, and pre-eminent, the brasserie Balzar, which has that sharp, informal style that cannot be transplanted into any other culture.

## Principal sights

**Eglise St-Julien-le-Pauvre** (12th century), rue St Julien-le-Pauvre: from where there is one of the best views of the cathedral of Notre-Dame, which was built at the same time.

    **Eglise St-Etienne-du-Mont** (late 15th-17th century), place Ste Geneviève: the shrine of the patron saint of Paris, this largely Gothic church is notable for its vaulting, the wonderful Renaissance rood screen and some stained glass rivalling that of Sainte Chapelle.

## Quiet hotels

**Hôtel de Notre-Dame**
*19 rue Maître Albert, 75005*
*Tel: 01 43 26 79 00*
*Fax: 01 46 33 50 11*
*E-mail: hotel.denotredame*
*@libertysurf.fr*
*www.hotel-paris-notredame.com*
*Métro: Maubert-Mutualité*
*34 rooms*
*Price: 154€ for a double room*
Located in a surprisingly quiet street and the better rooms (as above), which give onto an interior courtyard, are even quieter. Altogether a very civilised hotel.

**Hôtel les Degrés de Notre-Dame**
*10 rue des Grands-Degrés, 75005*
*Tel: 01 55 42 88 88*
*Fax: 01 40 46 95 34*
*E-mail: contact@*
*lesdegreshotel.com*
*www.lesdegreshotel.com*
*Métro: Maubert-Mutualité*
*10 rooms*
*Price: 115-170€ for a double room*
This will be one of the most interesting hotels you stay in. Theoretically all the rooms take two people but we recommend only the most expensive one (No. 51), a top-floor virtual apartment, with a view of Notre-Dame, plenty of space and an excellent bathroom. The 165€ room is on the second floor and is the width of the building with two good windows overlooking the street. Other rooms are either too small, too awkwardly configured or too dark – sometimes all three. There is no lift and you have to watch your feet on the stairs: this is a very old building.

    To get the best (or any) room

you need to book well ahead. Note that the price includes a generous breakfast in the adjoining restaurant.

### Hôtel du Collège de France
*7 rue Thénard, 75005*
*Tel: 01 43 26 78 36*
*Fax: 01 46 34 58 29*
*E-mail: hotel.du.college.de.france*
*@wanadoo.fr*
*www.hotel-collegedefrance.com*
*Métro: Maubert-Mutualité*
*29 rooms*
*Price: 99-120€ for a double room*
The best value in the area (and prices are even lower in the off season). A fairly plain but well-appointed hotel in a quiet street and those rooms that overlook the rue Latran are even quieter. An excellent base to enjoy this appealing quarter of the city.

### Hôtel-Résidence Henri IV
*50 rue des Bernardins, 75005*
*Tel: 01 44 41 31 81*
*Fax: 01 46 33 93 22*
*E-mail: reservation*
*@residencehenri4.com*
*www.residencehenri4.com*
*Métro: Maubert-Mutualité*
*8 rooms (2 AIR CONDI-*
*TIONED) and 5 apartments*
*with kitchenette*
*Price: 150€ and upwards for the*
*superior double rooms*
For a very small hotel the range of accommodation is remarkable, both in price and facilities. It is better to visit prior to staying there to be sure you get what you want. There are bedrooms and apartments on each floor and they vary in size and price.

Set in a quiet cul-de-sac, the hotel overlooks the square Paul Langevin. The 'cuisinettes' are only really suitable for preparing hot drinks and snacks, and your breakfast, but that can add up to a more comfortable (and economical) stay.

### Hôtel des Grands Ecoles
*75 rue du Cardinal Lemoine,*
*75005*
*Tel: 01 43 26 79 23*
*Fax: 01 43 25 28 15*
*E-mail: hotel.grandes.ecoles*
*@wanadoo.fr*
*www.hotel-grandes-ecoles.com*
*Métro: Cardinal Lemoine*
*50 rooms*
*Price: 110-135€ for a double room*
This hotel in its own private cul-de-sac is the best known secret in Paris. The owner, Mme le Floch, can be seen working at her reservations plan with pencil and rubber (no software spreadsheet for her) trying to accommodate the demands of tourists from around the world but particularly the United States. The rooms are good with decent bathrooms, and an additional pleasure is taking your breakfast in the cobblestone courtyard garden.

Remember: you need to book six months ahead; if not more.

## Breakfast

### Les Degrés de Notre-Dame
*10 rue des Grands-Degrés*
*Closed: Sunday*
*Open: from 7.30 am*
This place has a warm, friendly atmosphere: both hotel and restau-

rant (see p. 164) and the best choice in the area for breakfast. For 11€ you get as much baguette, jam and butter as you want, plus fresh orange juice, one croissant and coffee/chocolate/tea (free if you're staying in the hotel).

## Public gardens

### Square Paul Painlevé
*Location: backing on to the Musée de Cluny at the junction of the rue des Ecoles and the rue de Cluny*
A square dedicated to an eminent mathematician – the highest status academic profession in France – at the heart of things just opposite the Sorbonne. Its cool, shaded benches are crowded on hot days with refugees from the libraries, lecture rooms and laboratories.

### Place Marcellin Berthelot
*Location: on the south side of the rue des Ecoles, opposite the rue Thénard.*
There isn't much of a garden here. The grass is enclosed but there are benches surrounding a bust of Ronsard, where you may wish to read or spend a few thoughtful moments.

### Square Paul Langevin
*Location: facing the junction of the rue des Ecoles and the rue Monge.*
Long and narrow, shaped like a flattened triangle, this is the most dramatically beautiful of all the small 'squares' in the quarter. Facing north with the backdrop of a high stone wall, evergreen shrubbery and mature trees, grass

and flowers, it has an air of calm detachment.

### Jardin de la Bièvre
*Location: rue de Bièvre*
The best secret garden in this part of Paris and one you probably couldn't hope to happen on by chance. Small, roughly round in shape with seats set into the perimeter, trees, flowers and shrubs – and peace.

A good place to come after you've explored the market in the place Maubert.

### Square René Viviani
*Location: junction of the rue St Julien-le-Pauvre and the quai Montebello, facing Notre-Dame.*
The three-star situation means that this small garden is heavily patronised and therefore a bit worn: but the view is wonderful. The seats under the lime trees set back on the southern side are cool on a hot day.

A good place to sit even if you don't stay very long.

## Market

### Maubert
*Place Maubert, 75005*
*Open: Tuesday and Thursday 7.00 am – 2.30 pm; Saturday 7.00 am – 3.00 pm*
This small, popular and altogether excellent street market alternates with that held in the rue Monge (p. 153) but has a better balance of food stalls. It is very near the well-known baker, **Eric Kayser** at 8 and 14 rue Monge. The shop at no. 14 specialises in organic bread, and

there is another branch in the nearby rue Basse des Carmes.

## Fromager

**Fromager** (just that)
*12 place Maubert, 75005*
*Closed: Sunday afternoon*
*and Monday*
*Open: 8.30 am – 1.00 pm and*
*4.00 – 8.00 pm (9.00 am –*
*1.00 pm Sunday)*
A decent range of cheeses and adjacent to Eric Kayser's bakeries (and a good charcuterie) Fruit can be bought in the market.

## Glacier

**Les Gourmets de Notre Dame**
*1 rue des Grands-Degrés, 75005*
*Closed: Monday*
*Open: 11.30 am – 7.30 pm*
This tea salon was, until August 2007, the main retail outlet for Thomas Dammann, the son of a German icecream-maker, who opened his first shop in the rue du Cardinal Lemoine (now his 'factory') in 1987. The salon still sells his ice-cream (and, of course, Dammann teas) as do many other cafés and restaurants, because his wholesale business has expanded greatly.

Dammann is the intellectual of his profession with definite views – for example on 'excessively creamy' Italian ice-cream, which he thinks obscures the flavours. He is careful not to over-sweeten ice-cream and sorbets for the same reason. You can also sample his

product in the Tuileries gardens, where there is a kiosk near the octagonal pond.

## Neglected museums

**Musée de la Préfecture de Police**
*4 rue de la Montagne Ste*
*Geneviève, 75005*
*Métro: Maubert-Mutualité*
*Closed: Sunday and public*
*holidays*
*Open: 9.00 am – 5.00 pm*
*(Saturday from 10.00 am)*
*Entrance: FREE*
Not on everyone's list, and certainly under-visited: but a fascinating museum tracing the (tenuous) antecedents of the present police force. Police equipment, weapons used in crimes, numerous documents and assorted memorabilia related to great crimes and criminals. A rich feast for those with curious or morbid instincts; and it's free.

**Musée de l'Assistance Publique-Hôpitaux de Paris**
*Hôtel de Miramion*
*47 quai de la Tournelle, 75005*
*Métro: Maubert-Mutualité*
*Closed: Monday, public holidays*
*and the whole of August*
*Open: 10.00 am – 6.00 pm*
*Entrance: 4€ (FREE to under 13s)*
The title is hardly a crowd-puller but this is, in fact, a remarkable assembly of diverse exhibits relating to the development of hospitals in Paris since the Middle Ages, housed in an *hôtel particulier* that dates from the 17th century.

# Interesting shops

### La Maison de la Vanille
*8 rue du Cardinal Lemoine,*
*75005*
*Métro: Cardinal Lemoine*
*Closed: Monday and Tuesday*
*Open: 11.30 am – 7.00 pm*
*(Sunday from 2.30 pm)*
This shop-cum-café specialises in vanilla products from the island of Réunion. But you should also try their tea and pastries – particularly the sweet potato cake (highly recommended).

### Mayette
*8 rue des Carmes, 75005*
*Métro: Maubert-Mutualité*
*Closed: Sunday*
*Open: 10.00 am – 8.00 pm*
*(Monday from 2.00 pm)*
The magician's mecca, this shop has been in business for almost two hundred years. The range is enormous from those tricks suited to children, up to the level of the most advanced practitioner. They also have books, DVDs, videos – an amazing reference source.

### Etats d'Origine: Jouets Anciens
*5 rue St Victor, 75005*
*Métro: Maubert-Mutualité*
*Closed: Sunday and Monday*
*Open: 2.00 – 7.00 pm*
This small shop in an interesting side-street sells old toys of all descriptions and in superb condition. For collectors, of course, but the appeal of old toy cars etc. is such that you might appreciate them as decorative objects. The same is true of some of the doll's house furniture: I was particularly

taken by an old cooking range, complete with utensils. Don't be too shy to go in; you will find the owner expert and helpful, if a shade aloof.

### Bouddhas du Monde
*6 rue des Grands-Degrés, 75005*
*Métro: Maubert-Mutualité*
*Closed: Sunday and Monday*
*Open: 12.30 – 7.30 pm*
Béatrice d'Alexandry and her husband have assembled an extraordinary collection of statuary in all media and sizes, and from all the areas of the world where Buddhism holds sway. Their collection is quite different from the usual dubious offerings. They are intensely knowledgeable and are careful, for example, to point out that some of the Buddhas are not as old as they look. A lot of their stock is sold to antique dealers and interior decorators who may not be so scrupulous.

This is a shop that warrants more than a cursory inspection since original decorative objects of quality that will set off contemporary or 'Modern' or antique furniture are not easy to find.

# Bistrots

### La Maison de la Mutualité
*Square de la Mutualité, 75005*
*(corner of the rue Victor)*
*Métro: Maubert-Mutualité*
*Closed: Saturday and Sunday*
*Open: noon – 2.30 pm (lunch only)*
This isn't a bistrot or a brasserie but an art deco restaurant on the first floor of a community and

health centre. The food is entirely traditional and excellent value; pensioners appear to be the main clients. There is a two-course formule for 15€ *(boisson comprise)*, with three courses at 21€ and a menu-carte at 31,50€.

An experience not to be missed (in an exceptional setting) which offers an insight into the principled and rather formal strands of French character that you may not find elsewhere.

### Les Degrés de Notre-Dame
*10 rue des Grands-Degrés, 75005*
*Tel: 01 55 42 88 88*
*Métro: Maubert-Mutualité*
*Closed: Sunday*
*Open: noon to midnight for meals*
This is a restaurant with rooms, where the food is traditional French with imports from the former North African territories, all in large portions and freshly prepared. The three-course lunch menu at 12€ is much better value than the nearby tourist traps. There are dinner menus at 23€ and 25€; à la carte will not be much more but you are unlikely to need it.

A warm, friendly ambience – you will want to return.

### Chez René
*14 boulevard St Germain, 75005*
*Tel: 01 43 54 30 23*
*Métro: Maubert-Mutualité*
*Closed: Sunday, Monday, the whole of August, Christmas to New Year*
*Open: 12.00 – 2.30 pm and 7.00 – 11.00 pm*
I am old enough to remember René himself (he started here in 1957). His son, Jean-Paul, has recently retired and sold up. So there is a new owner, chef, and a 'directeur'. If the carte of classic dishes (including the famous coq au vin) remains, there are now no good-value menus, no daily specials the same from week to week. Gone also is the almost provincial charm; the ethos is sharper, more urbane, less sympathetic. Having said that, prices on the carte are not high – entrées from 4-16€, plats from 14-26€, desserts from 7-10€. Wines by the bottle are from 18-59€, by the half-bottle 13-26,50€, and glasses from 4-7,50€.

I reserve further judgement, but it is no longer on my list of favourites.

### Au Moulin à Vent (Chez Henri)
*20 rue des Fossés St Bernard, 75005*
*Tel: 01 43 54 99 37*
*Métro: Jussieu*
*Closed: Sunday, Monday (Saturday lunchtime), the whole of August, Christmas to New Year*
*Open: noon – 2.00 pm and 7.30 – 11.00 pm*
The most reassuring of restaurants: you go there with high expectations and they are always fulfilled. The professionalism, the reliability of the food, the discreet ambience give it something of the quality of a gentleman's club. What do you eat? Ideally start with the dried sausage from Lyon, brought to your table with a knife that has been sharpened almost to extinction: then help yourself. They weigh the plate before and after and charge accordingly.

For the main course you should try the beef (from Salers): ask for it *à point*. It comes with delicious sauté potatoes. It's not a place where you worry about the prix fixe (there isn't one at dinner anyway). Just be assured that you will dine well for less than 60€.

## Moissonnier

*28 rue des Fossés St Bernard, 75005*
*Tel: 01 43 29 87 65*
*Métro: Jussieu*
*Closed: Sunday, Monday, the*
*whole of August and Christmas*
*Open: noon – 2.00 pm and*
*7.30 – 10.00 pm*

You have a severe problem when you come here: how to avoid eating too much. Either have the 'starter' of saladiers lyonnais and don't have a main course, or vice versa. The term 'saladiers' is deceptive: you help yourself from a trolley bearing twelve large wooden bowls of 'salads' that are liberally mixed with various meats and fish; don't commit to a main course until you've checked the state of your stomach. The desserts are themselves substantial.

There is a lunch menu on weekdays for 23€; à la carte will cost about twice that, if you disregard our advice. The carafe wine from the region is the recommended option at 14€ a ½ litre.

## Chantairelle

*17 rue Laplace, 75005*
*Tel: 01 46 33 18 59*
*Métro: Cardinal Lemoine*
*Closed: Sunday (and Saturday*
*lunchtime)*
*Open: noon – 2.00 pm and*

*7.30 – 10.00 pm*

A slightly eccentric setting (recorded birdsong and other sounds of nature) with food from the Auvergne and wines from the region, and also a range of mineral waters including the sparkling Chateldon.

There are lunch menus at 15€ for two courses and 19,50€ for three, and a 28€ dinner menu of three courses (two choices for each course). A la carte is about a third more expensive than that but with a choice of dishes not generally on offer: chou farci and potée de porc, for example (both at about 15€). Wines from the Auvergne cost around 15-23€ a bottle, 10-11,80€ for a half.

A friendly place which displays endearing qualities: like an occasional menu devoted entirely to cabbage!

## Brasserie

### Balzar

*49 rue des Ecoles, 75005*
*Tel: 01 43 54 13 67*
*Métro: Cluny-La Sorbonne*
*Open: DAILY noon – 11.45 pm*

For many this is *the* brasserie of the Latin Quarter. Inevitably it has been taken over by the Flo Group but it does have a quite different ethos from the others that have been gathered into the fold. Straightforward food with no prix fixe until an hour or so before closing: but it's not expensive – you'll eat well for around 40€. Ask for a table on the terrace in summer and watch the world go by.

# 14. Odéon/St Michel
# (and for the Ile de la Cité)

This is an area of, and for the young. They cluster in front of the fountain in the place St Michel chattering like so many excited starlings at all times of the day and night. Theirs is an unanalysed and unreflective state of mind: they are excited just to be there. They eat *crêpes* and *sandwiches* from the nearby stalls and they are having a good time; you cannot but envy their self-assurance and sense of being centre-stage. The old (that is, anyone over twenty) have to accept a subordinate role.

But whatever your age there is much to discover and enjoy in this tightly compacted area because it's not expensive, even good value. Here you will find a pastiche of the Latin Quarter (life imitating art?) ready and waiting: roughly the streets immediately around the rue de la Huchette. And yet if you can approach it with an innocent eye there is excitement here too: just don't eat in the restaurants.

Together with the Maubert quarter it is the oldest part of Paris, the site of the Roman settlement of Lutetia, of which survives part of the vast Roman baths now incorporated into the Musée de Cluny. The Hôtel de Cluny itself is one of only three medieval houses extant in the city. The Sorbonne is here too dating back to the 13th century, although the main building just south of Cluny is a late 19th century reconstruction. The Sorbonne and associated colleges make up the University of Paris, and its influence is everywhere, not least in the appeal of the student image: an aspiration in France's meritocratic educational system.

So the legacy of history runs deep, in a district of a thousand perspectives, particularly towards the river. The embankments are lined with the green boxes of the bouquinistes; and along the quais and bridges you'll find yourself compelled to stop again and again as yet another prospect comes into view.

The Left Bank is also the place from which to explore the Ile de la Cité; there is only one hotel on the island, Henri Quatre in the place Dauphine, and it is of the ultra-unmodernised variety. All you have to do is cross a bridge (Pont Michel), which will bring you to the flower market in the place Louis Lépine (it's a bird market on Sunday). And of all the historic sights on the island the most beautiful is the Sainte-Chapelle, concealed within the grim exterior of the Palais de Justice.

## Principal sights

**Hôtel de Cluny** (late 15th century), place Paul Painlevé: one of the oldest buildings in Paris housing one of the most interesting museums, with outstanding religious statuary and treasures of medieval art and crafts, tapestries in particular.

**Eglise St-Séverin-St-Nicolas** (13th-16th century), rue des Prêtres St-Séverin: with a history much earlier than the date of the present building, there is a great deal to admire in this small church including some fine 15th century stained glass.

And on the Ile de la Cité:

You need hardly be reminded that the island boasts one of the most famous sights in the Western world, the cathedral of **Notre-Dame** (12th-14th century), whether viewed from the parvis (the great west front with rose window), from the quai de Montebello across the river or, from the perspective of the Ile St-Louis, the chevet with its flying buttresses. However, two others that are sometimes missed have world-class qualities of their own:

**La Sainte-Chapelle** (13th century), boulevard du Palais: only the slender Gothic spire advertises its whereabouts and nothing prepares you for the splendour of its stained glass (largely original). If you plan to devote time to sightseeing on the island, this should be the priority.

**La Conciergerie** (14th century), quai de l'Horloge: similarly embedded but equally surprising with its magnificent Gothic halls. Notorious as the prison for thousands who crossed the bridge to the Right Bank (and the guillotine) during the Revolution, Marie Antoinette amongst them.

## Quiet hotels

**Grand Hôtel des Balcons**
*3 rue Casimir Delavigne, 75006*
*Tel: 01 46 34 78 50*
*Fax: 01 46 34 06 27*

*E-mail: resa@balcons.com*
*www.balcons.com*
*Métro: Odéon*
*50 rooms*
*Price: 110-150€ for a double room*
This is an excellent hotel, well maintained by its owners, the Corroyer-André family. Some rooms are much bigger than others and the upper price range is recommended. As also is the exceptional self-service buffet-breakfast – eat all you can for 10€. A pleasant and fairly quiet street despite the central location.

### Hôtel du Lys

*23 rue Serpente, 75006*
*Tel: 01 43 26 97 57*
*Fax: 01 44 07 34 90*
*E-mail: hoteldulys@wanadoo.fr*
*www.hoteldulys.com*
*Métro: Odéon*
*22 rooms*
*Price: 120€ for a double room*
In a fairly quiet street, this hotel represents exceptional value for style and location. Note that breakfast is included in the modest room rate.

### Hôtel de la Sorbonne

*6 rue Victor Cousin, 75005*
*Tel: 01 43 54 58 08*
*Fax: 01 40 51 05 18*
*E-mail: reservation*
*@hotelsorbonne.com*
*www.hotel-paris-sorbonne.com*
*Métro: Cluny-La Sorbonne*
*39 rooms*
*Price: 110€ for a double room*
*with shower, 130€ with bath*
Passing through an archway you come to a cobbled interior court-yard, which most rooms overlook:

so it's quiet, although the street itself sees little through traffic. Rue Victor Cousin is the sort of narrow street which will have you peering at maps: it's parallel with, and in between the rue St Jacques and the boulevard St Michel.

Essential to book well ahead because the hotel is well-known and good value for its peaceful location.

### Hôtel Cluny Sorbonne

*8 rue Victor Cousin, 75005*
*Tel: 01 43 54 66 66*
*Fax: 01 43 29 68 07*
*E-mail: cluny@club-internet.fr*
*www.hotel-cluny.fr*
*Métro: Cluny-La Sorbonne*
*23 rooms*
*Price: 90-95€ for a standard*
*double room; 110-150€ for a*
*larger one*
Next door to the Hôtel de la Sorbonne but built right up to the street so it's not as quiet. Nonetheless, well-maintained and much in demand. The cheaper rooms although technically double are a bit cramped; one of the larger rooms on an upper floor is the recommended option.

### Hôtel Parc St Séverin

*22 rue de la Parcheminerie,*
*75005*
*Tel: 01 43 54 32 17*
*Fax: 01 43 54 70 71*
*E-mail: hotel.parc.severin*
*@espritdefrance.com*
*www.esprit-de-france.com*
*Métro: Cluny-La Sorbonne*
*27 rooms AIR CONDITIONED*
*Price: 150-160€ for a double room*
On a traffic-free street this beauti-

fully maintained hotel is itself modern but surrounded by vintage Paris, adjacent to the church of St Séverin and within sight of the Musée de Cluny. There are more expensive rooms with a terrace (at 195€ and upwards) but the difference will buy you a decent dinner.

**Hôtel Villa des Princes**
*19 rue Monsieur le Prince, 75006*
*Tel: 01 46 33 31 69*
*Fax: 01 43 26 30 04*
*E-mail: villadesprinces*
*@wanadoo.fr*
*www.villa-des-princes.com*
*Métro: Odéon*
*12 rooms*
*Price: 119€ for a double room*
*(109€ for single occupancy)*
Formerly the Hôtel des Ecoles, it has been taken into new ownership and was entirely renovated in 2004. In a street which sees little through traffic this is a very good quality hotel for the price. Two of our recommended restaurants are in the same street so you wouldn't have far to walk after taking your dinner on board.

There is a good buffet breakfast at 10€. And note that low season prices (some 10€ lower) apply from mid-November to the 1st March, as well as the usual summer discount.

## Breakfast

**Paul**
*14 boulevard St Michel*
*Closed: Sunday*
*Open: from 8.30 am*
This busy branch has an excellent first-floor café where you can take the usual breakfast formules. *(See also the other breakfast places in the immediately adjacent St Germain/St Sulpice area, p. 177).*

## Gardens

**Square André Lefèvre**
*Location: junction of the rue St Jacques and the rue de la Parcheminerie, behind the church of St Séverin.*
A small shady garden largely given over to a children's play area with surrounding benches; a little oasis in a stage setting.

Since it's easy to go and sit by the banks of the Seine and absorb the view, the relative lack of gardens is not a severe problem. On the Ile de la Cité, however, you'll find the **Square Jean XXIII** which lies behind and to the south of Notre-Dame: very busy as you might expect but with a good children's play area. Much less crowded and an excellent spot with a fine view down-river from the Pont-Neuf, is the **Square du Vert-Galant** at the west side of the island behind the statue of Henri IV (and beyond the queues for the *bateaux vedettes*).

## Market

**Rue de Buci/Rue de Seine, 75006**
The exact opening times vary from one shop to another but the pattern of closure – Sunday afternoon and

all day Monday – on the whole still applies.

Over the years this cross-roads market street (it's mainly the rue de Buci) has become less of a market area as the cafés and art galleries have taken over. So it's nothing like the rue Cler or the rue Mouffetard; it does have the basic ingredients, however, and there is still something of that buzz especially in the morning.

## Fromager

### La Fromagerie 31
*64 rue de Seine, 75006*
On the border with St Germain so described in that section (details p. 178).

## Glacier

### Amorino
*4 rue de Buci, 75006*
As above (p. 179) with branches elsewhere, including the Ile St-Louis (p. 64).

## Neglected museums

### Musée de la Monnaie de Paris
*11 quai de Conti, 75006*
*Métro: Odéon/Pont Neuf*
*Closed: Monday and public holidays*
*Open: DAILY 11.00 am –*
*5.30 pm (Saturday and Sunday from midday)*
*Entrance: 5€ (FREE to under 16s)*
The museum of the Paris Mint displaying thousands of coins,

medals and tokens along with working machines, sculptures, documents, pictures, showing the evolution of coin-making. Very well-organised with a 'discovery' area for children.

### Musée d'Histoire de la Médecine
*Université René Descartes*
*12 rue de l'Ecole de Médecine, 75005*
*Métro: Odéon/St Michel*
*Closed: Thursday, Sunday and public holidays*
*Open: afternoons only,*
*2.00 – 5.30 pm*
*Entrance: 3,50€*
A varied collection going back to the earliest recorded stages of medicine, including a range of surgical instruments which will make you thankful you didn't need an operation in those times.

## Interesting shops

### Shantala
*3 rue de l'Odéon, 75006*
*Métro: Odéon*
*Closed: Sunday and Monday*
*Open: 11.00 am – 7.00 pm*
The owner of this shop travels to Southern India to buy her stock which has a fresher, more personal appeal than the usual range from wholesalers.

Here you can find old and antique objects in wood, bronze and pottery. But it is the coloured lithographs decorated with beads and sequins that stand out. These date from 1900-1930 and are of traditional religious subjects. All in their (rather battered) original frames, they are distinctive in their appeal. Priced variously 100-150€ depending on size and subject.

### Maison de la Lozère (Maison du Tourisme)
*Opposite the restaurant in the rue Hautefeuille, 75006*
If you don't know anything about the region of Lozère (almost 600 km from Paris) all you need to know is here, or you can find out more by checking the website: france48.com. The tourist office is included under this heading for its range of regional products – a mini-épicerie of jams, rillettes and the like.

### Arts et Autographes
*9 rue de l'Odéon, 75006*
*Métro: Odéon*
*Closed: Sunday and Monday*
*Open: 11.00 am – 12.30 pm and 2.00 – 6.00 pm*
The window display of this fascinating shop is enough to stop you for ten minutes; there is even more in the interior which is set out like an exhibition – and you are welcome to browse. Autograph letters are the staple of their stock: Napoléon? Marie Antoinette? Bizet? They're all here and many more, along with miniatures, dedicated books signed by their authors, drawings and so on.

Prices are from less than 200€ upwards so you might just be tempted to buy. The owner, Jean-Emmanuel Raux, is very knowledgeable and generous in sharing his expertise.

### San Francisco Book Co.
*17 rue Monsieur le Prince, 75006*
*Métro: Odéon*
*Open: 11.00 am – 9.00 pm Monday to Saturday; 2.00 – 7.30 pm Sunday*
Run by a laconic American this doesn't sound very Parisian, and yet it is.

There comes a time when you feel you've had enough of wandering around Paris streets and what you want is to lie on your hotel bed and read an undemanding English language paperback. This is where you'll find them, priced at a modest 3€; the vintage stock is an excellent source of green Penguins – on a recent visit a couple of Ed McBains. There's a good range in boxes outside: many more inside.

## Bistrots

### Allard
*44 rue St André des Arts, 75006*
*Tel: 01 43 26 48 23*
*Métro: Odéon*
*Closed: three weeks in August*
*Open: DAILY noon – 2.00 pm and 7.00 – 11.30 pm*
This once-famous restaurant founded over sixty years ago gradually slipped into decline with the demise of the original owners until it was rescued in the late 1990s. The signature dish of canard aux olives looks dramatic and tastes good if you like duck – it is Challands duck in any case – and all the ingredients here are top quality: Salers beef, poulet de Bresse, lamb from the Limousin. But it is one of the restaurants the French

seem to have deserted (like Chez Dumonet, p. 187).

Prices are not high for what you get: the three-course 32€ menu includes the daily special but not the big classic dishes (which are for two people anyway). There is even a two-course *formule midi* at 24€ so no-one is being robbed. The plats du jour (same each week) are two in number and carrying over to the next day – as follows:

Monday: boeuf bourguignon; cassoulet Toulousain

Tuesday: cassoulet Toulousain; veau à la Berrichonne

Wednesday: veau à la Berri chonne; mijoté de porc aux pruneaux

Thursday: mijoté de porc aux pruneaux; navarin d'agneau

Frida : navarin d'agneau; boeuf braisé carottes

Saturday: boeuf braisé carottes: coq au vin.

Their coq au vin is famous rivalling that at **Chez René** (p. 164). Wines are 23€ plus for a decent basic variety – but a reasonable choice.

### La Maison de la Lozère
*4 rue Hautefeuille, 75006*
*Tel: 01 43 54 26 54*
*Métro: St Michel*
*Closed: Sunday, Monday and the whole of August*
*Open: noon – 2.00 pm and 7.30 – 10.00 pm*
I'd never heard of Lozère until I visited the tourist office opposite the restaurant (both owned by the Region). It is a rugged province in Central France and the cuisine has

something of that character.

The restaurant is a great success and booking is essential. As it is next to a branch of the boring Chez Clément chain, the contrast is marked. Cheeses (goats' and ewes') are a speciality and even appear in the desserts. There are dinner menus at 21,90€ for three courses and 25,50€ (plus cheese); and bargain lunch menus at 14,90€ (two courses and a glass of wine) and 16€ (three courses and a ¼ litre of wine). Vin de Pays de Cévennes is 4,60€ a ¼ litre or 2,90€ a glass, and there are intriguing aperitifs of the region. A bottle of chilled water (free) is brought to the table as standard, and a large quarter loaf of country bread, complete with bread-knife, for you to help yourself.

A very complete meal will cost around 30€ and you won't need to eat for another twenty-four hours.

### Chez Maître Paul
*12 rue Monsieur le Prince, 75006*
*Tel: 01 43 54 74 59*
*Métro: Odéon*
*Closed: Christmas, and Sunday and Monday during July/August*
*Open: otherwise DAILY 12.15 – 2.15 pm and 7.15 – 10.30 pm*
This is the kind of restaurant that induces a sense of well-being with relaxed, attentive service. The food and wines are primarily from the eastern edge of France: Savoy and the Franche Comté, not generally available in Paris and here done supremely well.

Start with a glass of vin jaune, the sherry-like wine from the Jura which also forms the basis of the distinctive coq au vin. Unusual regional wines are indeed a strength and as they tend to be little-known you should ask for advice. Hearty reds predominate – good with the equally robust cassoulet and the prince of cheeses, Vieux Comté, which here deserves that title.

There are menus at 29€ and 35€ which are fine if they contain what you want; though à la carte doesn't cost much more.

## Brasserie

**Vagenende**
*142 boulevard St-Germain,*
*75006*
*Tel: 01 43 26 68 18*
*Métro: Odéon*
*Closed: August*
*Open: otherwise DAILY noon*
*through to 1.00 am*
Founded in 1904 this classic brasserie is a listed historic monument. The interior is magnificent belle époque, but you can choose to eat outside on the pavement terrace in fine weather.

The food tends not to get a good write-up: my own experience is that it's as good as any other brasserie, and it's not expensive.

There is a 23€ three-course menu, available all day, which includes the daily special known as *Le Semainier*. A sample menu could include:

Entrées:
*six oysters (huîtres)*
*soupe à l'oignon gratinée*
Plats:
*daily special (as below)*
*poularde au bouillon*
Cheese
Desserts:
*crème caramel*
*carpaccio d'oranges*

You get an amuse-bouche (tapenade), and a ½ litre of wine en pichet costs around 10€. There are plenty of bottles in the range 18-30€.

*Le Semainier* (daily specials):
Sunday: coq au vin, pâtes fraiches (fresh pasta)
Monday: saucisse au couteau, purée de pois cassés
Tuesday: pot au feu et son os à moelle (bone marrow)
Wednesday: pied de cochon grillé béarnaise
Thursday: gigot d'agneau
Friday: aïoli de morue provençal
Saturday: cassoulet au confit de canard.

# 15. St Germain/St Sulpice

One occasionally comes across magazine articles with titles like 'Secret Paris' or 'Hidden Paris' which at one level is an absurd pretension on the part of the authors. Take the case in point: the St Germain quarter – indeed all of the area between the curved length of the boulevard and the Seine – is the most intensively scrutinised sector of Paris. Even outside the main tourist areas, can anything have escaped the city's five or six million visitors a month and those who write guides for them?

The answer is that Paris is always changing, at the same time always contriving to remain the same. The cliché is right: the process of getting to know the city is never finished. And so the first-time visitor is only to a degree at a disadvantage, as guide writers driven by the demon of updating know to their cost.

St Germain is expensive territory, not in the luxury goods and deluxe hotel sense of the 8th and 16th arrondissements (though these are to be found here as well) but in the area of the arts and antiques – easily demonstrated by an attentive stroll along the rue de Seine which runs up to the embankment. No museum of modern art can equal this exposure to the commercial edge (the term here is not derogatory) of creative practice. But do go back and visit the galleries that appeal. Not everyone is expected to be a major buyer with a large budget, and you will be received with courtesy.

St Sulpice, south of the boulevard, is different again: less thronged with tourists, while the hotels though generally more expensive have a quality of exclusiveness that is not just about price. It goes without saying that this is a very smart area in which to live and the people who do lend something by their presence. It also has what many regard as the best café terrace in the city: the Café de la Mairie overlooking the church and the square with its opulent fountain and pink chestnut trees.

You'll see the fashionable here and in the superlative pâtisseries of Gérard Mulot (good value); and of Pierre Hermé and Pierre Marcolini whose pastries are so expensive that, to use the phrase of an elderly aunt of mine, it's like eating money.

## Principal sights

**Eglise St-Germain-des-Prés** (11th century – but earlier and later in parts): the elaborate history of this, the most famous church in Paris, is a book-length topic. Mainly in the plain Roman style its severe beauty lends distinction to the quarter. The interior is on a smaller scale than one might expect, reflecting its original purpose as the church of the abbey.

**Place de Fürstenberg** (late 17th century): the stuff of picture postcards, a quiet and dignified square where the painter Eugène Delacroix had a studio. The artist who epitomised the spirit of Romantic revolt lived and died at No. 6, now a museum (which doesn't qualify as 'neglected').

**Institut de France** (17th century), quai de Conti: the home of several 'academies' devoted to the preservation of France's cultural heritage, the best known being the Académie Française – guardian of the French language. Because surrounding buildings are on a smaller scale the famous dome is a dominant feature of the area.

The church of **St-Sulpice** (17th to 18th century): this massive parish church almost overwhelms the place of the same name; recently cleaned and restored its impact is powerful. The vast interior (compared with the abbey church of St-Germain) is extraordinary in scale. Murals by Delacroix amongst others adorn the walls of the transept and there's the mysterious obelisk with its *ligne de cuivre merédienne* (shades of *The Da Vinci Code*). Outside stands the 19th century fountain, a masterpiece of design excess if nothing else.

## Quiet hotels

The three hotels listed north of the boulevard are in the rue Jacob which is the heart of the St Germain quarter and so not cheap. Even the less expensive hotels hover around the upper boundaries of our price range and advance booking is essential. We suggest at least six months ahead, especially for key periods.

### Hôtel des Marroniers
*21 rue Jacob, 75006*
*Tel: 01 43 25 30 60*
*Fax: 01 40 46 83 56*
*E-mail: hotel-des-marroniers*
*@wanadoo.fr*
*www.paris-hotel-marroniers.com*
*Métro: St-Germain-des-Prés*
*37 rooms (24 double rooms) AIR CONDITIONED*
*Price range: 161-176€*
The caution about advance

booking applies especially to the Marroniers, one of the most sought after hotels, and although the room tariff pushes up relentlessly year by year it remains good value. Rooms are small but pleasant. From the upper floors (at the back) you get a view of the church of St-Germain.

### Hôtel des Deux Continents

*25 rue Jacob, 75006*
*Tel: 01 43 26 72 46*
*Fax: 01 43 25 67 80*
*E-mail: continents-hotel@wanadoo.fr*
*www.continents-paris-hotel.com*
*Métro: St-Germain-des-Prés*
*41 rooms (27 double rooms) some AIR CONDITIONED*
*Price: 167€ for a double room, courtyard side*

Rooms at the front of the hotel – made up of three 18th century buildings – are larger, but also noisier than the rest. The smaller, quieter rooms overlook an interior courtyard.

### Hôtel du Danube

*58 rue Jacob, 75006*
*Tel: 01 42 60 34 70*
*Fax: 01 42 60 81 18*
*E-mail: info@hoteldanube.fr*
*www.hoteldanube.fr*
*Métro: St-Germain-des-Prés*
*40 rooms (25 double rooms) and one suite*
*Price: 140-175€ for a double room*

The quietest rooms here overlook an interior light-well, which means they are a bit gloomy at the bottom. So, preferably: *au dernier étage et au fond.*

South of the boulevard in the St Sulpice quarter there are some expensive hotels but recommended are a couple of reasonably priced ones:

### Hôtel le Clément

*6 rue Clément, 75006*
*Tel: 01 43 26 53 60*
*Fax: 01 44 07 06 83*
*E-mail: info@hotel-clement.fr*
*www.hotel-clement.com*
*Métro: St-Germain-des-Prés*
*28 rooms AIR CONDITIONED*
*Price: 120-140€ for a double room*

For the area this hotel is exceptional value in a price-range which does not usually have air-conditioning. Although at the centre of things the street does not get much traffic, nor other activity. The rooms on the 'courtyard' side are not recommended except for the top floor. Those on the street-side top floors have a view of St Sulpice.

### Hôtel Perreyve

*63 rue Madame, 75006*
*Tel: 01 45 48 35 01*
*Fax: 01 42 84 03 20*
*E-mail: perreyvehotel @gofornet.com*
*www.hotelperreyve.com*
*Métro: Odéon*
*30 rooms*
*Price: 90-119€ for a double room*

Near the Luxembourg Gardens and in a quiet street, this hotel has basic but decent bedrooms, some of which overlook an interior courtyard. Rooms on the upper floors are the best choice: great value for the area but no frills.

# Breakfast

## Paul
*77 rue de Buci (corner of the rue de Seine)*
*Open: DAILY from 7.30 am*
Look no further: this is the best and best value breakfast café in the St Germain area. Unusually for Paul it is more café than boulangerie. Apart from the café tables (inside and out) there is an elegant salon-de-thé where you can get an inexpensive lunch, as well as afternoon tea.

A stimulating place to start the day.

## Gérard Mulot
*76 rue de Seine*
*Closed: Wednesday*
*Open: from 7.00 am*
The celebrity pâtissier (with customers to match) provides breakfast of the stand up or perch variety so neither the space nor the place to linger. But it is a bargain especially for such high quality: 2,70€ for fresh orange juice, 1,50€ for a café crème and 0,90€ for a croissant. For around 6€ you can get a delectable *kouglof* (their spelling) which you can take away to finish off later.

## Les Deux Magots
*6 place St-Germain-des-Prés*
*Open: DAILY from 7.30 am*
For reasons of inverted snobbery I almost didn't include this famous café. It's more attractive and less crowded than its equally famous competitor **Flore**. Where it scores is in the large sunny terrace on the square facing the church; choose a table on the pavement or the semi-interior covered terrace.

It is mainly a tourist venue but you get café crème served properly with two jugs (at 4,80€) and a croissant for 2,20€: so what is there to complain about?

## Bistrot Mazarin
*42 rue Mazarine*
*Open: DAILY from 8.00 am*
This is not a place for café crème with little jugs. Go instead for café allongé (dilute expresso) and a tartine beurrée and you'll feel like a real Frenchman (or woman) for less than 4€.

## Café de la Mairie
*8 place St-Sulpice*
*Open: from 7.00 am Monday to Friday (8.00 am Saturday; 9.00 am Sunday)*
A café with a splendid view of the church (and the florid fountain). Go here only when the weather is good enough to sit at a table on the extensive terrace. The interior is quite ordinary and you don't get much of a view.

A café crème and a croissant cost 6€.

## La Palette
*43 rue de Seine*
*Closed: Sunday, one week in February and three weeks in August*
*Open: from 8.00 am*
At the corner of the rue de Seine and the rue Jacques Callot this is a busy café with plenty of outdoor tables (and powerful heaters), situated in a street of art galleries. A café crème costs 4€, a croissant or a

tartine beurrée 1,50€; the bottled pasteurised fruit juice is robbery at 4,50€ but this is a well-situated place to have breakfast.

## Public gardens

### Square Gabriel Pierné
*Location: at the top end of the rue de Seine, behind the Institut de France.*
Trees and benches but no grass: a cool, quiet spot with the gilded dome of the Institut in the background.

### Square Laurent Prache
*Location: on the place St-Germain-des-Prés to one side of the church.*
Often unnoticed, this small garden with good seating is in a very busy area where you might find yourself taking an (expensive) café seat to rest your legs. Here's the alternative.

### Square Félix Desruelles
*Location: on the boulevard St Germain in front of the church.*
Not large, the garden is trapezoidal in shape, screened by trees from the boulevard. On the east wall is a Sèvres-tiled ceramic that looks like the backdrop to a fountain but isn't. Sandy gravel underfoot, and a small play area.

### Square Taras Chevtchenko
*Location: the north-east corner of the junction of the rue des Saints-Pères and the boulevard St Germain.*
A bit gloomy, perhaps to reflect the spirit of the Ukrainian poet of whom you and I have never heard. Small with no grass but good seating and well-screened from the busy boulevard.

## Markets

### Rue de Buci/Rue de Seine, 75006
A market street clustered around the crossroads and included in the previous section: Odéon/St Michel – see pp. 169-170.

### Le Marché St-Germain
### Rue Mabillon, 75006
There used to be a traditional covered market here, now redeveloped as an urban shopping mall of no merit whatsoever. For a while there were some stalls under the arcades; these have been cleared to make way for café tables. A planning disaster in one of the most attractive parts of the quarter.

## Fromager

### La Fromagerie 31
*64 rue de Seine, 75006*
*Closed: Sunday and Monday*
*Open: Tuesday to Thursday, 10.00 am – 3.00 pm and 4.30 – 8.00 pm; Friday and Saturday, all day*
This is an excellent fromagerie and a speciality café as well, offering cheeses in various combinations to eat on site (plate of five cheeses for 9,80€). There are soups and desserts too. A good place for a (fairly) light lunch. A glass of wine to wash it down will cost from 3,50€ or you can get a ½ litre pichet from 13,50€.

# Glacier

## Amorino

*4 rue de Buci, 75006*
*Open: DAILY noon to midnight*
Queues form at this very popular branch of the famous Italian glacier. One enormous serving, called 'moyen' costs 4€: you won't need any more. (See entry for Montparnasse for details, p. 137.)

# Neglected museum

## Musée des Lettres et Manuscrits

*8 rue de Nesle, 75006*
*Métro: St-Germain-des-Prés*
*Closed: Monday and public holidays*
*Open: Tuesday to Friday, 10.00 am – 8.00 pm; Saturday and Sunday 10.00 am – 6.00 pm*
*Entrance: 6€*
More than 250 historical documents and autograph letters including the luminaries of French history, arts and sciences in a building dating from 1608. The exhibits go back much further than, for example, those on display in the gallery **Autographes et Manuscrits** in the rue de l'Odéon – but then that's free.

# Interesting shops

## Comptoir de Famille

*34 rue St Sulpice, 75006*
*Métro: St Sulpice/Mabillon*
*Closed: Sunday*
*Open: 10.00 am – 7.00 pm (from 11.00 am Monday)*

A French 'country kitchen' shop with a huge selection: the total effect is a bit overpowering and some of the stock displays the worst excesses of the genre. It is included here for the kind of tablecloths and napkins (variants of check reds and blues on natural linen) that you see in provincial style restaurants like D'Chez Eux (p. 205) and La Fontaine de Mars (p. 204). A 180 cm square tablecloth costs 46,50€ which enables you to gauge the price range.

There is another branch in the passage Jouffroy (p. 102) but this one is more extensive.

## La Vaissellerie

*85 rue de Rennes, 75006*
*Métro: St-Germain-des-Prés*
*Closed: Sunday*
*Open: 10.00 am – 7.00 pm*
Another branch of the shop selling cheap but stylish plain white tableware; it would go well with tablecloths from the above, which don't need competition.

## La Chine Ancienne

*15 rue Guénégaud, 75006*
*Métro: St-Germain-des-Prés*
*Closed: Sunday and Monday*
*Open: 11.00 am – 7.00 pm*
In a slightly out-of-the-way location but of the St Germain arts and antiques community, this is a superlative collection of Chinese antiques in bronze, marble and ceramic. Gérard Santolini is a great expert in an area where fakes abound. The quality of what he sells is manifest: I retain a clear image of a green marble bust of a man's head (18th century) which

would have cost me 5600€ if I'd had the money. Prices range from the high hundreds to the tens of thousands but you shouldn't let that frighten you off; as in all these galleries, visitors are courteously received.

## Bistrots

### Le Petit St Benoît
*4 rue St Benoît,*
*75006*
*Métro: St-Germain-des-Prés*
*Closed: Sunday, and two weeks in August*
*Open: noon – 2.30 pm and 7.00 – 10.30 pm*
Traditional, competent food served by amiable no-nonsense matrons who write your order and your bill on the paper tablecloth, just as they do at Chartier. For an expensive neighbourhood this is extraordinary value. Lunch on the pavement terrace is the ultimate unsmart, civilised experience – and all for less than twenty euros for a complete meal.

We don't give a telephone number because they can't be bothered with reservations.

### Aux Charpentiers
*10 rue Mabillon,*
*75006*
*Tel: 01 43 26 30 05*
*Métro: Mabillon*
*Closed: Christmas*
*Open: DAILY noon – 3.00 pm and 7.00 – 11.30 pm*
Booking is essential as this is a well-known and good value 'bistrot de quartier'. It is particularly

recommended for its daily specials (costing 14-19€):

> Sunday: gigot d'agneau rôti
> Monday: veau Marengo
> Tuesday: bocuf mode
> Wednesday: petit salé aux lentilles
> Thursday: jarret de veau
> Friday: aïoli de morue
> Saturday: chou farci

– and as you can see an entirely traditional establishment.

There is a lunch menu at 19€ and a dinner menu at 26€, which include the daily specials. Wines are correspondingly inexpensive. The desserts are not recommended; the cheeses are a better option.

### Bistrot Mazarin
*42 rue Mazarine,*
*75006*
*Tel: 01 43 29 99 01*
*Métro: Odéon*
*Open: DAILY 8.00 am through to half past midnight*
Also recommended for breakfast, this is more café than restaurant with its large terrace. But on a summer's evening it is a pleasant place to eat outside or there is an attractive small dining room at the back.

Certainly good value with entrées in the range 6,50-9€, plats 11-18€, cheese (camembert) 3€, desserts 6-8€ and the entire carte seems to be copied from a list of traditional dishes. Wines by the glass cost from 3€, and a ¼ litre carafe from 4,50€.

Cheerful service of the mildly impertinent variety.

## Brasserie

### Lipp
*151 boulevard St Germain, 75006*
*Tel: 01 45 48 53 91*
*Métro: St-Germain-des-Prés*
*Closed: Christmas*
*Open: DAILY noon through to*
*1.00 am*

The myth here is that the maître d' assigns you to the ground floor (good) or the first floor dining room (bad) depending on whether he knows your (famous) face or thinks you look as though you might qualify. The myth is half-true and I challenge you to be indifferent to it. The in-between state (and only if you've reserved) is to be offered a table at the back of the ground floor dining room. If he rates you higher (much higher) you get a table at the front among the regulars and celebrities.

You come here for the meats (not the sauerkraut) and these are excellent, and cooked as you ask. If you skip the first-course, which you won't need, but take a calorie-laden dessert (mainly imports from top pâtissiers) you should get away with 50€ plus the cost of your wine. But you're not just paying for the food: the total experience is worth the money, not least the expert, case-hardened waiters who give a performance an actor couldn't hope to match.

Put on your best suit, assume nonchalance, and go...

*Parisian pet-lover*

# 16. Sèvres-Babylone

This may not be the first part of Paris you will visit; but after you have 'done' the sights, and discharged your tourist obligations in that respect, it is one you are likely to return to again and again.

The focus of the quarter is the crossroads of the boulevard Raspail, rue de Babylone and rue de Sèvres, with the Left Bank's only grand hotel, the Lutétia, rearing its bulk like a trans-Atlantic liner: an analogy with some depth to it as you penetrate the gleaming art deco interior of the brasserie and piano bar, the foyer and the restaurant. This so impressed the Nazi hierarchy that during the occupation they were quick to commandeer it for their own use.

Almost opposite, you will find the first department store in Paris, Le Bon Marché, with its internationally famous food hall: La Grande Epicerie (p. 187). One of the building's hidden features is the iron framework designed by Gustave Eiffel; the tower that bears his name subsequently gave him the chance to make visible his skill as a structural engineer.

*Baker in the marché biologique in the boulevard Raspail (Sundays)*

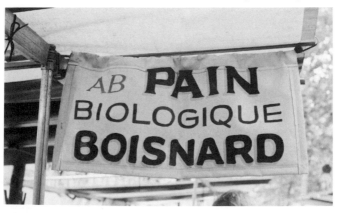

The area is also rich in small specialist shops and restaurants. One street, the rue du Cherche-Midi, is enough evidence of this. You could spend a whole day exploring what some argue is the most interesting shopping street in Paris. On Tuesday and Friday mornings the boulevard Raspail has a lively street market; and also on Sunday morning when it acts as a showcase for the *marché biologique*, crowded with dedicated shoppers from all over the city and the suburbs – not to mention eager tourists in search of they are not quite sure what.

## Principal sights

In the historic sense there aren't really any 'sights' of note: the big attractions here are to do with the pleasures of living.

## Quiet hotels

### Hôtel Lindbergh
*5 rue Chomel, 75007*
*Tel: 01 45 48 35 53*
*Fax: 01 45 49 31 48*
*E-mail: infos*
*@hotellindbergh.com*
*www.hotellindbergh.com*
*Métro: Sèvres-Babylone*
*26 rooms*
*Price: 136€ for a standard double/twin room; 160€ for a larger room*
In a quiet side-street but near the boulevard Raspail and the rue de Babylone this is a well-appointed hotel, particularly the 'superior' rooms which are worth the extra cost. About half of them give on to a narrow interior courtyard so those on the lower floors are distinctly gloomy. We only recommend those on the top floor.

Very centrally placed but a bit expensive for a hotel without air-conditioning.

### Hôtel Mayet
*3 rue Mayet, 75006*
*Tel: 01 47 83 21 35*
*Fax: 01 40 65 95 78*
*E-mail: hotel@mayet.com*
*www.mayet.com*
*Métro: Duroc*
*23 rooms*
*Price: 120€ for a double room with shower, 130-140€ with bath*
In a very quiet street this is a hotel in contemporary style which is competitively priced. Breakfast is included in the room rate.
Strongly recommended.

### Hôtel Ferrandi
*92 rue du Cherche-Midi, 75006*
*Tel: 01 42 22 97 40*
*Fax: 01 45 44 89 97*
*E-mail: hotel.ferrandi*
*@wanadoo.fr*
*www.parisby.com*
*Métro: Vaneau*
*42 rooms AIR CONDITIONED*
*Price: 145-160€ for the smaller double rooms*
Set in a handsome 19th century

block, this is a beautifully maintained bourgeois hotel where prices for the larger double rooms go above our limit. It is located immediately opposite the Museé Hébert (p. 186). The best choice for the summer (when rates come down anyway) on account of the air conditioning.

### Hôtel de Sèvres

*22 rue de l'Abbé-Grégoire, 75006*
*Tel: 01 45 48 84 07*
*Fax: 01 42 84 01 55*
*E-mail: hotel@sevresazur.com*
*www.hotelsevresazur.com*
*Métro: Saint Placide*
*31 rooms*
*Price: 110-130€ for a standard double room with bath or shower; 130-150€ for a 'supérieure' with bath*

Not as cheap as it used to be, this is still a bargain for the area, a well-maintained hotel in a fairly quiet street. There is the usual narrow 'courtyard' so top floor or street-side rooms are to be preferred.

## Breakfast

### Le Nemrod

*51 rue du Cherche-Midi*
*Closed: Sunday, and two weeks in August*
*Open: from 6.30 am*

With its large pavement terrace Le Nemrod is an excellent spot for breakfast on this street which is prime terrority for people-watching. Café crème and a croissant will set you back 5,40€.

### Brasserie Lutétia

*45 boulevard Raspail*
*Open: DAILY from 8.00 am*

There are tables at the front on the covered terrace overlooking the busy crossroads, and a few inside where you can take a banquette and watch the waiters gearing up for the lunchtime crowd. For 10€ you get a large café crème (or equivalent), orange juice, five mini-viennoiseries and petits pains and a wide choice of jam and honey.

### Le Confiturier

*20 rue du Cherche-Midi*
*Closed: Sunday and Monday*
*Open: 8.00 am – noon for breakfast*

A pleasant pavement terrace for an open-air breakfast. Two formules are on offer: *Le Boulanger* at 5,60€ which comprises coffee etc., bread, butter, jam; and *Le Continental* at 9,80€ for the above plus a croissant and orange juice.

## Public gardens

### Square Boucicaut

*Location: junction of the rue de Babylone and the rue de Sèvres with the boulevard Raspail.*

A well-stocked garden and bigger than most, this is a good spot to eat the lunch you have bought in the immediately adjacent Le Bon Marché (Aristide Boucicaut was its founder).

There is a very large sandpit for children with play equipment inset so if they fall they won't hurt themselves; and separately a small permanent carousel at 1,50€ a ride.

## Jardin Catherine Labouré

*Location: on the south side of the rue de Babylone near the junction with the rue Vaneau.*

A walled garden which retains a cultivated kitchen garden and so is unusual for a public space. It is a favourite with local children and so not entirely peaceful; a water fight was in progress the last time I was there (boys *v.* girls). To one side, there is a shady vine-covered walkway with benches overlooking flowerbeds.

## Square des Missions Etrangères

*Location: on the rue du Bac between the rue de Babylone and the rue de Commaille.*

This small garden is but a step from the famous glacier Le Bac à Glaces (see below) so you can sit here to enjoy your ice-cream.

## Square Chaise-Récamier

*Location: at the end of the rue Récamier cul-de-sac on the north side of the rue de Sèvres.*

Truly a secret garden. Even standing at the entrance to the street it's not easy to tell that it is there: perhaps why one rarely finds more than a dozen people, including the statutory pair of entwined lovers. A wealth of trees and flowers, and it *is* quiet.

# Market

## Boulevard Raspail, 75007

*Tuesday, Friday and Sunday 7.00 am – 2.30 pm*

This street market is to be found on the boulevard Raspail between the rue du Cherche-Midi and the rue de Rennes. Always an animated setting, it is on Sunday that it comes into its own as the first, and best organic market in Paris. This quarter is prime shopping territory in a prime residential area so the market really is crowded: patience is required. Stall-holders come from all over the Ile-de-France (and beyond) and customers from all over the city.

The range of organic products is both impressive and expensive: fruit and vegetables, dairy produce (sweet-tasting unpasteurised butter), andouillettes, poultry, every type of bread imaginable. In addition there are craft stalls of the superior kind where, for example, you can treat yourself to one of those long mohair scarves still favoured by French intellectuals or those who aspire to that status.

# Fromager

## Fromagerie Quatrehomme

*62 rue de Sèvres, 75007*
*Closed: Sunday and Monday*
*Open: 8.45 am – 7.45 pm*

There is a good range of cheeses in the nearby Bon Marché foodstore but this popular specialist has the edge on quality and variety. Unusually for a fromagerie it does not close for lunch.

## Glaciers

### Le Bac à Glaces
*109 rue du Bac, 75007*
*Closed: Sunday, and the first*
*three weeks in August*
*Open: 11.00 am – 7.00 pm*
Wonderfully fresh-tasting ice-cream with 44 different flavours to choose from – not all available in cornets, but you can buy them by the half-litre. The list changes slightly from year to year (a recent new flavour is green tea sorbet). Inventive and original but the 'classics' – like their coffee ice-cream – are the favourites.

There is a small café where a complicated assortment is available for around 7-9€, including a fine peach Melba. Cornets cost from 2,20€ for one boule to 4,40€ for three.

### Il Sorrentino
*19 rue de Sèvres, 75007*
*Closed: Sunday afternoon*
*Open: 10.00 am – 8.00 pm*
*(Sunday to 1.00 pm)*
This Italian grocer's shop sells first-class ice-cream (their own make): 16 flavours and 3€ for a cornet – as large as you will need.

## Neglected museum

### Musée Hébert
*85 rue du Cherche-Midi, 75006*
*Métro: Sèvres-Babylone*
*Closed: Tuesday*
*Open: 12.30 – 6.00 pm (from*
*2.00 pm weekends and public*
*holidays)*
*Entrance: 3€*

Although his name is now less well-known, Ernest Hébert (1817-1908) was, in his time, much sought after as a painter of portraits of society beauties, also landscapes especially of Italian scenes.

A skilful craftsman, his work does look very dated: part of the artistic world thrown into oblivion by the Impressionists. But worth a visit if you have a free afternoon.

## Interesting shops

### Almandine
*72 rue de Babylone, 75007*
*Métro: Sèvres-Babylone*
*Closed: Sunday, and Monday*
*morning*
*Open: 11.00 am – 7.00 pm*
*(Monday from 4.30 pm)*
The sign reads *De Père en Fille*; for twenty years until 2002 Almandine (fille) had a stall on the first floor of Le Bon Marché, which was the best antiques market in Paris until new owners cleared them out.

This former butcher's shop (the name P. Blat is still on the façade) now holds the large stock – some of it going back years – of old and antique jewellery, watches and small silver, and what the French call *bibelots*, which warrant careful attention. Prices are fair and Almandine is open to negotiation.

### Le Palais des Thés
*61 rue du Cherche-Midi, 75006*
*Métro: Sèvres-Babylone*
*Closed: Sunday*
*Open: Monday 10.30 am –*
*6.00 pm; Tuesday to Saturday,*

*10.00 am – 7.00 pm*
Entering this shop – one of several branches in Paris – is to enter a delicately perfumed environment that rivals any parfumerie. The company is owned and run by dedicated enthusiasts who offer some 250 teas from around the world, including rare varieties from such countries as Iran, Turkey, Nepal, costing as much as 38€ per 100g. However, there is a large range of modestly-priced teas: packets of these would make welcome gifts.

Free tea-tastings are only part of what is on offer. Go and see.

### A la Reine Astrid

*26 rue du Cherche-Midi, 75006*
*Métro: Sèvres-Babylone*
*Closed: Sunday*
*Open: 10.15 am – 7.00 pm*
The beautiful Queen Astrid of Belgium, well-loved by the French and who died in a car accident in 1930, is celebrated here in the name of this confiserie, famous in its own right for its *nougat tendre (peu sucré)* which is sold in large cake-like slices and looks (and is) wonderful: at 42€ a kilo but one slice (about 150g) is enough.

### Le Bon Marché (La Grande Epicerie)

*38 rue de Sèvres, 75007*
*Métro: Sèvres-Babylone*
*Closed: Sunday*
*Open: Monday, Tuesday, Wednesday, Friday,*
*9.30 am – 7.00 pm;*
*Thursday 10.00 am – 9.00 pm;*
*Saturday 9.30 am – 8.00 pm*
By common consent the best food hall in Paris: there is nothing you cannot find here, though you may have to ask because there are tens of thousands of different products from all over the world, including wines. Prices are competitive, often cheaper than the famous institutions of the Right Bank like **Hédiard** – but they're represented here anyway.

### Depôt Vente Enfants

*64 rue Vaneau, 75007*
*Métro: Vaneau*
*Closed: Sunday and Monday*
*Open: 10.30 am – 6.30 pm*
'Depôts Ventes' are a major feature of the retail fashion scene; that is, shops where well-heeled women take their surplus clothes to be sold: many of them distinctly up-market (that little Chanel suit...) with prices to match.

High quality clothes for children in Paris can also be expensive – and soon outgrown. This shop has a huge selection, some more ordinary than others, but includes those beautifully made smocked and embroidered dresses for the under-3s that typically cost, new, around 150-200€: offered here at little more than a third of that.

### Poilâne

*8 rue du Cherche-Midi, 75006*
*Métro: Sèvres-Babylone*
*Closed: Sunday*
*Open: 7.15 am – 8.15 pm*
This is a surprisingly modest establishment for the most famous baker in France. The reputation is entirely justified: the choice is great, but try the much copied small *seigle aux raisins* at 1€.

### Le Passé d'Aujourd'hui
*43 rue du Cherche-Midi, 75006*
*Métro: Sèvres-Babylone*
*Closed: Sunday and Monday*
*Open: 10.00 am – 2.00 pm and*
*3.00 – 7.00 pm*

The owner of this shop, specialising in art deco jewellery, glass, furniture and 'classic' handbags, speaks excellent English and is helpful in a general as well as a specific way. His prices are reasonable and I once bought a favourite pair of cuff-links here. Incidentally, Paris is a great hunting ground for this item of male jewellery – now increasingly in fashion for the modern woman. But then didn't Marlene Dietrich wear them?

## Bistrots

### Chez Dumonet
*117 rue du Cherche-Midi, 75006*
*Tel: 01 45 48 52 40*
*Métro: Vaneau*
*Closed: Saturday, Sunday and*
*the whole of August*
*Open: 12.30 – 2.30 pm and 7.30 –*
*11.00 pm*

This is a classic bistrot which the French appear to have deserted entirely. When I last dined there, mine was the only accent that wasn't American. Where were their French clients? The waiter shrugged: *Peut-être demain?* and he got on with the business of serving those who were there.

The food is good, even excellent and makes no concessions to Anglo-Saxon tastes: you can have your game *bleu* or *saignant* but not otherwise. The wine list is outstanding, particularly of clarets (nothing under 36€ and up to 1,600€). Elsewhere on the list there is nothing under 20€.

Service is courteous, the tables well-spaced. The dining room is in three sections, one near the service doors at the back: don't let them put you there.

You can take the entrées in half-portions (at not quite half the price). Your total bill for one person, including modest amounts of wine, is going to be around 75€: that's considered too much by most Parisians these days even though it would be cheap by London standards for a meal of this quality.

### Chez Germaine
*30 rue Pierre-Leroux, 75007*
*Métro: Duroc/Vaneau*
*Closed: Saturday, Sunday and*
*the whole of August*
*Open: noon – 2.15 pm and*
*7.00 – 10.00 pm*

This authentic-looking (grained woodwork) bistrot is worth the money and the experience: just don't expect too much and then you might be surprised. Located in a quiet side-street it is very well-known; no reservations, you take your chance on getting a table.

In Paris really cheap meals are largely a thing of the past so this is a survivor. There is a two-course lunchtime formule (eat and go) for 12€ but you can always spread yourself and go for the 14€ menu *(au choix)* which might include pâté de campagne, boeuf bourguignon and compôte de pommes.

In other words, nothing fancy but sound. If you insist the à la carte will cost around 25€.

Oh, and it's been non-smoking since 1967.

### Au Pied de Fouet
*45 rue de Babylone, 75007*
*Métro: Sèvres-Babylone*
*Closed: Sunday, public holidays and the whole of August*
*Open: noon – 3.00 pm and 7.00 – 11.30 pm*

This is a tiny bistrot even if it is on two floors, and definitely one that time forgot. It would have looked mildly bohemian in the 1950s and has clients to match (elderly gentlemen in carmine corduroys). Perhaps the prices remind them of days gone by as well, because the entrées range from 3-5€, the plats 7,90-10,70€, with cheese or dessert for 3-4€. Wine prices are equivalent. You'll get a full meal for 25€ all in: but get there early to secure a table.

Traditional food? What else?

## Brasseries

### Brasserie Lutétia
*45 boulevard Raspail, 75006*
*Tel: 01 49 54 46 76*
*Métro: Sèvres-Babylone*
*Open: DAILY noon – 2.30 pm and 7.00 – 10.30 pm*

Part of the largest traditional hotel on the Left Bank (dating from the Edwardian era), the brasserie has a dazzling 'Modern' décor and is famous for its seafood offered in a variety of formats. There is a range of seafood salads at 15€ which make an excellent light luncheon with a glass of Alsace riesling: a half-bottle costs 14€ (from a distinguished wine list).

They offer menus of two courses for 29,50€ and three for 35€. There is also a special menu for a table of four to include tiny multiple desserts to taste.

Recommended for a meal on any day of the week but especially good after you've trudged round the market on a Sunday morning.

*One of the many plaques all over Paris commemorating those who died in July/August 1944, when the Resistance rose against the Occupation*

# 17. Faubourg St Germain

As it extends towards the west the boulevard St Germain changes character: slowly at first, but once past the rue du Bac the transformation is almost complete. We are into an area of embassies, government ministries and official residences often occupying the fine *hôtels particuliers* of the quarter. At one time the Faubourg St Germain housed the kind of upper and upper-middle class strata where Marcel Proust engaged in his rarefied preoccupations with self. It still retains something of that ethos. Walking along the rue de Grenelle and the rue de Varenne one has a strong sense of a way of life being pursued out of sight, behind those massive double doors which open, just occasionally, to reveal vast courtyards.

It is in the side-streets that you will encounter the more usual version of Paris life, if at a bourgeois level, catering for the senior staff of ministries and other institutions of government. Hence, restaurants tend to be more formal and more expensive; this is not bistrot territory though there are exceptions – like Le Basilic (p. 195) which has a winning informality.

You have to stay in this part of the quarter if you are to assimilate its quieter charms, penetrate the reserve: a hasty walk through is not enough. Something to come to, perhaps, as a change from the obvious attractions of the more popular districts.

One problem is access: for example, you won't be able to see the splendid gardens of the Hôtel Matignon – the biggest in the area – but that's the Prime Minister's residence, and so understandable. Yet access generally is restricted: not merely on grounds of security but partly the obsession with privacy characteristic of the upper echelons of French society. And although it may seem perverse to say so, going to the Rodin Museum, the 18th century Hôtel Biron, is as much an opportunity to see the interior of one of the finest houses in the area – and its garden (p. 192) – as to view the lifetime's work of the master.

## Principal sights

**Palais Bourbon** (18th century), quai d'Orsay: originally a royal palace, now the home of the Assemblée Nationale, one of the two houses of the French parliament (the Sénat in the Palais du Luxembourg is the other). Not open to visitors but good views from the quai d'Orsay and the Pont de la Concorde of the often photographed classical façade, with the tricolour much in evidence (as outside every public building in France).

**Musée d'Orsay** (20th century), quai Anatole France: the conversion of the obsolete Gare d'Orsay (1900) into a museum in the 1980s caught the popular imagination and has been besieged by crowds of tourists ever since (expect to queue). The interior designed by the Italian Gae Aulenti, making powerful use of the open central space, is unequalled as a show-case for the development of art in France over the past 250 years.

## Quiet hotels

### Hôtel de Varenne
*44 rue de Bourgogne, 75007*
*Tel: 01 45 51 45 55*
*Fax: 01 45 51 86 63*
*E-mail: info@hotelvarenne.com*
*www.hotelvarenne.com*
*Métro: Varenne*
*24 rooms AIR CONDITIONED*
*Price: 137-177€ for a double room*
The hotel is set back around a leafy courtyard where you can take breakfast (until midday!). The best

rooms overlook this. Highly recommended; with excellent quiet air conditioning.

### Bersoly's St Germain Hôtel
*28 rue de Lille, 75007*
*Tel: 01 42 60 73 79*
*Fax: 01 49 27 05 55*
*E-mail: hotelbersolys*
*@wanadoo.fr*
*www.bersolyshotel.com*
*Métro: Rue du Bac*
*16 rooms AIR CONDITIONED*
*Price: 106-122€ for a double room (single occupancy)*
A charming, characterful hotel (each room is named after a painter). Very good value for the area: the better rooms are worth the modest extra cost.

### Hôtel de Lille
*40 rue de Lille, 75007*
*Tel: 01 42 61 29 09*
*Fax: 01 42 61 53 97*
*E-mail: hotel-de-lille*
*@wanadoo.fr*
*www.hotel-paris-lille.com*
*Métro: Rue du Bac*
*20 rooms*
*Price: 105-110€ for a double room (single occupancy)*
Remarkable value for the area but the larger rooms are the best value (as usual). A neat, pleasant, competent hotel at the heart of things. Breakfast is included in the room price.

### Hôtel Saint Thomas d'Aquin
*3 rue du Pré-aux-Clercs, 75007*
*Tel: 01 42 61 01 22*
*Fax: 01 42 61 41 43*
*E-mail: hotelsaintthomasdaquin*
*@wanadoo.fr*

*www.hotel-st-thomas-daquin.com*
*Métro: Rue du Bac/St-Germain-des-Prés*
*21 rooms*
*Price: 120-130€ for a double room*
I remember coming across this hotel by accident and being struck by how quiet the street was: a backwater with no through traffic. Its peaceful situation and modest price for the area give it a strong appeal.

# Breakfast

### Rollet-Pradier
*6 rue de Bourgogne*
*Closed: three weeks in August*
*Open: DAILY from 8.00 am*
This is a very posh place for breakfast; as well it might be positioned almost next door to the Palais Bourbon, the seat of the National Assembly. Since those well-fleshed, well-dressed men at adjoining tables could be deputies fuelling themselves up for debate, you must understand that a respectable appearance is necessary just to survive the scrutiny of the waitresses.

Having said that, breakfast is a delight, at 12€ for the usual combinations. They also offer a substantial *menu d'affaires* at lunchtime featuring a daily roast. And it's a good place to buy *sandwiches* of a superior kind.

### Le Roupeyrac
*62 rue de Bellechasse*
*Closed: evenings and all day Sunday*
*Open: from 9.00 am*

This ordinary but pleasant little café-bistrot in a side-street offers a good value breakfast for 6€: orange pressé, café crème and a tartine (beurrée or bring your own jam).

# Public gardens

### Square Samuel Rousseau
*Location: between the rue St Dominique and the rue Las Cases, opposite the church of Ste Clothilde.*
This garden square is not usually marked on maps although it is the best in the immediate area. Facing the church with its attractive Gothic façade and adjacent to the recommended brasserie Le Basilic, this is the prototypical Parisian small park, much patronised by locals especially at lunchtime. Plenty of grass, and you can sit on it.

### Hôtel Biron (Musée Rodin)
*Location: 77 rue de Varenne*
*Open: (except Monday) 9.30 am – 5.45 pm (4.45 pm winter months)*
The largest garden in the area (open to the public) is that of the *hôtel particulier* that houses the collection of Rodin's sculpture, with some of his most famous works requiring the open spaces of the garden. Entrance to this costs only one euro, and despite being heavily visited there is ample seating. Monumental sculptures surround you (including, of course, the brooding figure of *Le Penseur*) and overlooking it all the gleaming dome of the Invalides.

A handsome setting for a discreet picnic, though the café is open during the spring and summer months.

## Market

**Boulevard Raspail, 75007**
*Tuesday and Friday 7.00 am – 2.30 pm; Sunday 7.00 am – 3.00 pm*
The market runs between rue du Cherche-Midi and rue de Rennes so a little southeast of our quarter, but one of the best including much that is home-made: jams, cakes and the like. The Sunday market is Paris' most important organic market with many specialist stalls (see also p. 185).

## Fromagers

**Barthélemy**
*51 rue de Grenelle, 75007*
*Closed: Sunday and Monday*
*Open: 7.30 am – 7.30 pm*
One of the finest fromagers in Paris, Roland Barthélemy is an authority on cheeses world-wide but sees France, rightly, as pre-eminent. This small but beautifully organised shop sells cheeses at the peak of perfection.

Get your bread from **Gérard Besnier** at 40 rue de Bourgogne and eat it in the square Samuel Rousseau.

**Androuet**
*37 rue Verneuil, 75007*
*Closed: Monday, and Sunday afternoon*

*Open: Tuesday to Friday, 9.30 am – 1.00 pm and 4.00 – 7.30 pm; Saturday all day; Sunday 7.30 am – 1.30 pm*
A branch of the well-known chain selling a wide range of cheeses in good condition. Not in Barthélemy's league but convenient if you are staying on the eastern side of the quarter.

## Glacier

**Le Bac à Glaces**
*109 rue du Bac, 75007*
*Closed: Sunday*
*Open: 11.00 am – 7.00 pm*
As we've defined it, this is outside our area (see Sèvres-Babylone, p. 186) but we are not victims of our own categories. Choose from 44 different flavours from one of the best ice-cream makers in the city.

## Neglected museums

**Musée Maillol (Fondation Dina Vierny)**
*61 rue de Grenelle, 75007*
*Métro: Rue du Bac*
*Closed: Tuesday*
*Open: 11.00 am – 6.00 pm*
*Entrance: 8€ (6€ under 16s)*
There are regular (and high-profile) temporary exhibitions here but the neglected aspect is the work of the sculptor Aristide Maillot (1861-1944), who specialised in female nudes (you can see some in the Jardin des Tuileries). The bonus here is the private collection of his model, Dina Vierny, which includes lesser-known works by

Dufy, Cézanne, Matisse, Gauguin, Kandinsky and other contemporaries of Maillot.

## Interesting shops

### A la Mine d'Argent
*108 rue du Bac, 75006*
*Métro: Rue du Bac*
*Closed: Sunday*
*Open: Monday to Friday, 10.00 am – 7.00 pm; Saturday 11.00 am – 6.00 pm*
There is not much antique silver for sale in Paris and what there is is expensive. It can be bought more cheaply in London where 'foreign' silver is little regarded. Indeed you pay as much for 19th century electroplate in Paris as you would for the silver equivalent in England.

However, if you hanker after the rather more elaborate designs produced in France (and not just in the past) this is probably the best place to look. But it won't be cheap.

### Madeleine Gély
*218 boulevard St Germain, 75007*
*Métro: Rue du Bac*
*Closed: Sunday and Monday*
*Open: 10.00 am – 7.00 pm*
These days their stock is wider-ranging, but this is still the place to go for umbrellas of traditional style – as well as canes. The Paris equivalent of Swaine, Adeney and Brigg in London, their umbrellas do have something that marks them out as distinctively French: at a price, of course.

### Depôt Vente
*39 rue de Lille, 75007*
*Métro: Assemblée Nationale*
*Closed: Sunday and Monday*
*Open: 10.00 am – 6.00 pm (usually closed for lunch 1.00 – 3.00 pm)*
A small shop with an extraordinary range of bibelots (bric-à- brac). Like a mini flea market it is an excellent place to spend an odd half-hour.

## Bistrots

### Tan Dinh
*6 rue de Verneuil, 75007*
*Tel: 01 45 44 04 84*
*Métro: Rue du Bac*
*Closed: Sunday, and the whole of August*
*Open: noon – 2.30 pm and 7.30 – 10.30 pm*
Established in 1978 this is the pre-eminent Vietnamese restaurant in Paris and it's here partly for that and largely because it has one of the best wine cellars anywhere in the city. Robert Vifian is an acknowledged expert and he will proudly show you his list of classic clarets (some of which are very big money). But even the 'ordinary' wines are excellent and carefully chosen to go with the delicately spiced food which is not over-elaborate. The carte is comparatively simple and you will be given advice; portions are not large – part of their delicacy. For dessert try the mango fritters. And finish with preserved ginger, kumquats and tea.

A delectable experience which is unlikely to cost you more than 55€.

### Le St Laurent
*38 rue de Varenne, 75007*
*Tel: 01 45 48 79 64*
*Métro: Varenne*
*Closed: Sunday (Saturday and Monday lunchtimes), four weeks late July to late August, Christmas to New Year*
*Open: 12.30 – 2.30 pm and 7.30 – 10.00 pm*

A bistrot in every respect except the décor and ambience which is feminine-bourgeois-elegant, and may not be to your taste. It is what the French call *feutré* (literally 'felted') and the setting does have a cosseted, insulated-from-reality feel to it. But it would be churlish not to appreciate the beautiful table settings and the way the (good sized) tables are well-spaced. And the food? Last time I had some excellent coq au vin served with fresh tagliatelle.

The menu gourmand which includes cheese and coffee is the recommended option at 45€ but you could manage on less than that.

### Bistrot de Paris
*33 rue de Lille, 75007*
*Tel: 01 42 61 16 83*
*Métro: Musée d'Orsay*
*Closed: Saturday lunchtime, Sunday, Monday evening; mid-July to mid-August; Christmas to New Year*
*Open: noon – 3.30 pm and 7.00 – 11.00 pm*

This 'bistrot' which is more like a brasserie attracts an enthusiastic rating. The cooking is very good indeed: classic dishes of grilled meats and fish with the kind of sauté potatoes you could never make yourself. The cheeses are first-rate, Vieux Comté, St Marcellin amongst them; and you should leave space for the tarte tatin.

A truly professional Parisian ambience. No menus but à la carte won't cost more than 50€ unless you're greedy: portions are large.

## Brasserie

### Le Basilic
*2 rue Casimir-Périer, 75007*
*Tel: 01 44 18 94 64*
*Métro: Solférino*
*Open: DAILY noon – 2.30 pm and 7.30 – 10.30 pm*

The most attractive place to eat in the immediate area. There is a peaceful covered terrace overlooking the church of Ste Clothilde, and heated so you can eat outdoors much of the year, even for dinner. The food is entirely straightforward (steack au poivre, crème brûlée) but very good and there are decent, reasonably-priced wines. A complete meal including wine and coffee is unlikely to exceed 45€. A relaxed atmosphere and friendly service.

# 18. Rue Cler–Rue St Dominique (and for Passy)

It is easier to fix the focus of this quarter than to determine its boundaries. The rue St Dominique passes across the northern end of the rue Cler and you will likely be staying, breakfasting and dining (and shopping) mainly in these two streets. Their influence pervades the surrounding district which is as attractive to Parisians as it is to tourists. For this has become an area of choice to live, with rents and prices for apartments as high as almost any other part of central Paris.

The outer boundaries to the east and west are provided by the Invalides on the one side, and the Champ-de-Mars/Eiffel Tower on the other. The Eiffel Tower is, of course, the ultimate cliché of Paris, but what the countless images cannot prepare you for is the sheer scale of the thing: so enormous as to seem always nearer than it is. The best time to see it is at night when it's illuminated to create an object of fantasy; a leisurely stroll after dinner will bring you to appreciate the great engineer's achievement in the right frame of mind.

A different perspective is provided by the classical elegance of the Hôtel des Invalides whose gilded dome, like the Eiffel Tower, seems always to be in view, rather as Sacré-Coeur does in other parts of the city. This pervasiveness is more than that of a recurring image because their presence is sensed even when not seen.

In general, and at 'ground level', as you move to the perimeter the character of the district changes. Here are offices and embassies, government buildings and the kind of anonymous apartment blocks to which those with a great deal of money seem to like to retreat. A good example is the avenue de Saxe that runs directly at right angles to the south face of the Ecole Militaire. This is a street with no apparent life except on Thursday and Saturday mornings when a pleasantly animated market is held on the central reservation. Its lively character only serves to emphasise the bleakness of the surroundings: there is no better witness to the folk wisdom of Paris as a city of contrasts.

## Principal sights

**Hôtel des Invalides** (late 17th-18th century): this majestic building dominates the area and the dome with its lantern tower is, indeed, one of the great sights of Paris. The original purpose of caring for the nation's war wounded is still maintained in the administrative sense. Notable also for housing the remains of Napoleon (from 1840) in the chapel beneath the dome, and for the église St-Louis-des-Invalides (Chapelle des Soldats).

The layout of the building demonstrates the French love of perspective, as do the Esplanade lawns bordered by lime trees stretching down to the Seine.

Within the Invalides is the **Musée de l'Armée**: an extraordinary collection of arms and armaments and galleries providing extensive coverage of military campaigns, including France's role in the two World Wars.

**La Tour Eiffel**, Champ-de-Mars: when erected (1889) the tallest man-made construction in the world, a symbol of French technological progress – and a subject of fierce controversy. Now accepted as a landmark and romantic symbol of Paris, the tower offers visitors exceptional views of the city and its suburbs, and is the focus for celebrations from the Millennium to sporting triumphs.

**Musée du quai Branly** (21st century): the most recent major museum in Paris, which incorporates the relocation of non-Western arts and crafts and opened to a mixed reception. The exterior is curiously shabby, the interior confusing, hard to read and somehow unwelcoming: an interesting conception that fails at the level of implementation. Having said that, the exhibits are stunning – in particular the bronzes from the former empire of Bénin (Nigeria).

You can of course cross the flamboyant pont Alexandre III to admire two buildings long neglected but now impeccably restored. The **Petit Palais** (1897) houses the art collection and bequests of the city of Paris, 19th century painting in particular, and attracts travelling exhibitions of European artists of the period (recently Sorolla and John Singer Sargent). Facing it, the **Grand Palais** (1900) was built for the Universal Exhibition, its enormous metal structure hidden behind a classical façade. Worth a visit to see the magnificent glass roof, quite apart from major exhibitions in the adjacent galleries.

**Les Egouts** (mid-19th century), entrance at the junction

of the quai d'Orsay and pont d'Alma: the sewers of Paris, part of the vast programme of recon-struction during the Second Empire. The streets above are mirrored below ground, even to the blue enamelled name plaques. Visitors can see a small part of the system on a guided tour. A power-ful experience but perhaps not for the fastidious.

## Quiet hotels

### Grand Hôtel Levêque
*29 rue Cler, 75007*
*Tel: 01 47 05 49 15*
*Fax: 01 45 50 49 36*
*E-mail: info@hotel-leveque.com*
*www.hotelleveque.com*
*Métro: Ecole Militaire/*
*La Tour-Maubourg*
*50 rooms*
*Price: 102-112€ for a double room with shower; 118-125€ for a twin with shower*
I have happy memories of staying here with my younger son in the 1980s: the hotel remains much the same, prices apart (see the framed reviews covering the past twenty years in the entrance hall). Much of the hotel's charm comes from its location in the pedestrianised market street of the rue Cler, so it is not *very* quiet (markets start early).

There are some rooms over-looking a narrow courtyard but these, although cheaper at 97€, are smaller (and gloomy on the lower floors); the price given above is for street-side rooms. You need to book well ahead, particularly to get a room on one of the upper floors, as this is a popular hotel with high occupancy at all times of the year.

The tiny and very slow lift takes only one person and a case (or two good friends): quicker to use the stairs – better for the heart anyway.

### Hôtel de France Invalides
*102 boulevard de la Tour-Maubourg, 75007*
*Tel: 01 47 05 49 15*
*Fax: 01 45 56 96 78*
*E-mail: hoteldefrance @wanadoo.fr*
*www.hoteldefrance.com*
*Métro: Ecole Militaire*
*60 rooms*
*Price: 110-140€ for a double room*
Face aux Invalides says the brochure and that's exactly right: you'd pay a fortune for an apart-ment with a view like this (and it's worth specifying the view when booking). The situation is surpris-ingly calm and is next door to the upmarket regional bistrot D'Chez Eux (p. 205).

This hotel is a bargain not just for the area (smart) but anywhere in the capital. It is exceptionally well-maintained, and there is even a bar. Their breakfast is recom-mended largely because there are no convenient alternatives in the vicinity at the price (9€, but free for childen under 12).

### Hôtel Muguet
*11 rue Chevert, 75007*
*Tel: 01 47 05 05 93*
*Fax: 01 45 50 25 37*
*E-mail: muguet@wanadoo.fr*

*www.hotelmuguet.com*
*Métro: La Tour-Maubourg/*
*Ecole Militaire*
*48 rooms AIR CONDITIONED*
*Price: 135€ for a double room*
Although close to some busy main roads this is a quiet side street with little traffic noise. It is, in fact, one of those corners of Paris that tend to be overlooked. Approximately half of the hotel rooms give on to the light interior courtyard, and unusually in this price range all rooms are air-conditioned.

More expensive rooms (180-190€) on the top (6th) floor have excellent views – some of the Eiffel Tower.

### Hôtel de Londres Eiffel

*1 rue Augereau, 75007*
*Tel: 01 45 51 63 02*
*Fax: 01 47 05 28 96*
*E-mail: info@londres-eiffel.com*
*www.londres-eiffel.com*
*Métro: Ecole Militaire*
*30 rooms AIR-CONDITIONED*
*Price: 175€ for a double room*
*(high season)*
In a quiet street between the avenue Bosquet and the avenue de la Bourdonnais, this is a well-appointed hotel in a smart area of the quarter: good value nonetheless. Rooms that overlook the courtyard are even quieter. More expensive ones have a view of the Eiffel Tower: you have to judge whether that's worth an extra 15€ a night.

### Hôtel Saint Dominique

*62 rue St Dominique, 75007*
*Tel: 01 47 05 51 44*
*Fax: 01 47 05 81 28*

*E-mail: saint-dominique.*
*reservations@wanadoo.fr*
*www.hotelstdominique.com*
*Métro: La Tour-Maubourg/*
*Invalides*
*34 rooms*
*Price: 93-121€ for a double room*
This charming hotel is made up of two buildings with a pretty central patio garden which most of the rooms overlook; those that give on to the street should be avoided (even though double-glazed) as the rue St Dominique is a main thoroughfare and can be noisy.

Attractively decorated and well-maintained, it is almost opposite the excellent brasserie **Thoumieux** (p. 205).

# Breakfast

**Pâtisserie Jean Millet** LE GRAND PALAIS
*103 rue St Dominique*
*Closed: Monday, and the whole of August*
*Open: from 9.00 am (8.00 am Sunday)*
Highly commended for their croissants (particularly aux amandes), the café has tables set out on one side of the shop. As a tea salon it is good at any time of day but perfect for breakfast. It's not cheap: fresh orange juice, café crème, croissant and jam will set you back 12€ but worth it. They also sell a range of luncheon dishes and for those with a sweet tooth wonderful marshmallows at 13,70€ a kilo.

### Le Café du Marché

*38 rue Cler*
*Open: DAILY from 7.00 am*

Normally open until midnight (although closing at 4.30 pm on Sunday), the café serves food all day but this entry is not for that. Breakfast is another matter. Especially on market days the terrace is a splendid spot to see the street at work. Even late in the year (or early) you can sit on the heated terrace and enjoy a breakfast that will cost around half what you pay at Millet. Specifically, orange juice costs 3,20€, café crème 2,50€, croissant etc. 1,50€. If you can make do with a café allongé and a tartine beurrée you'll get away with just 3,20€.

An excellent place with friendly service.

### Lenôtre
*40 rue Cler*
*Closed: Sunday*
*Open: from 8.00 am*
The firm of Gaston Lenôtre produces pastries and 'savouries' that are almost design objects – a trend that was established by Lenôtre.The minimalist interiors of his shops are the setting for what he sells.

When you're feeling cool and elegant this is the place to come for a minimalist breakfast: modest in quantity but delectable in quality. For 9€ you can get a ¼ litre of fresh fruit juice, coffee etc. and three mini-viennoiseries.

## Public gardens

### Square d'Ajaccio
*Location: north-east of the Invalides at the junction of the rue de Grenelle and the boulevard des Invalides.*
The finest garden in the area with a range of specimen trees and shrubs, well-kept lawns and flowerbeds: little used and carefully maintained rather in the manner of a house garden. Even the children's play area, with its diminutive sandpit has that domestic quality.

### Square Santiago du Chili
*Location: northwest of the Invalides at the junction of the avenue de la Motte Picquet and the boulevard de la Tour-Maubourg, adjacent to the Métro station.*
A garden backing on to the Invalides with fine mature trees, lawns and flowerbeds and ample seating. The **place Salvador Allende** opposite is smaller, less appealing and acts as a kind of traffic island.

To one side there is a discreet memorial to the writer and aviator, Antoine de Saint-Exupéry (1900-1944) who lived nearby.

### Jardin de l'Intendant
*Location: the south corner of the Invalides at the junction of the avenue de Tourville and the boulevard de la Tour-Maubourg.*
A large formal garden surrounding a central *bassin* with fountain. To sit here is an almost hypnotic experience such is the degree of ordered calm broken only by the birds swooping and strutting around. Splendid in summer; and if it gets too hot you can retreat to the benches under the severely

regimented trees where there is a memorial fountain *aux victimes du terrorisme.*

### Parc du Champ-de-Mars
*Location: between the Ecole Militaire and the quai Branly.*
A military parade ground in the 18th century, then chosen as the site for world exhibitions in the 19th, the present gardens were laid out in the early 20th century: some in the formal style of French parterres, some landscaped in the English style.

On a fine day you can't do better than spread yourself out on the lawns, with a world-class backdrop for your picnic.

## Markets

### Saxe-Breteuil, 75007
*Open: Thursday 7.00 am – 2.30 pm; Saturday 7.00 am – 3.00 pm*
The market runs along the avenue de Saxe (from the avenue de Ségur to the place de Breteuil, southeast of the Ecole Militaire). One of the lesser-known and less regarded markets yet one of the most enjoyable.

Displays of spices perfume the air and ethnic food stalls (from the Antilles, North Africa etc.) sell the kind of hot snacks you can eat as you wander round. There is a good range of regional products – apples and cider from Picardy, for example – and a fine selection of charcuterie, especially the grilled sausages made from unmentionable parts of the pig and known as andouillettes.

### Rue Cler, 75007 (market street)
*Tuesday to Saturday 7.30 am – 1.00 pm and 3.00 – 7.00 pm (and Sunday morning)*
It is the southern half of the rue Cler between the rue de Grenelle and the avenue de la Motte Piquet which makes up the market street section. The level of activity has to be experienced to be believed. It has an almost provincial quality in contrast to the remote urban style of much of the surrounding area. And apart from a complete range of food shops there are several excellent cafés: from the always busy Café du Marché to the high-toned branch of Lenôtre – impeccable and a bit expensive – which seems curiously out of place.

The entertainment is mainly watching the action but this is one of the few places in central Paris where you still find street singers (one with a hurdy-gurdy on Sunday mornings).

## Fromagers

### Fromage Rouge
*83 rue St Dominique, 75007*
*Closed: Sunday and Monday*
*Open: Tuesday to Friday, 9.30 am – 1.00 pm and 4.00 – 7.30 pm; and all day Saturday*
This used to be a branch of the old-established chain of fromagers Androuet but the ethos here is bang up-to-date. The range is not large but carefully chosen, and there is an equally thoughtful selection of wines to go with the cheeses. Part of their service is to

provide trays of cheeses for dinner parties or festive occasions.

The two reliable market street fromageries are closed on Sunday afternoon and Monday, otherwise open 7.30 am – 1.00 pm and 3.00 – 7.00 pm:

**Fromagerie**, 31 rue Cler
**La Fermette**, 38 rue Cler
– no competition for Marie-Anne Cantin but if you're operating in basic mode these will meet your requirements at a modest price. No. 31 has the bigger range.

### Marie-Anne Cantin

*12 rue du Champ-de-Mars, 75007*
*Closed: Monday, and Sunday afternoon*
*Open: 7.30 am – 1.00 pm and 2.30 – 7.30 pm*

There are perfectly adequate fromagers in the nearby rue Cler but the exquisite shop of Mme Cantin is like haute couture to prêt-à-porter. The cheeses are all in a superlative state; and if you want to know more you can buy her book (see p. 34).

Supplier to many of the leading hotels and restaurants in Paris, as well as the Elysée Palace, Mme Cantin and her husband have recently opened branches in Japan.

In the seven cellars under her shop, cheeses are brought to a state of perfection which justifies their relative high price. Superbly aged Vieux Comté, but also such rarities as the finest of all blue cheeses, *bleu des Causses* which is produced in small quantities and becomes rarer each year.

## Glacier

### Martine Lambert

*192 rue de Grenelle, 75007*
*Closed: Monday and Tuesday*
*Open: Wednesday to Friday, 10.00am – 1.00 pm and 3.00 – 7.00 pm (Saturday to 8.00 pm; Sunday to 1.30 pm)*

The sign reads *Glaces de Normandie*, and so they are with flavours like *Quiberon (lait confit ou caramel au beurre salé), mûre sauvage* (wild blackberry) and *pomme à cidre et Calvados du Pays d'Auge*: plus a range of the more usual but still exceptional (*marron glacé, rhubarbe* and so on).

Based in Deauville and Trouville, Mme Lambert is an obsessive specialist, emphatic about quality and freshness. She uses unpasteurised juices for her sorbets, the milk and cream comes from Normandy and they manufacture almost all their ingredients.

A lot of fuss about ice-cream? Just try some and you'll be a convert. Competitively priced at 2,10€ for one boule, 3,50€ for two, 4,40€ for three. My advice is to take them one at a time.

## Neglected museums

Nothing much to report under this heading except that the Musée des Plans-reliefs on the top (4th) floor of the Musée de l'Armée attracts little attention. All those scale models and layouts formerly used in military training look just a little sad at first, until you give them the attention they deserve. You can be

sure that few of the tourists who crowd the lower floors have the stamina for that – if they get so far.
*Métro: Invalides*
*Open: DAILY except for public holidays, 10.00 am – 6.00 pm*
*Entrance (to the museum as a whole): 8€ (FREE to under 18s)*

And in Passy (across the pont d'Iéna, and turn left) you find:

### Musée du Vin
*5-7 square Charles Dickens, 75016*
*Métro: Passy*
*Closed: Monday and public holidays*
*Open: 10.00 am – 6.00 pm*
*Entrance: 8,50€ (but free if you buy lunch, served from noon to 3.00 pm)*
*www.museeduvinparis.com*
This museum concerned with the making and cultivation of wine is set in a terrace that looks doll's house size in comparison with the surrounding bulging apartment blocks of this bourgeois residential district.

It is best to arrive for the inexpensive lunch (three courses for 23€, glass of wine 2,90€) served in the ancient ecclesiastical cellars – with a medieval tableau at one end. The food is excellent traditional bistrot fare which will put you in a good mood for wandering around the fastidiously arranged exhibits afterwards.

Strongly recommended.

### Maison de Balzac
*47 rue Raynouard, 75016*
*Métro: Passy*
*Closed: Monday and public holidays*
*Open: 10.00 am – 6.00 pm*
*Entrance: FREE to the permanent collection*
You go along a street of opulent 20th century apartment blocks to reach the low-lying house where Balzac, hiding from his creditors, wrote many of his works. There are occasional exhibitions related to Balzac (a fee for these) but his small study is left undisturbed, the table having an example of his obsessive correction of proofs (a printer's nightmare). In truth, not a lot to see but with a presence, nonetheless.

## Interesting shops

### Florent Monestier
*47 bis avenue Bosquet, 75007*
*Métro: Ecole Militaire*
*Closed: Sunday*
*Open: 10.30 am – 7.00 pm*
A crowded shop with decorative objects from all parts of the world but especially tableware and furnishings from Provence: attractive in themselves but it is the traditional bedcovers from the Midi which catch the eye.

Glassware is there in great variety, some of it remarkable, some OTT. There is also an unusual range of well-made wooden toys. The initial impression of organised clutter is not favourable but you will almost certainly find something to your taste among Mme Monestier's eclectic stock.

### A la Mère de Famille
*47 rue Cler, 75007*
*Métro: Ecole Militaire*

*Open: Monday to Saturday, 9.30
am – 8.00 pm; Sunday 10.00 am –
1.00 pm*
Another branch of the famous
confectioners though the original
in the rue du Faubourg Montmartre is beyond compare (p. 103).
However, the usual excellent range
of sweetmeats from all over France
is to be found here.

### Thanakra

*170 bis rue de Grenelle, 75007
Métro: La Tour-Maubourg
Closed: Sunday and Monday
Open: Tuesday to Friday, 1.30 –
7.00 pm; Saturday 11.00 am –
1.00 pm and 3.00 – 6.00 pm*
Henri Crouzet specialises in
Moroccan tribal rugs and textiles
which he imports directly from
original sources. The rugs are not
cheap – anything from 600 to 3000
euros – yet when you examine
them you can appreciate that the
quality justifies the price. The bold
simple designs and colours would
look very effective in a modern
setting. He also sells a range of
boxes and carvings from the same
tribal areas.

### Bonsai Rèmy Samson

*10 rue de la Comète, 75007
Métro: La Tour-Maubourg
Closed: Sunday and Monday
Open: 10.30 am – 1.00 pm and
2.00 – 7.00 pm*
One cannot but admire the owner
of this shop. His dedication to his
specialism is manifest: this is no
high-design setting to inflate the
prices. Everything he sells is the
product of the infinite attention
that bonsai require. Forget the

visual clichés: some of his stock
is stunning in its style and compo-
sition.

The shop is small but you can
pass through to a conservatory
filled with hundreds of bonsai in
different styles and forms. They
range in price from 15€ up to
1200€ for a superb specimen that
has taken 45 years to reach its
present state.

## Bistrots

### La Fontaine de Mars

*129 rue St Dominique, 75007
Tel: 01 47 05 46 44
Métro: Ecole Militaire
Open: DAILY noon – 3.00 pm
and 7.30 – 11.00 pm*
This is an enormously successful
bistrot with, during the summer, a
delightful open-air terrace under
the arcades surrounding a fountain. So the prices have gone up,
and you need to book a week or
two in advance.

The food is straightforward
and with a *tendance sud-ouest*: the
predominant regional emphasis in
Paris these days. There is a lunch
menu for 23€ (three courses with
a fair choice); à la carte only in the
evening. We suggest you bypass
the starter because main courses
are large – including the inevitable
cassoulet – but also because here
you can get *tourtière Landaise aux
pruneaux et armagnac* (prune pie,
for short, served warm with prune
ice-cream) and it is not to be
missed.

Wines from the South-West
figure largely (cahors, madiran)

and these cost from 18€ a bottle; but you can get a ½ litre of house wine for 11€ and there are wines by the glass. Main courses are in the range 20-30€ e.g. lapin à la moutarde for 22€; entrées around 13€ and desserts 9-14€.

### D'Chez Eux
*2 avenue de Lowendal, 75007*
*Tel: 01 47 05 52 55*
*Métro: Ecole Militaire*
*Closed: Sunday, and three*
*weeks in August*
*Open: noon – 2.30 pm and*
*7.30 – 10.00 pm*
This is a bourgeois bistrot at its very best: formal, courteous but friendly. You will likely be welcomed by the owner, M. Jean-Pierre Court, who has the demeanour of a senator; and encouraged to eat and drink even as you inspect the carte, with a complimentary kir and a slice or two of *saucisson*. You will be wise to skip the entrées (served from a laden trolley) to leave room for the 'farandole des desserts' where for 10€ you can have as many different desserts as you wish.

Apart from the lunch menus at 35€ and 40€, there is a six-course 'menu gastronomique' at dinner (99€), which includes accompanying wines and is serious eating. On the 'ordinary' à la carte you could start with the 'chariot de salades' at 17€ which has things like salade aux queues d'écrevisses or pot-au-feu en salade – almost a meal in themselves. The main course trademark cassoulet is 30,20€; côte de boeuf (for two) is 66€. House wines (brouilly, madiran) are

around 26€ a bottle.

Simple arithmetic will tell you that a two-course choice à la carte will cost 40-50€ plus wine, with three courses pushing the price up to 60€.

## Brasserie

### Thoumieux
*79 rue St Dominique, 75007*
*Tel: 01 47 05 49 75*
*Métro: Invalides*
*Open: DAILY noon – 2.30 pm*
*and 7.00 – 11.00 pm*
If you want soupe à l'oignon gratinée or cassoulet (served in its cooking pot) you come here: the carte reads like our list of traditional dishes. And these are cooked and served in the traditional manner which means without a lot of flim-flam. The only changes I can detect, in the twenty-five years I've been eating here, are that they accept reservations; and the prices have gone up in real terms.

Not that it's expensive: the dinner menu at 33€ which includes a ¼ litre of wine, is normally adequate, but you can eat from the carte for around 45€ with a wide choice. Wine by the bottle costs from 14€ (for the Cuvée Thoumieux) and if you don't drink it all they'll give you a bag to take it away.

Very much a family establishment: you can see the different generations operating in their different roles. A friendly sort of place where you talk to the people on neighbouring tables.

# Special restaurants for luncheon on the day of departure

This is the way to finish your holiday – on a high instead of the anticlimax of packing, snacks at the airport – and so on. What makes a restaurant 'special' is a matter of one's own taste and style; with this in mind our suggestions are divided into three categories:

**Haute cuisine luxury**: top Paris restaurants in a sumptuous setting. You need to book well in advance, and this is normally jacket-and-tie territory. We have picked out five which are quite different from each other.

A caution: note that the price given is for the set lunch (the *menu*) and here even a modest expenditure on drinks will double the size of the bill. You may need to be emphatic that you don't want the *carte* (which could be at least three times the menu price) so: *on va prendre le menu.*

**Restaurants of character**: difficult to define in the abstract but easily recognisable when you experience it – something about the personality and style of the place combined with good food – at a less daunting price than the above. Here you should usually go for the carte (which will be about the price of an haute cuisine menu). So your meal will end up costing about the same.

**Open-air restaurants**: each of these has a unique setting – in some ways the most satisfying option of all, if the weather is right.

# Haute cuisine

### Le Meurice
*228 rue de Rivoli, 75001*
*Tel: 01 44 58 10 55*
*Métro: Tuileries*
*Closed: Saturday lunchtime,*
*Sunday and the whole of August*
*Open: noon – 2.30 pm*
*Lunch menu: 75€*

For those with long memories it is much changed. The old cocktail bar where you could watch expensive women being suitably rewarded is gone. Drinks are served in the large salon (and where those not heading for the restaurant gastronomique – like you – will be lunching). Service is impeccable from the moment you are relieved of your coat until you are escorted out. Allow 30 minutes to people-watch before taking your table.

Your three-course meal (perhaps langoustines followed by Scotch beef and subtle desserts) is of extraordinary delicacy. Portions are not large but you have two amuse-bouches and a pre-dessert of four items including an adult version of a lollipop. The sommelier will guide your wine choice and there are plenty of half-bottles for around 35-60€.

Your total bill will amount to no more than 150€ for a memorable experience, even for the case-hardened.

### La Tour d'Argent
*15 quai de la Tournelle, 75005*
*Tel: 01 43 54 23 31*
*Métro: Maubert-Mutualité*
*Closed: Monday, Tuesday*
*lunchtime, and first three weeks*
*in August*
*Open: noon – 1.30 pm (note that*
*the hours are for starting your*
*meal)*
*Lunch menu: 75€*

Always full, always in a state of excitement emanating from the tourists who are having the time of their lives, this restaurant with its three-star view of Notre Dame is difficult to be objective about. Sober judges agree the food is good, though not outstanding. For a supplement of 22€ you can get the famous pressed duck (*canard au sang*) and a numbered postcard (each duck has its own number).

Even the staff appear to be enjoying the occasion and the serving of the wine is a performance in itself with a cellar of the finest clarets to back it up. Claude Terrail, the elderly owner used to come round to each table, smiling as well he might. But no more: at the time of my last visit in May 2006, shortly before his death, he was seated at a table near the entrance, as well-groomed as ever, but very frail.

### Le Grand Véfour
*17 rue Beaujolais, 75001*
*Tel: 01 42 96 56 27*
*Métro: Palais-Royal-Louvre*
*Closed: Saturday, Sunday, Easter*
*week, the whole of August,*
*Christmas to New Year*
*Open: 12.30 – 2.00 pm*
*Lunch menu: 88€*

If ever a restaurant displayed unobtrusive confidence in itself, it is this one. The discreet setting – wine-red curtains on brass rails –

and the character of the stunning décor of gilt and painted glass with nothing of excess about it, can make other places seem to be trying too hard.

Impeccable, under-played service and food to match: very much of the *cuisine inventive* genre but here sometimes dazzlingly successful. Everyone takes the menu which, although based on inexpensive ingredients (crab, cod, tête de veau, etc) is of exceptional delicacy and imagination. The selection of cheeses is conventional, yet with a glass of young (and inexpensive) Syrah they are beyond compare and almost a meal in themselves; but keep going for the petits fours, the incredibly light *gâteau Savoy,* and chocolates to conclude.

### Lasserre

*17 rue Franklin D. Roosevelt, 75008*
*Tel: 01 43 59 53 43*
*Métro: F. D. Roosevelt*
*Closed: Sunday, and the whole of August*
*Open: for lunch, Thursday and Friday only, 12.30 – 2.30 pm*
*Lunch menu: 110€*

Lasserre represents the luxury of the 1950s and '60s (with much use of expensive ingredients like truffles and foie gras, even on the menu). The unchanging quality is part of its fascination: one could imagine Cary Grant eating there with Audrey Hepburn, under the sliding roof that is open to the sky in summer.

The lunch menu is not exactly cut price and, with care, you may find you can eat from the carte for only a little more. Superb wines at superb prices (nothing under 60€ a bottle, and very few under 100€).

### Taillevent

*15 rue Lamennais, 75008*
*Tel: 01 44 95 15 01*
*Métro: George V*
*Closed: Saturday and Sunday*
*Open: noon – 2.30 pm and 7.30 – 10.00 pm*
*Lunch menu: 70€ - but see below*
With its discreet entrance in a side-street off the Champs Elysées and an equally low-key interior this is one of the great restaurants. There is a lunch menu but you may feel a cheap-skate taking it; the 140€ *menu dégustation* (seven delicate courses) is so good as to be its own justification. And you won't feel you've eaten too much: each course ranging from the solidly traditional (duck with marinated cherries) to the highly inventive (rocquefort and prune ice-cream) is a few delicious mouthfuls. The superb wine list has bottles from as little as 30€ and more than a third of the list at under 100€ – with a good range of half-bottles at rather more than half the cost of a full one.

One tip: book well ahead and they will ask you to confirm the day before. If you do not you will lose your table.

## Restaurants of character

### Hôtel Lutétia
*45 boulevard Raspail, 75006*

*Tel: 01 49 54 46 90*
*Métro: Sèvres-Babylone*
*Closed: Saturday, Sunday, public holidays and the whole of August*
*Open: noon – 2.30 pm*
*Lunch menu: 37€ (but consider going à la carte at around 75€)*
The lunch menu is certainly a bargain, not just because of the food but because it gives you entrée to this famous art deco restaurant modelled on one of the interiors of the 1930s transatlantic liner Normandie. Great fun: the adjacent brasserie deserves a similar accolade (see p. 189).

**Benoît**
*20 rue St Martin, 75004*
*Tel: 01 42 72 75 76*
*Métro: Châtelet*
*Closed: public holidays and the whole of August*
*Open: otherwise DAILY noon – 2.00 pm*
*Lunch menu: 38€ (but go à la carte for around 70-80€)*
Secreted behind bay-trees and velvet curtains this classic bistrot is situated in one of the most strident areas of Paris. You wouldn't think that from the calm of the interior. Of its kind you find here some of the best cooking the capital offers. But, having been in the same family ownership since 1912, the restaurant was taken over in 2006 by the ubiquitous chef-entrepreneur, Alain Ducasse.

If it retains its character you will have an outstanding experience: the à la carte is so much better than the menu that it would be foolish to opt for the latter. What you get is haute cuisine bistrot food at big hotel menu prices. Let's hope it stays that way.

**La Closerie des Lilas**
*171 boulevard du Montparnasse, 75006*
*Tel: 01 40 51 34 50*
*Métro: Vavin*
*Open: DAILY noon – 2.15 pm*
*Lunch menu: 48€ (includes coffee and a half-bottle of wine)*
The glass-roofed restaurant (next to the brasserie) exudes an atmosphere of professionalism. The sommelier, who looks like a junior cardinal, will show you your prix-fixe half-bottle as gravely as if it were the rarest vintage. The food is resolutely traditional; the best choice for the main course is from the trolley (a roast except for Friday). However, if your day of departure is a Sunday, go for the carte, because this is the great day for the bourgeois to eat out *en famille*, and you'll feel out of it if you don't follow suit. It'll be twice the price of the menu but a great occasion.

**Au Pressoir**
*257 avenue Daumesnil, 75012*
*Tel: 01 43 44 38 21*
*Métro: Michel Bizot*
*Closed: Saturday, Sunday and the last week in April*
*Open: noon – 2.30 pm*
*Lunch menu: 76€*
This is not a part of town where you find many Michelin-starred restaurants. The price of the (all-day) menu matches that of the august restaurants of the chic arrondissements; but you will eat better here.

Henri Seguin is a chef who plays no tricks but is subtle in his treatment of traditional dishes. Quantities are copious: you may find the menu too much for you. In which case (omitting the entrée, for example) you could spend no more on the carte.

### Le Train Bleu

*Gare de Lyon, place Louis Armand, 75012*
*Tel: 01 43 43 09 06*
*Métro: Gare de Lyon*
*Open: for Sunday brunch 11.30 am – 2.00 pm*
*Brunch menu: 35€*

Brunch is for some reason a smart thing in Paris. Here it is served in the bar area (you need to make that clear at the time of booking otherwise they'll put you in the more expensive restaurant). It is essential to book as this is a popular venue and splendid value: the price includes mineral water, fruit juices and coffee.

The food is self-service, buffet-style with a wide choice of salads, charcuterie, smoked salmon etc. – plus the very English bacon and eggs, cooked for you. Altogether an animated place to fuel up for your return journey (if it's on a Sunday).

Waiters clear your empty plates and bring what drinks you want (wines extra). The bar area is very pleasant and you can wander along and look at the splendours of the restaurant (see also p. 59).

## Open-air restaurants

### Ziryab

*Institut du Monde Arabe*
*1 rue des Fossés St Bernard, 75005*
*Tel: 01 53 10 10 19*
*Métro: Jussieu*
*Closed: Monday*
*Open: 12.30 – 2.00 pm*
*Lunch menus: 26€ and 34€ (à la carte at 45-55€)*

The terrace of this restaurant on the top floor of the Institut offers interesting but not wonderful food from North Africa for a modest outlay, with an unparalleled view of the Seine and Notre-Dame. Altogether a very civilised experience – at civilised prices.

### La Maison de l'Amérique Latine

*217 boulevard St Germain, 75007*
*Tel: 01 49 54 75 10*
*Métro: Solférino*
*Closed: Saturday, Sunday, the whole of August, Christmas to New Year*
*Open: noon – 2.30 pm*
*Lunch menus: 37€ and 50€*

On the right day the perfect setting. When booking you should specify a table in the garden – others are further back on an open terrace.

From the outside you would never guess there was a restaurant here. The austere 18th century façade (and the name) is what you might expect of a cultural centre, which it is. The garden is a delight and you can walk round it after your meal. The food is contemporary which means I can never remember what I've eaten: but it's always pleasant and suitable to a summer's day.

## La Cigale-Récamier

*4 rue Récamier, 75007*
*Tel: 01 45 48 86 58*
*Métro: Sèvres-Babylone*
*Closed: Sunday, and Christmas to New Year*
*Open: noon – 2.30 pm*
*Lunch carte (no menu): around 50€*
This used to be a favourite Burgundian restaurant for serious and hearty eaters. It now specialises in soufflés (both sweet and savoury), omelettes and what are best described as tea-salon dishes. The soufflés are astonishingly light, the omelettes ditto: all very well if you like eggs.

The restaurant is included here for its fine open-air terrace, set in a pedestrianised cul-de-sac with a small public garden at the end of the street (see p. 185).

A complete meal including a couple of drinks (wines by the glass) will cost you in the region of 50€; but remember you're here for the setting.

## Jardins Plein Ciel

*Hôtel Raphael*
*17 avenue Kléber, 75016*
*Tel: 01 53 64 32 30*
*Métro: Kléber*
*Closed: October to April*
*Open: weekdays only, May to September, noon – 2.30 pm*
*Lunch menu: 70€*
Paradise: this seventh-floor roof terrace provides an outstanding buffet-style luncheon and at the same time one of the best panoramic views of Paris. It has a relaxed, informal but smart ambience. On a warm summer's day, with a cooling breeze, it can scarcely be bettered.

# Some practical details

**What to say when making an initial telephone reservation to a hotel or restaurant  214**
Hotel 214
Restaurant 214
Spelling your name in French 214
Giving the date in French 214
'Model' fax, e-mail and letter formats to confirm a
    hotel reservation 215

**Getting around in Paris  216**
Public transport 216
Buying a Carte Navigo 216
Vélib 217
Street maps 218
Other guides 218

**A word to the wise...  219**
Social behaviour 219
What you need to know about lavatories in Paris 219
French time 220
Carrying your passport 220
Credit cards  221
Paris postcodes  221
Telephones  221

**Free concerts and classic films  222**

**Antiques  223**

**Holiday accommodation for families  224**

**Top five special trips for children  226**
Paris Plage 227

# What to say when making an initial telephone reservation to a hotel or restaurant

## Hotel

Start off in French:

*Bonjour. Je m'appelle -_____, je suis anglais(e), américain(e), etc. Je vous téléphone d'Angleterre, des Etats-Unis, etc. Vous parlez anglais?* (If they do, no problem except that of spelling your name – see below.)

If they don't have good English, you continue:

*Je voudrais réserver une chambre (avec grand lit/ deux lits jumeaux/pour une famille, etc.) pour les* (number) *nuits commençant le* (day, date, month) (e.g. *le lundi seize février*). *Une chambre:*
  - *avec douche/salle de bains*
  - *climatisée* (air-conditioned)
  - *non-fumeur* (see hotel entries)
  - *au dernier* (top) *étage/aux étages supérieurs* (upper)
  - *au fond/sur la rue* (at the back/overlooking the street)
  - *si possible.*

*Ça me coûtera combien?*

*Je vous épelle mon nom:* (......)

*Je vous enverrai un fax/e-mail pour confirmer ma réservation avec le numéro de ma carte de crédit.*

*Merci, au revoir.*

## Restaurant

*Je voudrais réserver une table pour* (number) *personne(s) pour le* (day, date, month) *pour le déjeuner/le soir à* (time e.g. *treize heures/vingt heures trente*).

*Je vous épelle mon nom* (particularly important in restaurant bookings). *Je suis (je serai) à l'hôtel _____ dans la rue _____. Le numéro de téléphone est _____.. Merci, au revoir.*

## Spelling your name in French

Even those French people whose English is quite good have trouble with the English alphabet – and vice-versa for English-speaking people. Here goes:

| | | | |
|---|---|---|---|
| a | ah | n | en |
| b | bay | o | oh |
| c | say | p | pay |
| d | day | q | coo |
| e | er | r | air |
| f | eff | s | ess |
| g | jhay (soft j) | t | tay |
| h | ash | u | ooh |
| i | ee | v | vay |
| j | gee (soft g) | w | dooblevay |
| k | kah | x | ix |
| l | ell | y | eegrek |
| m | emm | z | zed |

If there are two letters the same and together in your name e.g. ll, mm, tt, you say *deux* – not double, as we do. And if they begin with a vowel sound you elide the '*deux*' e.g. duzell for double l. It's worth practising: I was once almost refused a restaurant table because the waiter had written my name in the book in what seemed like a Russian version.

## Giving the date in French

Not so simple...You do it in

this order:

definite article first *(le)*

day of the week next *(lundi, mardi, mercredi, jeudi, vendredi, samedi, dimanche)*

date next *(premier, deux, trois, quatre, cinq, six, sept, huit, neuf, dix, onze, douze, treize, quatorze, quinze, seize, dix-sept, dix-huit, dix-neuf, vingt, vingt-et-un, vingt-deux, vingt-trois, vingt-quatre, vingt-cinq, vingt-six, vingt-sept, vingt-huit, vingt-neuf, trente, trente-et-un)*

month last *(janvier, février, mars, avril, mai, juin, juillet* (jweeay), *août* (oot), *septembre, octobre, novembre, décembre)*

so, for example: *le mardi premier janvier.*

Days of the week and months of the year do not have initial capitals.

## 'Model' fax, e-mail and letter formats to confirm a hotel reservation

*E-mails/faxes* For whatever reason I find electronic missives (e-mails more than faxes) to France somewhat unreliable. It is important to ask for confirmation. The fact that you have made an initial reservation by telephone means nothing – hotels get many such. If you don't receive confirmation of your e-mail/fax send a letter by secure postal delivery (in the UK *Airsure*). It is no joke (particularly at peak times) to arrive at a hotel and find they don't have your booking. Also, if you expect to arrive after 6.00 pm let them know, otherwise they can legally let your room (*arrhes* or not).

You should give:

Date:

*Nombre de page(s):*

*A l'attention de:* (to)

*Emetteur:* (from)

*Objet:* (subject)

Fax/e-mail: (yours)

*Monsieur/Madame,*

*Je vous écris pour confirmer la réservation que j'ai faite par téléphone aujourd'hui:*

– *d'une chambre (avec grand lit/deux lits jumeaux/de famille),*

– *pour les* (number) *nuits commençant le* (day/date/month).

– *Si possible une chambre*

– *au dernier étage/à un étage supérieur,*

– *au fond/qui donne sur la rue,*

– *avec douche/salle de bains.*

*Veuillez trouver ci-dessous les détails de ma carte de credit:*

*Carte:* card type (e.g. Visa)

*Numéro:*

*Valable jusqu'à:* (expiry date)

*Au nom de:*

*Je serais heureux (heureuse) de recevoir votre confirmation.*

*Avec mes remerciements.*

*Letter format:* This is essentially the same but with a conventional heading (use headed paper if you have it). For a letter the above terminal courtesy would be regarded as a bit abrupt. So, flowery though it may seem you should use the following:

(to women) *Veuillez agréer, Madame, l'expression de mes sentiments respectueux, ......*

(to men) *Veuillez agréer, Monsieur, l'expression de mes sentiments distingués, ......*

Fulsome, yes, but in France it is better to err on the side of courtesy and formality.

# Getting around in Paris

## Public transport

The city has one of the most efficient and least expensive public transport systems in Europe. The Métro in particular is both quick and easy to understand (French logic at its practical best): just look for the terminal destination and *correspondances* (connections) where necessary. The bus system requires more study but does allow you to see Paris. The Métro closes down at 1.00 am; after that you have to rely on the Noctambus (look for the blue signs with an owl and yellow moon). Take a taxi as a last resort – and if you can get one... Parisian taxi-drivers are a byword for surly unhelpfulness. This guide suggests you make limited use of either by 'living' in your local area so that, for example, after dinner you can simply walk back to your hotel.

The Métro links up with the RER (Réseau Express Régionale) but as the name suggests this mainly serves suburban and out-of-town commuters. Most of the Métro lines were built more than 70 years ago (line 1 in 1900) but in 1998 the new Méteor line (14) was opened, now running from St Lazare to Olympiades, with high-speed driverless trains like those in Singapore.

For functional travel the Métro is best: a *carnet* (ten single journey tickets) costs 10,90€ and as the tickets have no date limit you can keep them to use on your next visit. Moreover all tickets can be used on buses as well as the Métro.

You can buy a *Paris Visite* card for one, two, three or five days, costing 8,50€, 13,95€, 18,60€ and 27,20€ respectively, which allows unlimited travel within zones 1 to 3. As simple arithmetic will tell you these are not good value unless you plan to do a great deal of travelling. Better value for one day is a *Carte Mobilis* which costs 5,50€ for use in zones 1 and 2 – as much as you'll need (zone 3 is beyond city limits). For longer stays, you should get a *Carte Navigo* - see below.

Tickets are available from any Métro station but only the larger ones have a ticket office. A recent innovation is that in smaller stations (which means most) you have to use a rather elaborate ticket vending machine. Payment is by credit card or cash (the latter is advisable). If you get it right then your tickets and change are dispensed. However, there is an adjacent information office where the helpful staff are used to instructing bewildered visitors. Incidentally remember to ask for a copy of the very clear free Métro map *(plan du Métro)*.

## Buying a Carte Navigo

The *Carte Orange*, which allowed you to buy a week's or a month's travel for a single price, has now been replaced by the *Carte Navigo*, an electronic touch-card like London's Oystercard. Needless to say the process for getting it is more complicated:

[1] Go the automatic ticket dispenser machines in the Métro; pick the one that takes bank notes.

[2] Using the roller at the bottom of the screen, scroll UP for the tickets menu and press the VALIDER button to the right.

[3] Scroll DOWN for the English language option and press VALIDER.

[4] Scroll DOWN for other ticket options – there are several screens – the last one gives the NAVIGO DECOUVERTE option: press VALIDER.

[5] You will be instructed to insert 5€, which will give you a paper ticket.

[6] Take this to the immediately adjacent information office.

[7] They will give you a plastic Navigo card plus the associated identity card (on which you stick a passport-sized photograph) and a rigid plastic wallet to keep them in. The (numbered) identity card validates the use of the travel card.

[8] To charge up your Navigo card you turn the roller DOWN and press VALIDER, placing the card on the sloping tray above the credit card slot (yes, I tried to put my Navigo card in there).

[9] You have to select the zones you want (1 and 2) and the period of use (a week or a month) and then insert your payment. A week costs 16,40€, a month 52,50€.

A week's charge starts from the following Monday (available from the preceding Thursday and up to Wednesday of the week in which it is in use) – still worthwhile because it gives you five days' travel for less than a three-day *Paris Visite* card. All this might seem a lot of effort but, once you've mastered the machine, it will make travelling easier and cheaper. Just don't try to do it for the first time when you're in a hurry.

## Vélib'

The ability of Parisians to assimilate innovation may be the reason why the city never appears to change in its essentials.

Vélo libre or vélo liberté (Vélib' for short) which makes available thousands of bicycles for hire across numerous sites in Paris was established in mid-2007 and by the end of the year seemed always to have existed. For full details check the website (velib.paris.fr) but, briefly, you can hire bikes in one location and leave them at any other, using your (charged-up) Vélib' card – the first half-hour is free – and there's a meter at each stand next to the row of uniform silver-grey bikes.

I haven't yet had the confidence to cycle in Paris but many (mainly young) Parisians do with the same assurance that they rollerblade on busy streets. Subscribers to the scheme receive a leaflet with safety advice and there are plenty of designated cycle lanes. One of the familiar sights is of trailers moving bikes from one location to another. And be assured: the whole thing is organised with the obsessive thoroughness of the French.

## Street maps

Paris is made up of myriad small streets which can seem hard to locate – even with the assistance of a map where, in any case, you need good eyesight and a clear head to spot them. Maps are no substitute for getting to know the local area; quite simply they are easier to read once you have an idea of the terrain. A useful tip is that Métro stations usually have an enlarged map of the locality displayed in the entrance. You should buy a broadsheet map showing the whole of Paris (to give you an approximate fix and to see how everything joins up) and a page-by-page book map which is more convenient to study on street-corners.

I have an elderly, much sell-otaped map (now out-of-print) which not only gives cross-references (G4, H9 etc.) but separately identifies each street within the sector with a number: I sometimes think I couldn't have done the research for this guide without it. But any map is only useful if it is in the right orientation: unless there are conspicuous landmarks you can easily lose your sense of direction. Absurd though it may sound, a pocket compass can be helpful.

## Other guides

The present book is not in competition with any other. Essential is the Michelin *Green Guide* which provides an impeccable, up-to-date, carefully researched account of the standard sights: nothing can compete with this. As an adjunct (rather than an alternative) Dorling Kindersley's *Eye Witness* guide is strong on visuals (pictures of everything) and easy to access. In addition you should buy the weekly *Pariscope*, on sale at news kiosks, which lists what's on from week to week – cinemas, exhibitions, sport, etc. (actually from Wednesday to the following Tuesday). At 40 centimes it is a great bargain. An alternative is *L'Officiel des Spectacles* at 0,35€.

Paris is in a constant state of flux even if it always appears the same, and nowhere is this more true than in the various forms of nightlife which can reinvent itself in a few months if not weeks. In this respect, accounts in guidebooks are out-of-date by the time they're published; which is why the present guide concentrates on the more stable (and more fundamental) aspects of a visit to Paris – in particular, where to stay and where to eat. Having said that, restaurants (more than hotels) change in quality and character so that a five-year old guide has to be used with caution, and a ten-year-old one is virtually useless.

# A word to the wise...

## Social behaviour

The French are easily offended if they feel you are not behaving properly. A few points:

1. What we may regard as 'friendliness', like the instant use of first names, is often not considered acceptable in France – at least between adults. So don't be too familiar in speech or manner: a degree of reserve is expected.

2. Even when you are on a friendly footing e.g. with a waiter, show this in a formal way – shaking hands on arrival and departure.

3. In a restaurant don't talk too loudly. You may address a remark (une plaisanterie) to someone at an adjoining table but don't expect to engage them in conversation: this is seen as an intrusion.

4. In shops (food shops in particular) don't pick things up. You will often see signs in English: Please do not touch (and whom are they aimed at?)

5. Address people by their title (monsieur, madame, mademoiselle). The title 'madame' is for (presumably) married women – though I know an eighty-year-old unmarried café owner who expects to be addressed as 'mademoiselle'. Waiters are called 'monsieur' not 'garçon' which is considered offensive.

## What you need to know about lavatories in Paris

Fifty years ago every 'suitable' wall bore the legend DEFENSE D'URINER which, on the Freudian principle that you don't have laws against things people don't want to do, said something about the male of the species at that time. Men were, in fact, well provided for by the vaguely gothic green-painted cast-iron urinoirs, pissoirs or châteaux de nécessité which were found in every street. Since little more than the offending portion of the male anatomy was screened, the upper and lower parts of the body were clearly visible: I remember seeing a (gentleman, no doubt) raise his hat to a passing female acquaintance.

These urinoirs have long gone, replaced by metallic silver and strangely futuristic windowless capsules which do at least cater for women. The door slides open and shut and I frankly find them claustrophobic: at least they are now free – you used to have to pay 40 centimes for the privilege. Métro stations sometimes have public lavatories – of the kind where there is an attendant and a small tray where you leave a tip (30 centimes is enough). As an aesthetic experience, and if you are in the area, the art nouveau subterranean lavatories in the place de la Madeleine (8th) are worth a visit.

In practice you often have to rely on private enterprise: go into the largest, most glittering café/brasserie you can see and look for the sign saying 'toilettes' or 'w.c.' (pronounced vay-say). They are usually in the basement and, if you're not sure, you should ask (in a confident tone): *Les w.c. sont en bas?* It is important not to behave in an apologetic manner as if you haven't the right to be there, and especially if you do not intend to buy a drink.

There are normally (but not always) separate lavatories for men and women. I suspect that Frenchmen find sit-on lavatories unmanly because it is often the case that the lavatory for men is of the hole in the floor variety – *à la turque.* In this situation I always go into the women's (usually a simple cubicle anyway). Whatever your sex there may be no choice – it's a hole in the floor or nothing. If you are not to experience a minor trauma you should note the following:

If, when you close the door, you find yourself in complete darkness with no light switch, don't panic – it will light up when you rotate the sliding bar lock.

Place your feet on the footrests and put one hand on the wall behind so that you don't fall backwards.

The canister-shaped cistern is normally high up on the wall with a lever marked TIREZ. When you pull this the water descends with explosive force and almost floods the floor: SO STAND WELL CLEAR or your blue suede shoes will look as though you've had an accident.

If you think this goes into unnecessary detail all I can say is that a bad experience in a Parisian lavatory can spoil your day; or at least put you off your meal.

## French time
This is always an hour later in France than the UK and will be shown on your air or other tickets accordingly. It used to be the case that French summer time didn't exactly synchronise with British Summer Time (clocks put forward an hour at the beginning of the period, put back at the end). But now the time differential is entirely consistent: one of the benefits of EU standardisation.

There is a difference in their use of the 24-hour clock, particularly in businesses, shops, restaurants and hotels, but increasingly in ordinary usage. It is less cumbersome and ambiguous: the French for am is *du matin*, and for pm *de l'après-midi* and *du soir*. You can say *huit heures et demie du soir* when booking a table but it's a lot simpler to say *vingt heures trente* (NB not *vingt heures et demie*).

## Carrying your passport
This is not just a useful habit – for occasional concessionary rates in museums (60+), getting a purchase tax rebate (*détaxe* – US citizens), changing travellers' cheques – it is also a legal requirement. French police have the right to stop *anyone* and ask for identification papers: *Vos papiers, s'il vous plaît...* This is exercised more often these days when the threat of terrorism is a constant preoccupation.

If you are asked for your papers, it is important to comply calmly and politely, however unreasonable or arbitrary the request may seem. You should not confuse the liberal attitudes of educated Parisians with the attitudes of the police who see themselves as having a job to do.

If you cannot produce your passport (because it's at the hotel) what happens will depend to a large extent on your demeanour which should be both respectful and apologetic. You address the policeman as *Monsieur l'agent* and you grovel *(je m'excuse…)*. If you feel the need to assert yourself you will likely be taken into custody; temporarily one assumes.

## Credit cards

The French have had 'chip and pin' credit cards *(la carte bleue)* for several years and so have always regarded cards which require a signature with some suspicion. Now that we have adopted the technology they are happier. However, although it is true that credit cards are widely 'accepted', they are by no means universally welcomed particularly in the lower price-ranges of the smaller, privately owned hotels, restaurants and shops included in this guide.

You will sometimes see a sign: *Nous n'acceptons pas les cartes de crédit/cartes bleues,* but even if you don't you shouldn't assume that they do – or like to do so. Simply ask: *Acceptez-vous les cartes de crédit?* I was once in a pâtisserie (Gérard Mulot) where a tourist was making a multiple order which was being elaborately packaged. When it came to payment he proffered his credit card: it was refused.

There is often a quite high minimum transaction level – which signals 'not welcome'. Many small entrepreneurs see credit card charges, not unreasonably, as a form of tax; and tax in any form is something that exercises French emotionality. Except in the case of more expensive establishments (and not always then), or for very big bills, you should assume that cash is preferred; and that in any case 'acceptées' does not mean 'bienvenues'.

## Paris postcodes

Throughout France the postcodes are given as five-digit numbers. The logic is simple once you understand it. The country is divided into 95 departments (French school children used to learn them by rote). The first two digits indicate which one; the remaining three the subdivision. Paris is unique amongst cities in having its own departmental number (75) so the postcode starts with that; then comes a zero, followed by the arrondissement number: there are twenty of these. So within each arrondissement the postcode is the same – in the first it's 75001; in the twentieth it's 75020.

## Telephones

If you're not using a mobile phone the easiest and cheapest way to make a call is from a public phone booth using a *télécarte* obtainable from any post office, tabac or news kiosk; coin boxes are a thing of the past. Ask for a France Télécom card for a *cabine publique*.

# Free concerts and classic films

## Free concerts

In case you think the present guide is not sufficiently concerned with things of the mind, this entry partly redresses the balance.

You may not be able to afford seats at the Opéra or the Salle Pleyel but a tradition in Paris is that churches mount concerts (not necessarily or particularly of sacred music) with no entry charge. The standard is extremely high with a wide variety of programmes, listed in *Pariscope*, so you can make your own choice. There is a whole section of Parisian society which patronises these concerts and attendance is always good: you need to get there early to secure a decent seat which is usually of the hard wooden bench variety – habitués bring cushions. An incidental pleasure is entry to churches and chapels not all of which are routinely open – like the Chapel of the École Militaire.

They are not entirely free (there is a collection) and five euros is considered respectable. If you don't contribute you can expect a look of disdain.

## The seventh art

Paris is the natural home for the cinéaste. There are over a hundred cinemas in central Paris (there used to be many more). They are often small, specialising in 'classic' movies, some of them rarities. But rare or not they give you the chance to see early talkies and the like on a (fairly) big screen and in the kind of audience atmosphere they were intended for. Whether your choice is the Marx brothers, the *films noirs* of the 1940s, Truffaut, Godard and the *nouvelle vague*, or those Hollywood musicals with their own idealised version of Paris, it's just not the same on a television screen.

These gems from the past are listed under *reprises* and where appropriate will be noted as *v.o.* ('version originale'). Your Parisian film buff is a fastidious client who doesn't want the goods tampered with; those dubbed into French will be marked *v.f.* ('version française') but in any case the very notion of Bogart speaking French is absurd. The films shown are always good copies (often advertised as *copie neuve*).

You will need to study *Pariscope* or *L'Officiel des Spectacles* because performances *(séances)* are often restricted, i.e. to one time in the day, as several films are shown in sequence from late morning to late at night.

So you haven't come to Paris to watch films? Well, if it's a wet afternoon and your feet are tired you might be happy to see one of the rarer Hollywood fantasies of Ernst Lubitsch – a favourite director – eclipsed only by the Master himself: I have never been in Paris when there wasn't a Hitchcock movie showing.

Apart from the pleasure of the films there are the cinemas

themselves, many of course plain and unremarkable. There are, however, survivors of varying sizes: **Le Grand Rex,** definitely large-scale, in the boulevard Poissonière (early 1930s art deco with starry night-sky ceiling); and in contrast, across the boulevard the smaller **Max Linder Panorama** (named after the film director) which offers original versions and art films. Then there is the delightful **Escurial Pano-rama** in the boulevard de Port Royal (convenient for Luxembourg and Montparnasse) or the idiosyncratic family-run **Studio 28** in the rue Tholozé in Montmartre. If you're looking for oriental splendour there's the **Pagode** in the rue de Babylone and if you are staying in the Latin Quarter then **Action Ecoles** in the rue des Ecoles will usually have something you'll want to watch.

Happy viewing for around 7€ (Wednesday is a good day for discounts), and in the smaller independent cinemas it's still good form to give a *pourboire* to the usherette (50 centimes is about right).

If you are a really serious student of the cinema you should make the pilgrimage to **Cinémathèque française,** the national museum of the cinema on the far edge of the 12th arrondissement at 51 rue de Bercy (Métro: Bercy). About six films a day are screened and there's a library and research centre/archive (www.cinematique. fr). And it's cheap with various formulas which make it even cheaper: a pity it's not more central, as it used to be.

# Antiques

There are antique shops of one kind or another scattered all over Paris: we have listed some of them in the relevant sections. Two well-known, but unappealing, large centres are the **Village Suisse** (a bit shabby) in the avenue de la Motte-Picquet (7th) and the **Louvre des Antiquaires** (glossy, over-priced and overwhelming) in the place du Palais-Royal (1st).

The rue St Paul in the 4th arrondissement has some interesting specialists; and in various courtyards between that street and the rue Charlemagne you find the **Village St Paul** (open Thursday to Monday 11.00 am– 7.00 pm) where most dealers are of the *brocante* variety – a good place to visit on a Sunday.

But the prime browsing territory – where you can indulge in that kind of window-shopping akin to fantasy – is the section of the Left Bank between the boulevard St Germain and the river, more or less bordered east and west by the rue Bonaparte and the rue de Seine, with many intersecting streets. Here are small specialised shops (medical antiques, old musical instruments, art deco sculpture) often staging selling exhibitions so that you may feel less inhibited going in to look around. And you just might buy something... Follow your nose.

# Holiday accommodation for families

One word of advice before we get down to detail: if any of your children (babies excepted) are still wetting the bed, defer your visit until they are safely dry. Otherwise you will need very good French and very strong nerves to cope with the consequences.

You have a choice:
– a 'family room' in a hotel which means all sleeping together;
– renting a flat;
– taking an 'appartement' with a cuisinette in a hotel.

My advice is to go for the last. With children there is more to accommodation than enough beds: they want drinks and snacks at all hours. Using room service or the mini-bar soon becomes expensive.

Flat rental agencies in Paris essentially cater for adult couples: the larger ones are as expensive as hotels and normally require a minimum stay of five days. Things like towels are unlikely to be in adequate supply, and general help/advice is not readily to hand.

Two good agencies, with English-speaking staff are:

**Roots Travel**
*85 rue de la Verrerie, 75004*
*Tel: 01 42 74 07 07*
*Fax: 01 42 74 01 01*
*E-mail: paris@rootstravel.com*
*www.rootstravel.com*

**Paris Appartements Services**
*20 rue Bachaumont, 75002*

*Tel: 01 40 28 01 28*
*Fax: 01 40 28 92 01*
*E-mail: info@paris-apts.com*
*www.paris-apts.com*

Both agencies have a large number of studios and apartments in the central areas of the Right Bank and the Left Bank, but you would still need to book well ahead to secure what you need for peak periods.

Here are four recommended hotels which have rooms or apartments with kitchenettes, as follows:

**Hôtel-Residence Henri IV**
*50 rue des Bernardins, 75005*
*Tel: 01 44 41 31 81*
*Fax: 01 46 33 93 22*
*E-mail: reservation*
*@residencehenri4.com*
*www.residencehenri4.com*
*Métro: Maubert-Mutualité*
This is a charming small hotel in a quiet cul-de-sac but in the heart of the Latin Quarter. There are five apartments with kitchenettes which can accommodate four people; these cost up to 260€ a night. All rooms are air-conditioned.

**Hôtel Résidence des 3 Poussins**
*15 rue Clauzel, 75009*
*Tel: 01 53 32 81 81*
*Fax: 01 53 32 81 82*
*E-mail: h3p@les3poussins.com*
*www.les3poussins.com*
*Métro: St Georges*
In a delightful part of the Right

Bank near good shops, bistrots and an excellent public garden, this hotel is strongly recommended. There are rooms that can take up to four people and fifteen of these have kitchenettes. Various combinations are possible e.g. two separate rooms, one with a kitchenette. Extra beds are also available. Family rooms cost up to 237€ a night. All rooms are air-conditioned.

### Home Plazza Bastille

*74 rue Amelot, 75001*
*Tel: 01 40 21 20 00/01 40 21 22 23*
*Fax: 01 47 00 82 40*
*E-mail: resabastille*
*@homeplazza.com*
*www.homeplazza.com*
*Métro: Bastille*
A big hotel (almost 300 rooms) and I wouldn't choose to stay here on my own or with another adult, but it has advantages for families like intercommunicating rooms,

as well as 'junior suites' with kitchenettes which can accommodate four people; all are air-conditioned. These cost up to 325€ a night but there are frequent *tarifs promotionnels* – ask about these.

Well-placed in the heart of the Bastille area, near the Marais and the islands.

### Hôtel Résidence Alba-Opéra

*34 ter, rue de la Tour d'Auvergne, 75009*
*Tel: 01 48 78 80 22*
*Fax: 01 42 85 23 13*
*www.parisby.com/alba-opera*
*Métro: Cadet/Pigalle*
This hotel is in a cul-de-sac and all 28 studios/apartments have kitchenettes and, by Paris standards, are large. The apartments cost 237€ a night. The owner-manager, Madame Alberola, assures me that children are welcome. Well-placed for shopping, public gardens and transport.

# Top six special trips for children

**Musée de la Curiosité et de la Magie, 75004**
*Métro: St Paul*
*(see details on p. 65)*

**Jardin du Luxembourg, 75006**
*Métro: Vavin*
The famous gardens have a lot to offer children but a particular attraction are the Marionnettes with hour-long shows on Wednesday at 3.30 pm; Saturday and Sunday at 11.00 am and 3.30 pm. Entrance: 4,40€. There is an attractive café, **La Buvette des Marionnettes,** next to the 'theatre', open daily from 8.30 am to early evening. The gardens have other attractions, not least the Grand Bassin for sailing yachts and other boats (and you can hire them).

**Piazza du Centre-Pompidou, 75004**
*Métro: Rambuteau*
The vast piazza in front of this no-longer-controversial cultural centre is a free show (which balances the surrounding tourist exploitation). Contortionists, acrobats, fire-eaters, sword-swallowers and mime artists perform all day and it is often eye-goggling stuff. However, it is also a magnet for petty criminals (especially pick-pockets); and keep an eye on your children (it is easy to get lost).

For seven to eleven-year-olds the Labyrinth in the nearby **Jardin des Enfants** at 105 rue Rambuteau,

provides a host of facilities for children who want to be active – mazes, tunnels, slides, climbing frames, etc. Open daily (except Monday) during school holidays from 1.00 – 4.00 pm; otherwise just Wednesday, Saturday and Sunday afternoons.

**Jardin d'Acclimatation, 75016**
*Métro: Les Sablons*
*Open: DAILY 10.00 am – 7.00 pm*
*Entrance: 2,70€*
It is a bit of a trek from the Métro station (the *Guide Michelin* has a good map) but this famous children's park warrants a day trip. Situated in the Bois de Boulogne, there is much here for children of all ages – a miniature railway, a go-kart track, a puppet theatre, a zoo, an 'enchanted river' and so on. Well worth the entrance charge (but not all the offerings are free).

**Canal Cruise (Canauxrama)**
*From: Port de l'Arsenal, opposite 50 boulevard de Bastille, 75012*
*Métro: Bastille*
*Departs: 9.45 am and 2.30 pm*
*No advance booking but you need to arrive at least 20 minutes before departure*
*Cost: 15€ (11€ for over 60s and under 12s)*
This long (2¼ hour) cruise is far more interesting for children (and adults) than the predictable and rather boring cruises along the Seine. The boat takes you through an eerie 2 km tunnel and along the

Canal St Martin and the Canal de l'Ourcq, with all the fascination of locks and close-in quais, up to the Bassin de La Villette. There in the adjacent park you'll find the **Cité des Sciences et de l'Industrie** (www.cite-sciences.fr), 'the largest science museum in Europe', with its multiple attractions: some free like the themed gardens and Mediterranean aquarium; others where you have to pay like the amazing **Géode** (8,75€) – see *Pariscope* for current details.

## Parc Zoologique de Paris (Vincennes), 75012

*52 avenue de St Maurice*
*Métro: Porte Dorée*
*Open: DAILY 9.00 am – 6.00 pm*
*(closing an hour earlier in winter)*
*Entrance: 5€*
A great bargain for what you get. The zoo itself is set in the vast park of Vincennes (study the Michelin *Green Guide*). An added bonus is the superb *Aquarium de la Porte Dorée* at 293 avenue Dausmenil (closed Monday, entrance 5.70€) which includes crocodiles in its repertoire.

### ...and when it's impossibly hot:

## Paris Plage(s)

*Paris, centre des loisirs créatifs* trumpets the publicity material and the claim is fully justified. The last few years (since 2002) have seen one of the most imaginative 'leisure' creations anywhere in the world – Paris Plage. For just four weeks and on a colossal scale, a two-mile stretch of the embankment of the Rive Droite, from the quai des Tuileries to the quai Henri IV, is transformed into a beach by vast quantities of sand and gravel. And it has all the back-up you would expect from the seaside: cafés, concerts, sports activities, swimming pools, children's entertainments, even a lending library (in French). There are witty touches (plastic palm-trees) and topical themes that change from year to year.

From 2007 the concept has been extended to the Port de la Gare, opposite the newish François Mitterrand Library in the 13th arrondissement and, more spectacularly, to the Bassin de la Villette in the 19th which has been turned into a marina of sorts (pedal boats and dinghies for hire, quay-side restaurants). A visit here could be combined with a trip up the St Martin canal.

The success of Paris Plages is so great that it seems set to change the habits of generations, at least amongst those who can no longer afford the traditional month-long summer at the coast. It transmutes Paris' great drawback, the unrelenting heat of late July to August, into an asset. Children love it. The only problem is they may want to go there every day; but so might you. And where did you get that tan?

One tip: if you're staying in an apartment be sure to take a large cool box to the Plage with freezer blocks *(pains de glace)* and as many drinks as you can carry; essential, anyway, but much cheaper than the *buvettes*.

# Acknowledgements

I couldn't have produced this book without a great deal of help. The main debt is to my wife Judith, who has waged unremitting war on my excesses of style as well as ensuring standardisation of details. Clare Cannon has word-processed innumerable drafts and thinks she'd like to go to Paris one day instead of just reading about it. Annie dal'Santo has dealt with my cavalier approach to the French language with her usual tact and firmness; while Anne-Claire Vilbert checked a late draft for remaining errors. Stephanie Black of Glasgow School of Art has transformed a rough sketch map with professional skill.

Finally Alexander Fyjis-Walker proved a sympathetic publisher; knowing my distaste for e-mails he has corresponded via a series of hand-written picture postcards.

B. G.

# Index

## Markets

## Fromagers

## Glaciers

**Museums (not all 'neglected'
but mentioned in the text)**

**Interesting shops**

## Bistrots

**Brasseries**

**Special restaurants
for luncheon on day
of departure**

PARISIANS' PARIS

UNIFORM WITH THIS VOLUME

# *An Hour from Paris*

ANNABEL SIMMS

A small classic: written with passion, perfectionism and
amusement, a guide that will make you see a Paris -
and a France - you would never have suspected.
Now fully updated and with extra walks.

Ground breaking work *Sunday Times*
A tremendously useful new guidebook *Paris Notes*
Delightfully erudite and idiosyncratic *Sunday Business*

This is a guide to the old-fashioned pleasures accessible within an
hour of Paris by train, if you know where to look:

- discovering half-hidden châteaux and writers' country houses
- walking, boating or dancing by the river
- exploring old towns and country footpaths
- eating in family-run restaurants with 1950s décor and prices
  to match

Written with an eye for the unusual and containing invaluable practical details and maps, **An Hour From Paris** describes 20 destinations
in the Ile de France, the fascinating yet little-known countryside
around Paris.

Better-known destinations include the châteaux of Chantilly and
Rambouillet and Maurice Ravel's house in Montfort-l'Amaury, but
the reader will also discover the Roman town of Senlis, the river-ports
of Conflans-Ste Honorine and St Mammès, the Gothic church and
medieval moats at Crécy-la-Chapelle, the old border-town and
water-mills of Moret-sur-Loing which inspired the Impressionist
painters, and the delightfully provincial atmosphere of Luzarches.

Published byPallas Athene
ISBN 1 873429 49 5/978 1 873429 49 5  £12.99

A psychologist and academic, Bill Gillham has written,
edited and translated over ninety books, ranging from
picture books for young children to research methods
texts for postgraduates. One of his children's novels,
*A Place to Hide*, was filmed as *Breakout* by the
Children's Film Foundation. The present
volume is a new venture and he now
has plans to write a children's
guide to Paris.

Cover, half-title and frontispiece:
Café Nemours, near the Palais Royal
p. 5 The famous fountain in the avenue de l'Observatoire
Back cover: café in St Germain
All photographs by Bill Gillham

Published by
Pallas Athene,
42 Spencer Rise,
London NW5 1AP
For further information on our books
please visit
WWW.PALLASATHENE.CO.UK

Series editor: Alexander Fyjis-Walker
Special thanks to Barbara Fyjis-Walker

First edition 2008

ISBN 978 1 873429 81 5

Printed in China